# Susanna
## The Making of an English Girl

## S M Saunders

LEAF BY LEAF

Published by Leaf by Leaf
an imprint of Cinnamon Press,
Office 49019, PO Box 15113, Birmingham, B2 2NJ
*www.cinnamonpress.com*

Print Edition ISBN 978-1-78864-935-3
British Library Cataloguing in Publication Data. A CIP record for this book can be obtained from the British Library.

Designed and typeset in Adobe Jenson Pro by Cinnamon Press.
Cover design by Adam Craig © Adam Craig.
Cinnamon Press is represented by Inpress.

Editor's Note: Some of the names used in this book have been changed to protect the privacy of people referred to, though family names have been preserved.

## Acknowledgements

My heartfelt thanks to the editors Jan Fortune and Rowan Fortune for their encouragement and support when my confidence plummeted to an all time low. It is their interest which saved my book from being abandoned. Thanks also to Adam Craig for his cover design. Thank you, too, to my son Dan, and my daughters, Sarah and Sophie, for their advice, their faith in me and love. Not least, I pay tribute to my late husband Peter Davies who guided me, gave me strength and supported me through this difficult journey.

To the memory of my mother
Sophie Agnes Chmieloviec
and to my father

# Susanna
## The Making of an English Girl

Sorrow is a small beginning.
                    *Letters.* Vincent Van Gough


What cannot be said will be wept.
                              Sappho

.

1

# At The Horseshoe, Surrey 1947

An elderly couple stood side by side in the hall like salt and pepper pots waiting to greet us. My mother stretched her hand and they spoke words I couldn't fathom. The old man's shoes were black and bulbous, defined by the white square of the checked floor, his feet placed together like inseparable twins. The old woman wore glossy brown lace-ups with pointed toes facing away from each other. I could barely stand. My legs were giving way and my toes hurt in my outgrown ankle boots. I was irritable and hungry. We hadn't eaten anything all day but for a piece of rye bread early that morning. I pulled at my mother's coat and asked to go home. The old woman looked alarmed and stepped back. The old man stared down at me and pinned me to his gaze.

Then the stranger, Leonard, guided my mother and me up the stairs. Candles on the dressing table in a back bedroom transformed the world to a little space. Papery figures presided over me as I lay helpless on the bed floating on the wave of half sleep. Too exhausted to protest, I felt my mother untying my bootlaces and pulling off my damp coat and dress. She tucked me in the cold double bed in my vest and knickers. Then whisperings at the door and the candles were blown out. The burnt waxy odour of the smouldering wick I would always associate with a fear of being left, helpless and adrift. I tried to lift myself up to follow her when I heard footsteps descending the stairs, but I saw the burning eyes of the wolf in the forest. I lay timorous and defeated.

Our early days in England began with the scraping of the shovel collecting ash in the grate downstairs, echoing up through our bedroom's chimney piece. I watched from the safe distance of the top stair as the elderly lady padded through the hall to the front door with her bucket of dying embers to be scattered on the ice-capped paths. Afterwards, the men bustled in and out of their bedrooms and the bathroom, and the kettle whistled in the kitchen adding to the morning busyness that amounted to the daily deliveries of the early post, the milk, and newspapers.

The bustle looked promising. Once the men had left for the city, I was dressed, my hair brushed and re-plaited, a task my mother always performed impatiently, irritated by my whimpering. Weekday breakfast was a slice of white bread, thinly spread with margarine and warm milk, which I took in the kitchen while the old lady dusted the furniture. Weekends, we might have the treat of a boiled egg, but not often.

Meanwhile, my mother later told me, she awaited instructions, unsure of what was expected of her in her prospective in-laws' house. Dressed as a guest in her best skirt and blouse to show her respect to her fiancé's parents, I remember her shivering by the kitchen sink looking out through the window, the lower panes patterned with ferns and exotic flowers of hoar frost.

'Gut, *ja*? Be good. We must both be good,' my mother whispered. 'We're in enough trouble already.'

I didn't understand the precise nature of the trouble, but I understood the importance of obedience by the tone of her voice. Yet despite my efforts to be quiet, having already equated being good with not making a sound, it soon became clear the sight of me caused my step-Grandmother considerable anxiety. I noted her scowl of disapproval whenever her eyes settled on me. Then one day, while minding me during my mother's outing with Leonard, she cut off my plaits and gave me a rough pudding basin haircut. It was a truly short bob with a side parting and a hairclip in place to keep strands from falling over my eyes. That I allowed her to manhandle me was a measure of my fear and confusion and the importance of behaving well drilled into me by my mother. The 'delousing' and cutting of my hair was for me at least a relief, freed from the discomfort of plaiting.

But when my mother returned with Leonard, she let out a loud cry enough to disturb the neighbourhood. Later, she said, my changed hairstyle was tantamount to a personal assault. We were after all in possession of each other, and I belonged to her, and was not anyone's child to be interfered with in such an underhand way. She could barely contain her despair:

'*Gott im Himmel! Du armes Kind, was hat man dir getan?*'

God, what have you done to my poor child? She ran up the stairs. I remember we stood still as trees in the kitchen, listening to her sobs fill the house. My grandmother took a deep breath and pursed her lips as if to hold back her distain, or maybe sympathy. Confused and afraid, I climbed the stairs to comfort my mother lying across the bed.

'*Mutti, Mutti*, Mama, don't cry.' But the sight of me, shorn and ugly, only brought on a fresh wave of sobbing and left me feeling unloved for my looks.

Despite my new hairdo and effort at being quiet and

undemanding, Grandmother's intolerance of me intensified as the weeks wore on. If forbidden words flew out of my mouth by mistake and settled on Grandmother, she brushed them off with the slap of her hand like a swarm of plague-flies, clicking her tongue and shouting strange words. My mother turned away and didn't defend me. I was too young to judge her, or fathom her betrayal, although I felt it. My unhappiness was caused not so much by Grandmother, but my mother's necessary collaboration. It was only when Grandmother wrapped my lace-up boots in newspaper and threw them in the dustbin, removed my blue dress, and replaced it with a knitted skirt with shoulder straps, and a jumper of many colours made from her old, unravelled cardigans, that she probably allowed herself to feel I was partially cleansed of sullied traits. Her work on my transformation made me presentable to the outer world to avoid shame, embarrassment and ameliorate the affront to the unshakeable core of democratic principles. It didn't matter to me then how I looked. I had no idea which arrangement of features was considered ugly or beautiful. The human face had to be learned, especially the expression made by the mouth and in the eyes where I looked for love and approval. My mother would often suck on her cheek to hold back her waxing indignation. I knew nothing of my mother's plans or the reasons for her tolerance. I kept watch, trying to fathom the mystery of the bond between my mother and Leonard the stranger, and their bond with Grandmother. I wanted nothing more but to escape the flyblown house and be free of Grandmother's surveillance. I was frightened most of the time although never threatened. It was as if something terrible stalked the house and had its sights on me. My mother persistently lied to me when I asked, '*Mutti, Mutti*, Mama, Mama, when are we going *home?*' I could feel the scar on my leg burning with unhappiness.

'Ach! Soon. Soon,' she lied. Hope was rekindled, but it led to nothing but a worse kind of unhappiness. I knew we had been captured and I longed to be free again.

Meanwhile, in keeping with the adult insistence that I behaved as quiet and timid as a mouse, I was forbidden to run, jump, skip, tumble, laugh, cry or sing—the cardinal rule being that the English language was the *only* one tolerated 'inside these four walls.' The language my mother and I shared was 'filthy and vile'. The sound of 'G' words were enough to cause Grandmother to spit expletives into the broom cupboard next to the kitchen. She also had the habit of climbing the stairs, muttering under her breath. I soon picked up the habit since I had no one to speak to in my own language apart from secret whispers under the bed covers with my mother. I found it pleasurable listening to my own whispered words addressed to an invisible self equally exiled. As I was lonely, I made myself into two girls—my Other was mute and always a sympathetic listener. In Grandmother's case, talking to herself probably released tensions of having to do the decent thing for her son, and for her own sense of self as a fair-minded, tolerant English woman. But my mother and I later agreed, she probably found herself torn between the powerful, malicious urge to be rid of us, and her duty, which involved her campaign of over-meticulous care and training to make us good British citizens.

Mostly I ate in the kitchen alone, except on Sundays, when I was perched on a red velvet cushion covered in a napkin to protect it from my droppings as I tried to manoeuvre the two large instruments, which my mother later called a fork and knife—in that order—around the minefield called a plate. I was allowed in the sitting room at the back of the house overlooking a long garden, the snow-blooms turning blue in the midday twilight. But I was only allowed to occupy certain areas. Grandfather's chair to the right of the fireplace and Leonard's to the left, were out of bounds. Also, Grandmother's corner of the sofa was her precious territory. My mother was allowed to sit at the other end of the sofa, but I was always nudged out of the space between. Any prolonged proximity to Grandmother caused her brow to furrow. Instead, I would lean into my mother so she would take me on her lap until unable to bear me any longer, she let me slither down to sit by her feet.

There was a wicker stool by the French windows I could use, but I preferred to kneel beside it behind the sofa and pretend it was my very own table. It was here I turned the illustrated pages of a story book and gazed at little pictures depicting a bear living in a paradise of summer sunshine, and green hills I pretended were my true origins. I took pleasure in hiding because I was no longer under the critical eye of adults and relished the delicious sensation of freedom under the parsimonious glow of the crooked standard lamp, where I whispered my filthy words: *Liebchen... Mutti... Tante Minnie... kleiner Bär...* my darling Mama, Auntie Minnie, my little bear.

It was forbidden to go into the garden unsupervised. Unless you were a cat. But even then, rarely, for the neighbour's cat ventured there only at dusk. Once, I managed to slink off down the side of the house feeling daring and naughty, only to sense the burning smog in my throat and step inside before my crime was discovered. It was also forbidden to enter the larder or wander off into the dining room and lift the lid of the unused piano and tinkle the ivory keys. These rules were reinforced by the fact that Grandmother's face indicated there was little to be happy about in this world.

In the meantime, my mother was confined upstairs to our guest bedroom, which had consequences. Leonard's room at the front of the house was out of bounds. This would explain why he often tiptoed into our room in the evenings to sit at the foot of our bed close to my mother. I would pretend to sleep, opening my eyes a slit to catch them kissing and fondling. I imagined my mother didn't like him doing that because I wouldn't have liked it. Why she wanted to please him, I had no idea. I felt for her. Sometimes, she leaned away from him, and he would place his hand under her chin and draw her face close to his. It was difficult for my mother. She had to please everyone. I remembered her words that we had to be good because of the trouble we were in, and so I waited for some kind of outcome, for something momentous, either as a reward or a catastrophic failure. Every day dragged me towards the awaited moment. I could sense the anticipation thickening the air, the expectation, the promise, fear and excitement and the hope one day, now that we were captured, we would be set free to go home.

But my mother had her chores to do first, following her prospective mother-in-law with the carpet sweeper from room to room, pushing and pulling the tinny contraption over the carpets to squeak up the crumbs. After her first day at The  Horseshoe, when an attempt to sit prettily provoked Grandmother's sour look of disapproval, my mother returned her best clothes to the suitcase, and dressed in a darned sweater and an old skirt, did as she was told.

'It's impossible to get servants these days so we must all pull together,' said Grandmother talking to my mother as if she could understand. My mother, sensitive to context, understood the gist of Grandmother's words, and would try to smile while she dusted, brushed and swept, and washed the hall and kitchen floor on her hands and knees. I think it gave Grandmother a deep satisfaction to see my mother occupied in suitably lowly, contrite chores. But Grandmother suffered from bad faith. From her high moral ground, she relished her power over us; our daily submission, our futile efforts to please her reinforced her sense of a higher purpose compensating for the shameful burden put upon her to accommodate us. Her fear was almost as tangible as mine. You sensed she wanted to say, 'Leave my son alone. Go back to the misery you deserve!'

It was the neutral and transient territory of the stairs and its large square of landing with the plush red carpet and brass stair rods that became my special place, free from watchful eyes and instructions. From here in the soupy light pouring from the stained-glass window, a mosaic of sharp oranges and blues, I watched the domestic traffic below. Leonard, now less of a dark stranger, and Grandfather returning from work in the evenings, stamped their shoes free of freshly fallen snow on the doorstep; taking off their hats, and black coats, hooking them to pegs on the umbrella stand. Grandfather would tap the weather-clock on the wall, and with the evening newspaper rolled in his fist, went to warm his backside by the living room fire. Leonard always lingered to smooth his hair back in the stand mirror. My mother greeted him from the dining room doorway, his arms held her close insisting on a stolen kiss; Grandmother hissed along with a hot tureen folded in a kitchen towel.

Their habits and daily rituals helped me build a sense of security although what I desired was to be free of them. And yet despite the stifling rigor of Grandmother's routine, there was something new to learn every day. Not only did she try to conceal her emotions, but all bodily functions had to be performed behind closed doors. If she didn't have time to climb the stairs to the lavatory, she slunk outside along the covered passageway, closing the kitchen door behind her to pass copious wind. On Grandmother's return to the living room, my mother neutralized her amused face, and stared blankly at the wall. I copied her as it seemed the right thing.

Our capacity for duplicity matched Grandmother's in other ways too. On rare occasions when she went visiting in her fox-fur to take tea with her daughter-in-law Dolly in Purley, my mother would watch her departure from the dining room window and when she disappeared past the postbox on the corner, we broke the rules. In the larder we stole sultanas, cocoa powder mixed with sugar, thin slices of seed cake, bread and margarine, but only very little so the thefts were less likely to be detected. I would run around the house and enter forbidden rooms. I pounded the piano unheeded, and then ventured up the stairs to poke about in Grandmother's inner sanctum where I delighted in the pots of creams and lotions, the silver implements, the cut-glass scent bottles, the pins and pearls, the sumptuously soft powder-puffs, the photographs of ladies with tulle hats and men in butterfly collars.

In the mirror was an astonished face, a liquid portrait: large blue eyes, enormous fat cheeks and a baby mouth with tiny rows of almost transparent teeth. In the reflection you could also see an extraordinarily high bed, a little footstool at the side and two china pee-pots tucked underneath. The room reeked of Grandmother's personal odour, which matched nothing in this world; not entirely unpleasant, but heavy with her cloying musk of censure and condescension. I remember her smell permeated our clothes and hair like a reminder, so in her absence, she was always present. I gave a small shudder when I came across personal objects in the house imbued with her rancour: the fold-over pinny draped over the back of the chair, her shopping hat sagging on the hat peg in the hall, and her knitting bag tucked in the corner of her sofa.

But the best part was we didn't have to whisper. We could talk freely; my mother's language was like being kissed repeatedly. I craved the sounds and cadences. It satisfied a hunger for the world of home. When she spoke, I felt caressed and loved by her.

To keep warm on these liberated afternoons, my mother lit the gas cooker and kept the door open, so the hot air blasted over her legs. Then she fetched paper and pen, and a bottle of blue ink from the writing-bureau, and wrote letters home at the kitchen table. The iridescent ink from the pen made my mouth water. I asked my mother yet again when we were going home. It became my obsession. She found a pencil in the string drawer and told me I must write to *Oma* and *Opa*, my Grandma and Grandpa. I scribbled my message frantically in whirls. The request was clear: 'We are in bad trouble. Please come and take us home!' My mother showed me how to draw kisses and folded my letter and placed it inside her letter and sealed the envelope, which she hid in her apron pocket. Then she put everything back, switched off the gas and checked that all the rooms revealed no signs of our insubordination. We climbed the stairs and huddled on our cold bed under her fur coat. As I lay pressed beside her, I remembered sweet things that drop from trees in Grandpa's garden called *Äpfelchen*—little apples.

In time, I learned that our parcels and letters home over a period of many years were never answered and in awe of my mother's persistence, she taught me never to give up hope.

# Lüneburg, May 1936

What could be better than this moment to enjoy the beauty of abundant blossom and be enveloped in its sensual glow? At dusk, the blossom's whiteness intensified like a mass of stars. Sophie, my mother, just sixteen, turned her face towards its voluptuous layers, the branches creaking in the breeze, and breathed in the perfume in deep gulps, a glutton for its opiates. Returning to the house for supper it seemed nature's promise was more precious than politics. The conversation at the table was silenced by a familiar voice booming out of the wireless. It spat out the need for alliance with Britain to safeguard the interests of the Fatherland. The Lion and the Unicorn will lie with the Eagle in harmony.

Wasn't there a similar image in the Bible? Sophie recalled the words as she chewed on tough beef: 'And the wolf will dwell with the lamb, and the leopard will lie down with the kid, and the calf and young lion and fatling together, and a little child shall lead them.' At the table, the words, the voice from the mouthpiece—appeasement, sacrifices, glory, the protection of German blood—seasoned the boiled beef, red cabbage and mashed potato.

*Ordnung muss sein*—Order must prevail. The Führer insisted on a neat and tidy appearance and above all cleanliness. *Reinheit macht frei*—purity makes you free.

The Führer was always saying things full of wisdom. But like so many other young girls, Sophie realised that whatever the Führer spouted, it could easily be dismissed. After all he was a bit of an ugly old bore most of the time, insisting that women stay at home and cook and clean and bear housefuls of children. Instead, Sophie daydreamed of a different, exciting life; she didn't want to end up like her mother, worn down by farm-work. She saw herself free from toil on the land, from marital and maternal duties, enjoying the sophistication of city life, the clubs, theatre and restaurants. She was certain to be rescued from this domestic servitude by a wealthy, handsome man. It was what every girl wanted; to be loved to distraction, cosseted, to wear fine clothes and live a luxurious life. She looked across at her father at the table eating and listening anxiously to the wireless; he was concerned that the Führer's generous annual allowances to farmers might be rescinded. So far, the Führer was doing a good job: building fine roads, new houses for the poor, getting the economy moving again, making Germany a proud nation once more. Sophie's mother looked tired and pinched. Not only did she organize the farmworkers and their shifts, but she also worked with them, joining the band of workers that turned up every morning outside the back door. They came from old established farming communities fallen on bad times. And there were the apple and pear orchards to weed, the flower production to oversee, the potato, and vegetable plots to be nurtured.

Her mother looked up from her meal and gave Sophie a critical look. She wished she had a daughter less restless, closer to the land. She saw Sophie as heartless and selfish much of the time, only interested in her own pleasure. It was necessary to constantly rein her in, remind her of her thoughtless ways. That was the trouble with modern girls;

they had their heads in the clouds. She blamed the new politics, putting all kinds of ideas in girls' heads about romance, heroism and men in uniform. She worried her daughter would get into trouble with men who were always in pursuit. Close to her sat Erich her handsome son. He was destined to follow in his parents' footsteps. Although he dreamed of becoming an architect, he knew the land was in his blood and that he would inherit the large estate. But unlike his father, Erich was less optimistic. He knew about things going on in Hamburg and Berlin that made his blood cold, things he didn't tell his father about, or his mother or sister Sophie. He always filled his mouth to its capacity. This disgusted Sophie who was careful not to spill meat juice on her dress. She ate the way film stars did, placing delicate portions from the tip of her fork into her mouth, lips pursed, rotating in small movements, her nose twitching like a mouse.

# The Horseshoe, Coulsdon 1947

Grandmother at The Horseshoe would not tolerate a mouse in her house or any creature without a human face, so when Leonard found a black mouse leaping about in the bath, slithering, sliding down the sides to escape, my heart went out to it, especially when Grandmother approached wielding a rolling pin. To our relief, Leonard scooped the mouse up in his palm and held it upside down by its tail at arms-length. It broke into spasms, wriggling and squealing all the way to the back door.

The following day, after the morning's scouring and polishing, a visit to the ironmonger's became a priority. My Grandmother was impressed with his selection of mousetraps and the demonstrations that followed. My eyes widened as the old ironmonger demonstrated the power of the trap's springs. Using a pencil, he made squeaking noises, followed by tapping the end towards the trap. When the spring snapped down, I flinched which made him throw back his head and laugh. Then he had the audacity to tweak my nose, which made my eyes water. Indignant, I turned away.

Trussed up in my coat and a scratchy wool scarf Grandmother always wound round my neck and crossed over my chest at the front, tying the ends in a lumpy knot at the back, and my hair tucked in a knitted pixie cap with a strap under my chin, I retreated to feel the luxurious silky textures of various seeds slip through my fingers in open sacks by the door. Then guided away and bundled into a pushchair by Grandmother in her little wedge-shaped hat secured with a large needle-pin, I barely had time to contemplate the brown curls escaping from her delicate round face with its small doll-like features. I thought she looked rather pretty despite her grim mouth set against rodents and us, and of course, there were other looming dangers to consider.

Under stress, preoccupied with fear about how her association with us in public might arouse hostility, Grandmother made sure her *going out* rules were just as strictly adhered to as her *being in* rules. Now that she had, in her view, successfully Anglicized my appearance, I had already passed the test under her scrutiny by the hat-stand, although I registered the dismissive look she often gave my mother who failed miserably on several counts. My mother's fur coat was decidedly contemptible; excessively flamboyant and therefore vulgar. In Grandmother's estimation a fur coat was associated with mistresses and disreputable women. She was unaware that in Berlin, a fur coat commanded enviable approbation, and was much sought by most women. It was a pity, because my mother had bought the coat at an exorbitant cost on the black market—to my mind a nightmare place of dead animals rotting in the dark.

Later, long after the thaw, I remember watching my mother, sitting on the bed, cutting the coat into jagged pieces to make rugs for the floor. It disturbed me. The energy fuelled by anger as she used the scissors like a saw to cut the hide as if determined to blunt them. The tears flowing from her eyes told me this was not an act of domestic necessity, but of vengeance against herself, against the world. At moments, when she couldn't make

28

the scissors work, she tore at the cuts with both hands making an unearthly noise at the back of her throat. I was thrown into helplessness and dejection. On the bed were pools of silk lining. Staring down at them, I knew this was the end. I didn't understand why, but I knew we could never return home if my mother no longer had her fur coat. We were both doomed to remain prisoners. I never asked to go home again.

Before that incident, venturing out without a hat, gloves or handkerchief was forgivable in Berlin or Hamburg. Quite respectable, unlike here in Coulsdon. Bombed to brick-dust, the old sartorial customs and dress etiquette of German cities were buried among the rubble, renewed in a different way when the old buildings were replaced. My mother did eventually buy a hat Leonard called a 'titfer.' It was like a beret with a little upright piece of felt in the middle like a plum stalk. She could never bring herself to wear a scarf, which she associated with disreputable classes, the enslaved 'brick women' clearing rubble in German cities.

After inspecting our appearance in the hallway, Grandmother would sashay up the path with her shopping basket on her arm, ration books in her clip-up handbag, head in the air, with her dubious tenants in tow. She was confident she had the upper hand, for both mother and child had been instructed *not to utter a single word in public under any circumstances whatsoever*. With some trepidation and our mouths shut, we followed the diminutive figure in her everyday-battleship-grey-coat and black hat to the High Street down the hill.

After the mousetrap purchase, the next stop was the

sparsely stocked butcher's where the vile stench of dried blood mixed with sawdust on the floor, made my stomach churn. Next into the greengrocer's with its gratifying waft of wet cabbages and clods of earth—a pungent and more familiar fragrance than I had experienced at home—and then into the dark chemist's with its curious display of gigantic coloured vials in the window; down the splintering wooden steps into a wizard's den, the walls lined with numbered drawers from floor to ceiling and a forbidding counter, where a man smelling of chemicals in a white overall with bulbous eyes stretched across to deliver into Grandmother's tiny gloved hand a corked bottle of Tonic. This was given copiously to women suffering nerves or who felt off colour. We had to queue outside the baker's waiting for the bread van to arrive. I listened to the strange, sing-song utterances of the women, the tutting and spitting, coughing and grouching, my feet numb with cold, and my nose cut off by the icy wind.

The most interesting thing on these shopping expeditions was the sight of children dragged along by the arm or yanked forward by reins or sitting hunched in prams too small for them. Fascinated to encounter others as small as myself, I couldn't help staring. Eyes would meet in instant recognition as a species apart, and I grew excited stifling the urge to touch or speak. I had no idea that my separation from other children was against nature. Sometimes, children would gaze back without life in their eyes, strangely incurious, indifferent to their surroundings.

Home again, home again—to lunch of bread and margarine and sweet tea and put to rest in the double bed. Rest *from* what? Rest *for* what? I lay looking up at the ceiling rose and counted all the little stucco balls arranged in circles around the light: *Eins, zwei, drei, vier, fünf...* round and round, counting and recounting balls to twelve, believing numbers stopped at twelve, until my eyes grew weary of the demanding circuits.

Sundays were bad. It was a day of *Weltschmerz*—world-weariness—with a sprinkle of indulgence, marking the day sour with dinner-time tyranny. My mother took orders in the kitchen, improving her culinary vocabulary. Afterwards, the pans and the oven had to be scoured to perfection, a process that seemed to take her all afternoon.

It was also the day of the prolonged presence of men. In the morning, Leonard and his father, settled to read papers by the coal fire, lit early for their comfort while I had to be *seen*, which meant my presence was required in the living room where the men might indulge in a bit of horseplay to amuse themselves at my expense. Grandfather liked to play hide and seek and would sometimes chase me around the dining room table, wagging his white beard making roaring and grunting noises, while Leonard would magic sixpences out of my ears and pocket them for himself.

'Now then, now then,' said Grandmother carrying the gravy boat. 'Bertie, don't get the child too excited. You know it will end in tears.'

I couldn't fathom the function of men. They spent a great deal of time at work, whatever that was, and on their return were indulged with food and comfort, contributing very little, as far as I could see. As well as being bossed about, they were subject to variable and unpredictable mood swings, from the downright morose to the hilariously jovial on rarer occasions. One was expected to fit in with their moods and respond according to their expectations.

If it suited him, Leonard chose to be most provocative at my bedtime; he would tickle me under my armpits on the bed until my breathing stopped, or take delight in my screaming at the end of bath time, in fear of going down the plug hole. He also liked to tease me in the pushchair when we were let out for walks. I allowed only my mother to push me, but he enjoyed my cries of protest if he took over. Then, once in the semi-dark, leaning over me in bed, he showed me his upper set of false teeth, moving them up and down like a ventriloquist's dummy. He looked so repulsive and wicked, I burst into tears. Later, he sprang nursery rhymes on me, and there was one he thought particularly funny:

*It was Christmas day in the workhouse.*
*The snow was falling fast.*
*We don't want your Christmas pudding.*
*Stick it up your... jumper!*

Leonard's laughter was a wheezing 'he, he, he.' I listened dispassionately having no idea what the words meant. I bristled when he touched me and sulked when he paid me attention. No one told me his behaviour was rude and my reaction likewise.

Leonard's older brother, Harold, married to a lady called Dolly, was easier to endure since he didn't live at The Horseshoe. Whereas Leonard was tall and considered handsome, urbane and charming, Harold was stout, his face as broad as a spade topped with hair so fine, it showed his pink scalp. He shyly thrust his paunch before him, a barricade balancing on spindly legs. An insurance clerk, he loved the quiet, uncomplicated suburban life, tending his mixed variety of dahlias and taking his dog for walks.

And yet, every other weekend, his presence created a frisson, a kind of zip in the air of something at odds with the sedate ritual of tea-time. Looking through the banisters there was Harold transformed. Trussed in black leather, squeaking head to foot, his goggles thrust up onto his leather cap he looked like an enormous dung beetle stretching on its hind legs. Resting in the drive, stood his shiny monster, to which a sidecar was attached especially for Dolly who arrived with her bones shattered, escorted into the hallway by her elbow. In his leathers, Harold was cavalier, kissing his mother, bowing his head to his father, and slapping Leonard heartily on the back, before being released by Dolly from his squeaky carapace.

Grandfather called the proceedings 'a palaver' under his breath, and once the palaver was over, Harold sank into the sofa enervated, soft and pink as a peeled prawn, gazing into the fire, panting with the contortions of it all. The whole process would be reversed at dusk and we would wave at the gate, Leonard wheezing with laughter as Harold once more his plucky self, regressing, or progressing, depending how you looked at it, roared away on his silver beast, side-car lights blinking, and a giant glove waving farewell as he disappeared into the yellow smog.

Other visitors were rare, but there came a time when Grandmother succumbed to the pressure of friends and neighbours urging her to invite them to tea and encounter a *real* German. Believing my mother couldn't understand English, because she spoke so few words, Grandmother complained in her presence how difficult it was to live with Germans, their meticulous cleanliness, their sly greed and arrogance. The visiting ladies enjoyed commenting on my mother's appearance, trying to pin-point which aspects of her general makeup indicated she was still in all likelihood a member of the Nazi party. My mother later told me Grandmother had told nothing but lies about her, but she was unable to protest and this necessary acquiescence brought on bouts of depression and despondency.

It didn't help that the English women's ways were confusing to my mother. She hadn't yet picked up the art of English conversation, riddled with irony, double entendre, and other subtle nuances of tone, including knowing looks exchanged between the listeners, creating an atmosphere of disapproval and distaste that belied friendly expressions, the smiling, the polite nodding of heads of gratitude when offered a plate of bread-and-butter triangles. The German women were less diplomatic and circumspect. If they disapproved of anyone they said so or point-blank refused invitations so you knew where you stood. This kind of bluntness would be abhorrent to the English known for their impeccable manners.

Grandmother's friends also occasionally focused on me, but being young, silent, and exceptionally plain, it was my mother's gracious presence and good looks that held them awestruck right through to the second cup of tea. They enjoyed these meetings so much that afternoon tea with Grandmother became a regular feature of their uneventful afternoons. This was an entertaining change from their dreary parsimonious lives of make-do, patching, bottling, queuing, scrubbing, darning and knitting. They had suffered and were most likely good women with unappreciated talents. I imagine as they left The Horseshoe they were in no doubt about Grandmother's forbearance and kindness to her foreign intruders, leaving them equally delighted and horrified to have met my mother—the way one might feel after having taken afternoon tea with a notorious murderer or Hitler himself. Soon they hoped, they would be invited again to Rosa's. So exciting. They all looked forward to it. Of course, it wouldn't be the done thing to invite the German woman and her child to *their* homes. They watched. They were prepared to wait. It was as if they believed my mother's dignified exterior would crack under the pressure of their conviction, her black heart exploding behind the breast plate, splattering everything with spots of poison.

But nothing remained the same for long. The snow lost its flinty lustre and melted to slush, gutters became gullies, gurgling and sluicing away black ice. There were watermarks along the outside walls, lacing the lawns and paths. The trees sprang open their green umbrellas. Sunlight leaked weakly and settled in the corners, snaked along the sills and it seemed everything was reaching out to touch everything else. Grandmother said I had to keep my arms close to my side at the table, and I wasn't to slouch. She arched my upper body by pressing her fist into my back to make a hollow and I sprang up like a pale shoot.

Another important change was that my mother's

English was coming along well. We could venture out without supervision, lessening my Grandmother's burden.

The butcher, baker and grocer greeted my mother with enthusiasm. The butcher's face brightened when he saw her and he taught her new words: *sausages, minced beef, minced lamb, joint of pork* and *chop*, which she pronounced *shop*. Sometimes, when no other customers queued up behind her, he might say, 'All I've got for you today, my beautiful *Fraulein*, is spam,' and then he'd wink at her and hand over a blood parcel of pig's liver.

In the greengrocer's my mother knew how to ask for *potatoes, cabbage* and *carrots*. The greengrocer lady with a gold front tooth taught my mother how to count holding up her fingers, so I was learning, too. In the grocer's the man with a wart on his neck offered my mother a chair with a sweep of his arm. He was always trying to sell my mother things Grandmother had not written down on the list: a tin of peaches, or expensive date biscuits.

'*Ach, nein* no thank you,' my mother would say, mixing up English with a bit of German, her eye fixed on the golden slab of cheese under the glass dome. The grocer weighed everything, scoop in hand, ready to retrieve or pour out more sugar. 'A little extra for you,' he intimated with a smile. I liked the silvery rush of sugar falling into the blue paper bag and the way he folded the edges, so the corners stuck up like little mouse ears.

The grocer didn't care to teach my mother English. He preferred to touch her arm, even dared to stroke her shoulder. Grandmother would have told him to keep his arms to himself. I prided myself on knowing the rules. Sometimes the grocer took my mother to view the tins of precious fruit piled on the shelf behind the counter where I couldn't see what he was doing with his hands. My mother said he was always after her coupons.

There was one ugly incident that threatened to become dangerous. I remember it well because I held myself responsible. Liberated without Grandmother's presence, I became feckless and babbled in German outside the baker's empty shop in a long queue and my mother answered in a mixture of German and English.

Moments later, we became aware of an uneasy silence among the women waiting in the queue. My mother looked about her uncertain whether to remain. The women were moving away from us and the queue became broken into small groups all looking towards us. A low, swarming murmur became louder, the words mumbled, hooded, disguised as if muffled behind cloth.

Then a woman with a headscarf, forced her way towards us, and spat in my mother's face. My mother wiped her cheek with her glove. She was transfixed as if her whole system had shut down. They could have done anything they liked to her. The women, too, remained perfectly still, waiting. Then the other women shouted and hissed and one punched my mother's shoulder, so she almost fell but righted herself. I wanted her to push our way out of the crowd, but when I looked up, I saw her frozen expression, her eyes staring through the angry distorted faces, I could feel my scar prickling. Soon the women pressed, and all I could see were legs and feet and swaying skirts. My mother swayed too. I felt sick. A man's voice bellowed from the baker's doorway, 'What's going on out 'ere? The bread's in ladies. C'mon!'

The women turned their shoulders towards him; then paused as if their business with us could not remain unfinished, but then one woman let out a loud cheer. The spell was broken. My mother woke from her trance. Using me in my pushchair as a protective ram, she forced her way through the small dispersing crowd, the women stepping back so we could make our escape. My mother knew it was always dangerous to look back, to draw attention. She marched along Brighton Road, past Coulsdon railway station, and up the hill and into the safety of the empty park. Shaken, she sat on a bench under the cherry blossom trees and after parking me beside her, smoked one cigarette after another. I patiently sucked my thumb, my face whipped by the wind. I kept quiet. I knew I was to blame. Next time I must not speak when we go into the world. Grandmother was right all along.

And although the English spring was full of green promise, the idea that something beneficial and enthralling was about to happen became comforting. The world, indifferent to our skirmishes, got on with its business, dressing itself up for something unknown to me—the egg-shell blue of forget-me-nots and the trumpeting daffodils in garden among clumps of sprouting perennials, Grandfather pruning the roses, had the eloquence of a runaway tongue I envied.

Yet, incontrovertibly, at The Horseshoe we felt the chill of taciturn winter trapped inside, so the furniture did not bud or blossom, and Grandmother never opened the windows to let the wickedness out. She was fearful of cold draughts, of spiders, mice, midges, flies and bright sunshine that showed up the dust in corners and the shabbiness of the drapes and carpets. Without domestic servants these days the mammoth spring clean was out of the question and had to be abandoned.

Her hostility to nature and foreign guests became more palpable. It left marks on her face, and her mouth sagged. She winced at the slightest sound and yet snapped at us and raised her voice, slammed doors. Her suffering was like a cult around which her household revolved. Each person chafed against the other. My mother cried at the sink. She would turn the tap, water gushing into the tin bowl to disguise her sobs. She cried down the side of the house. My mother cried walking the streets. In the bedroom I leaned into her to comfort her. Sometimes I rested my head on her arm, and she would cry and stroke my hair while I hurt for her.

# Lüneburg, Summer 1936

School was over. It was time for daydreaming of when she would be free. Sophie saw herself as a girl with prospects. It was her ambition to rise above the farming community, looked down upon as a class of peasants by her classmates whose parents were in trade or the professions. As her older brother Erich would inherit the market gardening business, she believed marriage alone was her destiny. She decided the meeting with a man would occur at a dance. They would exchange a glance of recognition across the dance floor, and in slow motion she would watch him walk towards her and claim her. Love at first sight. A love to cherish forever. But first would be the months, maybe years, of toiling on the land; helping her mother in the fields and home, ruining her hands, the winds whipping and drying her skin. She wished her school life wouldn't come to an end.

Her heart lurched. The woman was there again standing opposite the school in the shadow of a tall house with its covered porch. Something about her made sixteen-year-old Sophie very much aware of her: an intensity of look, the expression of a person in search of someone else but not in a casual confident way, but anxious and stressed. Although, Sophie surmised, she was probably waiting for one of the pupils to come out of school and take her home, no one seemed to know her. And why stand back like that and not come towards the gate and look over the iron railings towards the main gate, where the pupils came pouring out into the street?

Her appearance added to her allure. The people of the little spa town of Lüneburg were country folk in the main, dressed in their old-fashioned clothes, more suited to the beginning of the century. Many travelled to Hamburg and other cities and knew how the fashionable townswomen dressed, causing amusement and astonishment, but no one looked like the attractive lady staring across at the school. It was June, but there was a fresh breeze wafting up in surges from the riverside quay, which meant the cream skirt with soft folds, and a long jacket to match that hung loosely around her hips, were perfectly appropriate. Her stockings were cream too and her shoes were white like her hat with its narrow brim shading her forehead. It was difficult to see the colour of her hair without staring, which would have been rude. Sophie tried to recall the last time she saw the woman in the exact same place. It must have been the previous year, but in the winter because the stranger had worn an ankle length coat with a fur collar.

As she and her friends, Lotte, Maria and Tia, left the school grounds, saying goodbye and going their separate ways, Sophie stopped at the kerb and looked across at the woman. For a split second there was a connection. Maybe Sophie just imagined it. The woman's face looked as if it would break into a half smile, but then remained impassive.

Sophie grew doubtful that the woman was a stranger at all. Maybe she was one of her father's customers. Maybe she had delivered plants or apples to her house. Her heart pounded when she thought of the secret police and spies, and the warning all mothers gave their daughters to keep them in check: if you don't behave, you could be reported by any family member and sent to a correction camp. Sophie had heard gossip about bad girls who went with boys in the woods and got pregnant. They went off to correction camps with their defiant heads held high and a belly big with a baby. But when the local girl Helena returned, she didn't have her baby with her and sat at home all day staring at a tree through the kitchen window.

With a start, Sophie stepped back from the kerb, and once she had reached the end of Rotestrasse, ran across the town square to arrive safely in the street that led to the bridge and home, breathless with a pain in her side. Sophie didn't tell anyone about the stranger. Her mother already called her a silly dreamer and as the woman never appeared again, Sophie didn't trouble herself about the last sighting, but she never forgot her. There remained a seed of hope, that this woman might be her real mother who would one day come to claim her and save her from a life of slavery on the land.

# Coulsdon, June 1947

Now I was ready to put an end to everything. It must have been a desperate Saturday afternoon when the impulse came to me in the High Street. Despite it being summer, I remember the wind had a chill and the air was laden with rain. My mother and Leonard had decided not to take the pushchair on the train to Croydon, so I walked beside my mother who urged me to pick up my feet and walk faster. The idea to run away, or cause a stir, came to me on impulse; like an unexpected visitor. I saw an approaching double-decker bus turning into the road as we waited to cross. A compulsive and unthinking opportunist, I slipped my hand out of my mother's grasp, stepped off the kerb and ran into the main road.

Unable to judge the speed of vehicles, I flung myself down onto the asphalt as the approaching bus droned towards me at considerable speed. My heart knocked hard against my chest, and my body tingled with anticipation and fear. I could feel the hot flow of wetness between my legs. I kept my head down, my eyes closed, and my cheek pressed into the asphalt waiting for deliverance. The red monster gobbled me up and spewed me out of its back end. This was my first resistance to life.

I heard screams. The bus came to halt further down the road. Someone lifted me up into his arms, and I fainted. When I woke, I found myself lying on a high shelf, lined with newspaper in the local hospital, my mother and Leonard and a young doctor in attendance. Were they going to wrap me up in newspaper and dispose of me the way Grandma wrapped my new boots, fish heads and meat bones to put out for the dustbin? I remember the off-white cracked wall tiles and a tall ceiling like a funnel and the glare of naked light bulb far off and the sour smell of my own sick. I was prodded all over by a doctor. Then he took hold of my limbs and bent them back and forth. Then he examined my head with both hands staring into my eyes. His gaze was too overpowering, so I let my eyes wander over his brow. The child before him, he observed, was in a dazed state and needed a good meal, but nothing was broken. He told my mother I was to be returned to home promptly and put to bed after a cup of tea. Grandmother made me a boiled egg with 'soldiers' when she heard of my accident. She admonished my mother and Leonard for not instilling road sense into the half-witted child. She hoped this would be a lesson to everyone concerned. On the doctor's advice I was put to bed. Tucked up, my shivering body pinned down by the top sheet, I was appalled to find myself, not on some adventure leading to home, but returned to Grandmother's unrelenting domain.

Despite the cold climate at The Horseshoe, and my failed attempt to escape, I remained a greenstick reed without roots, while unbeknown to me on August 12th, 1947 my mother, Sophie Agnes Groth, nee Chmieloviec, married Frederick Leonard Saunders in Epsom, Surrey. There were two witnesses, a German couple called Herr and Frau Lembke, who were resident in England since the 1930s and recently released from internment on the Isle of Man; they were introduced to my mother by Dolly who met the couple in church.

I have no recollection of this significant day because I was not invited to the wedding. Records show it was a bright mid-summer's day. There are no photographs of the newly married couple, so I don't know what my mother wore, certainly not her fur coat in August, but most likely her stylish cream and black striped jacket and black skirt. I don't know if she held a bouquet of lilies or wore one of those hats with a demure net over her eyes and took a lace handkerchief for tucking up her sleeve. As for her shoes, I can only imagine she wore her black suede high heels with ankle straps. It was, she told me later, a private affair, a euphemism I decided for everyone's disapproval so Leonard declined to send out invitations. There were no celebrations; no showers of paper rose petals, and no loved ones to wish the couple luck and happiness. They returned to The Horseshoe and life continued as it had before the event so you would never have known. Leonard remained in his room, and my mother and I slept in the back room allocated to us from the beginning.

Shortly after this, I became a problem. I was due to be sent to school not as a German girl, but in disguise as an English girl. I was not consulted of course, and everyone wondered if I could pull it off. 'She'll be strung up in the playground if we don't do something,' said my Grandmother who devised a damaging and yet protective strategy. She instructed my mother never to speak to me again in German. Grandfather Bertie, Leonard and Harold were all in agreement that this was the only solution. No one gave Dolly a chance to express her opinion.

'It makes sense. The more she is spoken to in German, the less likely she will learn English. It is time she was at school.' Grandmother was eager to gain everyone's support.

'If you leave it any longer,' warned Grandfather, 'it'll be difficult to explain her lack of knowledge at a late age. She'll fall behind and the authorities will want to know where she's been. You can't have them finding out what she really is.'

'And most certainly, she'll fall behind if we don't act now.' All this sounded frightening. Their words were enigmatic and threatening.

Grandmother's strategy was put into immediate operation and my mother spoke to me in her broken English while I chattered away in my mother-tongue when Grandmother was out of ear shot. As a consequence, my mother's refusal to speak to me in our shared indigenous tongue created a deepening schism between us. I was hurt, and perplexed. Our mother tongue was beautiful and precious to me, a link to our brief but shared past and lost family. The only time my mother had spoken to me in German was secretly under the bedclothes at bedtime. Now that our language was totally forbidden and as I couldn't speak English, although I was beginning to understand it, I had no choice but to remain silent. It wasn't long before my mute condition struck my mother with mortification and fear.

'*Ach Gott*, Heike! Speak to me,' my mother implored as I stood beside her bed witnessing her distress. She took me in her arms. *Meine Liebchen, Meine Mutti*—my darling Mama, I repeated silently in my head but dared not speak.

Grandmother was too practical to be waylaid by sentiment or melodrama. You had to admire her strength and pragmatism. 'The child must have English lessons. I'll put it to Dolly. She doesn't have children of her own. She's not a teacher, I know, but she's a patient soul and kind to animals.'

That summer, I was dispatched to Dolly's house. Grandmother took me by bus every day to learn English, although I had no idea of the purpose of the visits. I welcomed the change of house. Harold opposed the arrangement, but eventually relented and in any case, he was at work in the city, and the quicker something was done about the child, he reasoned, the quicker his mother would be relieved of her burden of having the Germans in her house. He would have to talk to his brother again about moving out, although he knew accommodation was hard to find.

Dolly's house was a semi-detached with green window frames and outside walls encased in grey pebbledash. In the large rooms, covered in white dust sheets, pieces of furniture resembled ice floes shifting their position in the downstairs rooms. Dolly liked to move the chairs and sofa around, but soon became dissatisfied with the new arrangement and put them back again. The rooms, with their old knotted wooden floors, were always flooded with a diffused light. Birdsong reverberated from wall to wall, and the sunlight flushed out adulterated nuances of shadow. Even when the rain fell and dark clouds pressed down on the pear trees and silenced the birds, the rooms retained a mellow, emollient glow. However, the small grand piano in the drawing room was never covered in dust sheets, its white teeth gleaming at the poplars lined up at the end of the garden. Dolly called them her warrior trees guarding her against easterly winds. There was another lovely surprise, too. It was Dolly's black spaniel, rather plump and lazy who liked to lie panting under the pear tree. He watched me condescendingly as I threw a cracked, bald tennis ball and then had to fetch it myself because he pretended not to understand my German command and refused to retrieve it. When I tried jumping over the flowerpots and rolling over and over on the moss-clogged lawn, he remained dispassionate and unimpressed. I bored him with shows of affection, stroking his fat neck and kissing the warm dip in his flat head between his ears, claiming him as 'Mein Hund—my dog', all of which he endured without complaint. I was so surprised how warm he was to touch, and quickly fell in love with him.

It was wonderful to have the run of the house and if Grandmother imagined for a moment I was receiving formal English lessons, she would have been mortified to find that I was left very much to myself, enjoying a newly found exuberance, jumping up and down on the armchairs, bouncing down the stairs on my backside, taking Mein Hund for a walk with Dolly, listening to her singing at the piano in the drawing room.

Lavender's blue, dilly dilly, lavender's green,
When I am King, dilly dilly, you shall be Queen…

The song filled me with a buoyant joy. At first, I liked Dolly, and then my feelings deepened, and I loved her. She was willowy and frail, and I was careful not to move sharply against her. She'd look down at me with goose-grey eyes, and her serious expression would break into a wide smile. Dolly was gentle in speech and manner and touched things delicately as she herself would like to be touched because everything was so precious and even the air and wind were kind to her. She reminded me of *Oma*, my grandma in Germany, who moved quietly in the house at home as if someone was sleeping nearby, although she had a firm tread in her boots outside. Dolly walked on the earth with a soft tread, her shoe ribbons fluttering. I was supposed to call her *Auntie* Dolly, which was the same as *Tante* in German. However, since I was mostly mute, her title was irrelevant. She never used my German name *Heike* but devised all kinds of other terms.

'Sweetie-pie,' she would say, 'little one, let's make a Gingerbread man, shall we?' And, 'Child, be careful sliding down the banisters,' and, 'Sweetie, fetch the lead. We are taking the dog for a walk.' Her voice was exceptionally caressing and mellifluous. She spoke to me in a manner halfway between song and speech. I later discovered the Germans have a name for it: *Sprechstimme*. No one else I knew had such a voice. It had a physical effect, a presence hovering over my head like a flock of butterfly-words, their counterpoint cadences fluttering in a delicate, colourful mesh while Dolly brushed my hair softly and I fell into a semi-trance.

In bed in the evenings at The Horseshoe, new words, delivered in Dolly's voice darted just beneath the surface of my mind. I fancied I could feel them swimming through my half-sleep, nibbling at my first language, weaving in its place unfamiliar patterns of sound according to a fixed design. Round and round new words resounded. Unable to sleep some nights with nothing to do, and no one to talk to in German, I put my lips against the inside of my wrist where the skin is sumptuously soft and practised the shape and feel of the new words as I whispered them onto my skin.

One day I returned from Dolly's house and held a simple conversation in English. My mother was astonished at my fluency. 'From that day on, you always spoke English,' she told me. 'You never spoke word of German again. It was if someone wiped the whole German language away with one wipe of a cloth.'

How did my mother feel about this? Was she pleased I was being changed into someone else? Was she proud of my achievement? 'Now you are safe,' she said. Her words in English always had a different intonation and pronunciation to others when she spoke. This distinctive difference made her English special, often with underlying meanings, and took the place of our once shared mother tongue lost in my forgetfulness.

As another winter approached, Grandmother's own taciturnity became contagious. My mother could only express her discomfort by remaining taciturn while Grandmother, tight-lipped and tense, released her malice on cupboard doors and the everyday dishes. The men, home from work, also remained silent behind their newspapers and so having just learned to speak the English language, albeit in a limited way, I couldn't see the point of having acquired it since no one wished to listen or speak to me. For months we lived like this with the presentiment of disaster.

It all came to a head. The increasing toxicity was resolved by violence. One wintry night, the doors crashed, and the bedroom walls shook as if the house was buffeted this way and that to loosen its roots. The windows rattled independently as cries and screams bounced from the walls and up the stairwell into the bedroom. Loud voices, barely recognisable, ripped up the night. In a half sleep, I recognised the distorted voice of Grandmother, her words wet and forced, and my mother's voice breaking into sobs and grandfather's anger booming so that you could no longer hear the grandfather clock ticking in the hall, or night-sounds of the wind's quiet hushing around the corners or the trees soughing.

I opened my eyes to meet the semi-darkness of the room. A thin streak of light crossed the foot of the bed from the door left ajar. I sat up in bed to listen more intently. I could make out Leonard's low voice and my mother's sobs and sniffling. Then a violent interjection of Grandmother's shrill, broken words. My heart held back for a moment before lurching into a gallop. Someone with a loud tread was on the stairs.

It was my mother. She switched on the light and reached up to the wardrobe for the black suitcase with the brass lock and threw it down at my feet on the bed and began to pack our few belongings. I sat upright; my eyes screwed up in the splintering light. I was afraid that she was going to run away with Leonard and leave me at The Horseshoe.

'*Komm. Schnell,*' she commands breathlessly breaking the no German rule. 'Coat on, little one. Over the nightie. No one will see. Shoes on. *Schnell. Schnell.* Good girl. Wake up. Wake up!'

I'm treading the pillow in my bare feet as she helps me with my coat and Leonard rushes in. He has packed already; I can see his suitcase on the landing. He is wearing a trench coat and his brown lace up shoes. 'Darling,' he says. But my mother ignores him and lifts me to the floor not properly buttoned so half my coat hangs lower than the other half. I'm certain Grandmother will not allow me to leave the house in this dishevelled state. I'm awake and startled. My mother snatches my hand, and we make our way down the stairs.

Grandmother storms out of the kitchen into the hallway. She is trembling and looks terrible. Her small, round face is blotchy and swollen, contorted in pain. I'm shocked.

'I've always said not in my house whether you are married or not. Never, never, never! I won't have it. I told you so and you agreed. Both of you agreed. Separate rooms, oh yes, you said. Then you broke your promise and lied to me. I've done everything I could to help you. It was all I asked…'

Her voice cracks to husky fragments crashing between Grandfather's soothing words. I have no idea what Grandmother means. I have tried so hard to please her. Tried exceptionally hard to be good. All I wanted from her was approval. I mistook her interest as love, believing it the English way, the unspoken nature of her cold love expressed through apparent care and concern. And now we are about to be cast out in the dark night, just as we came in the dark night and all that had lain between were layers of grey sediment and little shreds of hope for acceptance.

But now the buttons of my puckered coat are not done

up the right way, and my pixie hat is inside out, and the scratchy-scratchy scarf is not crossed over and tied at the back but hanging precariously around my neck. I want to show Grandmother the wrong way I have been dressed and ask her to help me. But I must remain empty of words because my heart is pounding fast with fear, and I keep my mouth wide to breathe in hungrily. Nevertheless, I'm disturbed that Grandmother's impeccable standards have been so easily abandoned. Her accusing eyes are fixed on my mother.

'You ask too much. I can't stand it anymore. All the sacrifices I've made for your benefit...'

'Now that's enough Rosa,' says Grandfather taking her arm. 'Look, they are going. Don't fret. There, there now.' He puts his arm around her hunched shoulders.

'My son... my son...' she sobs. Leonard stands close to his mother stupefied by the evening's outburst and remains silent.

My mother doesn't look back. She holds me by the hand and pulls me through the front door, up the path and into the lamp light on the wet pavement. Leonard follows closing the front door discreetly with a click. He picks up our black suitcase and his own small leather case standing in the porch, follows us onto the path. It occurs to me this is maybe an English custom: to visit for a while but not to prolong a stay. Then my heart lifts a little. Maybe my mother has seen sense and decided to leave these people to whom we have caused nothing but misery. I scratch my prickling scar that has come to life again. Maybe we are going home at last.

As we walk down towards the Brighton Road, past the

mock Tudor houses with their black gables like straps across their white fronts, blinking in the soft mist, I can't help feeling a little apprehensive about leaving Grandmother. Our departure was unfinished business. Everyone had forgotten the rituals of separation; we didn't wave or offer our faces for a peck on the cheek; we didn't call over our shoulders as we should: '*Auf wiedersehen!* Thank you for having us! It was so kind. We shan't forget. Goodbye!'

I assumed this, too, was the English way—the teeth-gritting harmony, this awful rupture of silences and sudden breach of sleep and dreams. How would my mother and I survive without Grandmother? What were we going to do now?

That same night, after a long conference in a dark porch, the rain falling in sheets of metal nuggets under the streetlamp, my mother hid by the hedge smoking a cigarette, while I held onto the hem of her coat, leaning against the black suitcase, both of us exhausted and in a trance. We were hiding outside a familiar house. Finally, Leonard's brother Harold relented. He released the chain from the lock and let us in. Dolly took off my wet clothes and rubbed me down with a towel and put me to bed in the box room all to myself. Leonard stole my rightful place next to my mother in the double bed in the bedroom next door. I was exhausted and unable to protest. It was a relief to have escaped the bitter quarrelling and crying, but we were all shaken up. My friend the dog and I were reunited, and he slept beside me all night. Like grandfather at The Horseshoe, the dog had grey hair, white whiskers and a pot belly. I woke early in the morning to his deep snoring.

We settled into a temporary routine at Dolly and Harold's pebble-dashed house, but I knew we were unlikely to stay long because my mother didn't unpack our black suitcase and Harold made no attempt to disguise his disapproval. My mother hid in the cold bedroom once he came home for the city office, her icy fingers darning holes in our clothes. I was put to bed early as usual, but the dog was warm company. I cast him two opposing roles in my secret games: the loyal and lovable dog who guarded me from the wicked people, Harold and Leonard, and the child-eating wolf from whom I hid. He always found me, of course, and wagged his tail and licked my laughing face.

Although Dolly's rooms were often cold without fires, it was sweeter in her house, cloying almost as the calming fluidity of a slower time drugged us and we wallowed in indolence, something unheard of in Grandmother's house. Nothing was urgent or pressing once the door slammed and the men went off to work. Dolly might sit at the kitchen table for two hours or more reading the newspaper or magazines, drinking tea with the wireless playing band music before she managed to get dressed and wander off, to meet friends in town at Lyons Corner House. Other times she might take me, unleashed, for a long walk leaving the old dog at home, and we would return tired from our excursion with sore, wind-thrashed faces.

She was good. We were allowed to follow her example, do as we please. She was perfectly happy to play the piano most afternoons, nothing too rousing, just the soft tinkling of Schumann's songs or nursery rhymes, especially for me.

I stopped seeking sanctuary on the stairs as I did at The Horseshoe and enjoyed the freedom of the house.

My mother stopped crying and with a renewed optimism and energy couldn't keep still enough to talk to me. She filled her time cleaning the kitchen and prepared dinner early to show her appreciation to Dolly. Then she would go off hunting a new home with her German friend, a Frau Lembke who had been a witness at her wedding.

'Now I go, Dolly. Frau Lembke is help me find a place to live.'

Dolly would simply look up at my mother in the doorway, and nod her assent, her eyes dreamy and intensely grey, her fingers working the piano keys; I would look up, too, from my picture book and nod, happy to let her go because Dolly and I were effortlessly at ease with each other. She never interrupted my imaginary games and would only intrude to announce a future event giving me time to prepare myself.

'If the rain stops, little one, we could go to the park and feed the ducks and then have a walk to the pet shop. They might have some kittens we could stroke.'

Her ideas and suggestions were so beautiful and encouraging and yet in many respects we were both *Weltfremd*—strangers to the real world, living in our own worlds, side by side, uninterrupted. I enjoyed talking. I talked to myself as Grandmother often did. I talked to the dog. I talked to little creatures in my picture books. I talked to the walls and the hollow wardrobe. I talked to the trees because in my world everything had ears and a mind connected to them; everything was my companion. Dolly understood. She respected my inner life. She respected my imaginative sphere and never mocked or demeaned me. And I watched Dolly in her world. I watched her knit and darn; watched her feed the birds with crumbs from the bread board. 'Come little birds,' she sang. I watched her read dress patterns out loud. I watched her shell peas. I watched her soak Sennapod seeds in a saucer on the windowsill. I watched her sleep, cradled in the whiteness of her sheeted chair. And yet, although I had found some happiness, I missed Grandmother, the way she fussed and brushed my coat before I went out and her constant reminders to obey her rules, and I missed the game of stalking her, creeping into her forbidden rooms, stealing from the larder and tinkling the piano when she went out. And I missed her precise step on the stairs and her sharp eyes and the way she always had a solution to everything.

That winter, our second in England, I remember nothing but the croaking gate, bare comatose trees, the snarl of cold draughts from under the doors and the threat of frost. The warrior-trees frothed in rainstorms. It was nature's attempt to disembody us, the wind jangling around the corners and everything unsettled and temporary. I ought to have known it meant something unpleasant was about to happen.

One morning, out of the blue, Harold said we had to leave.

He blamed Dolly, my mother said. He said her nerves couldn't take it anymore. She couldn't cope living with us because she was used to a solitary life. I was sorry to hear this especially as I mistakenly believed she liked us living with her. Harold thought not. He said her health was not good. It was a strain to have lodgers and he feared for her.

The truth was he was afraid we would become too settled and never leave his home.

I heard Leonard and my mother explain finding reasonably priced lodgings was difficult. There were signs up in the windows: *No dogs. No Irish*, and *No Children*. I had no idea people didn't want dogs or children or someone called Irish in their houses. It was a shock to me.

Early evening, eager for us to leave before Harold returned from work, Dolly gave me a cuddle and said she would see me again soon. I now understood *soon* meant 'never' and I could feel tears welling up. Then after seeing us off at the door, she closed it quietly and ran up the stairs to watch us from the window. When I looked up, she was there watching us behind the net curtains. I was certain she would sweep the curtain aside and beckon to us to return, but her dark shape moved away. I was sad to leave the dog. I wondered if he would miss us.

As we had nowhere to go, Leonard talked about returning to The Horseshoe certain his mother wouldn't have the heart to turn us away if he begged her to reconsider. 'Ach, Len. No. It is not good. Not good. The Horseshoe? No, please I can't…' my mother put down her suitcase. In the near distance, a figure emerged from the dark and walked towards us. As the man loped nearer a streetlight, we could clearly see it was Harold and instantly recognising us, he turned sharply to cross the road and walked briskly on the opposite side with his face turned towards a wall. My mother said she and Leonard fixed their eyes on this heartless brother. Leonard put his hand inside his coat, took out a cigarette from his silver case, tapping the cigarette end on the closed case, and put the cigarette to his lips and lit it. He gave it to my mother, and when she had drawn on it, she handed it back to Leonard. 'Wait here,' he told my mother, 'I'll be back.'

I looked up at my mother, her eyes fixed on him. She held my hand in hers. We had each other. It didn't matter where we were if we were together. We stood waiting in the street between two suitcases.

When Leonard fetched us, we followed him back to the house. What my mother would have given never to return to Dolly's house. It was an incident with a biblical theme buried in years to come: the betrayal and denial of a brother. My mother and Leonard swallowed their pride both wearing a lacerated look, heads bowed. Up the stairs again. Thrust into the tiny, box room. Undressed. Bread and jam cut into halves on a saucer. Drink of tepid tea. Tucked between cold blankets. Kiss from my mother. A dry kiss from Leonard. No kiss from Dolly. No dog allowed. Light off. My mouth closed in exhaustion, confusion and dread.

Downstairs, while I slept, Harold according to my mother, plotted to seal my fate as if his forced kindness sought recompense.

'Look, you are my brother,' said Harold, avoiding my mother's eyes,' and *she* is your wife, so you can both stay till you find a place of your own. I'll try to give you longer to search, bearing in mind your reduced circumstances. I didn't realise it would be so difficult.'

'Thank goodness,' said Leonard. 'Believe me, we'll do everything to find a place and leave you and Dolly in peace. We're so grateful to you both.'

Then, my mother said, Harold lifted his shoulders high

for a deep intake of breath. 'But I won't have the child living here. The child is no relation to our family. She can't stay here. One night will be allowed, but tomorrow she has to go.'

The children's home stood above substantial grounds of green fields sloping towards a high wooden fence obscuring the path and main road beyond. It was a late, red-bricked Victorian building judging by the tall gables, and once inside it was impossible to see the world beyond because the windows were high, and the inmates unable to view the large expanse of green grass and the trees along its eastern and western boundaries. It wouldn't do to put the idea of escape into their cunning little heads. It was as if they wanted you to forget the world existed. Day in and day out a grey mass pressed itself against the high windows and the sun loped off somewhere else, and when it dared cast a few paltry rays, it was not welcome inside the children's home, for black curtains were drawn across the windows consigning all living things to grey shadowy cubicles.

My internment probably began on a Saturday morning. Leonard and my mother walked me through the gate on the hill together and along the downward intersecting path in silence. My mother held my hand firmly, but nothing in her touch betrayed her intent. After an interminable walk through a warren of corridors with lumpy green walls and waxed wooden floors smelling of toilets and disinfectant, and my mother's footsteps echoing in a trail of flinty rhythms, a lady met us outside her office.

She was my mother's new German friend, Frau

Lembke, a large woman with extraordinary hair piled on her head in waves like small steps in a doll's house. Apparently, she ran the children's home. After a few brief words, they all took me into a large hall with high windows and tables placed end to end at one side. Frau Lembke lifted me in her arms and moved away from my mother.

'Look, *Liebchen*—darling,' she said. 'Look at all the little children eating their dinner.'

I trusted her because she spoke in a mixture of German and English and I was intrigued by the sight of so many little duplicates, spooning mashed food into their mouths. I ought to have paid more attention. I watched the children for some time in the arms of Frau Lembke. Some little mites were cadaverous faced with stones for eyes, silently eating without enthusiasm. Those in the far row looked up as they chewed, staring back at me, accusingly. After a while I suspected something strange, something in the feel of Frau Lembke's body, her spine stiffening. Slowly, because I was alarmed and suspicious, I turned my head.

The space behind us only a moment ago occupied by my mother and Leonard was empty. I looked to the doors. I returned my eyes to the empty space. I lifted my hand to my face. Just as it is possible to cry without tears, so it is to scream without a sound. The scream came up through the floor and speared my body like an electric charge. Afterwards my body slumped, and I entered into a state of shutting down.

But that first night I woke in a crowded dormitory. There was a single line of cots end to end filling the central aisle while either side were iron beds with little hillocks of bone under the blankets. At first, I was terrified, and then, when I remembered where I was, I called for my mother between bouts of sobbing. They had put me in a cot so I wouldn't escape, and I had woken with my feet sticking out of the bars to one side. Before I had time to contemplate climbing out, a young girl ran down the aisle afraid, no doubt, I might wake all the other babies and children.

'Mummy's coming,' she said. 'Mummy's coming. There. There.' And she laid me down again sobbing. I believed her. I believed in my mother. The girl reassured me that my mother would be coming.

Every hour for the first few days I told staff: 'My mummy is coming, you know.' They found this amusing and made a point of neither confirming nor disputing the fact.

But my mother didn't come.

I had nothing to cling to for comfort. No personal things were allowed. I watched the heavy doors open and close. I watched them as they were locked and unlocked and locked again. I listened for footsteps along the corridors. I looked up at the sky, aloof and pale, through the tall windows. I couldn't understand why I had been banished or abandoned. Everything was drained of colour, the dingy light, the children looking peaky and sickly with sores and scabs on their lips.

The daily regimentation, put into place to provide security and discipline, left little room for nurture or love, affection or warmth. The laborious routine was adhered to without exception. Little automatons rose at six-thirty and made the beds. The newcomers in cots remained incarcerated while the others went into the toilets to relieve themselves, endure a flick of a cold rag over their faces and then return to dress in silence. Then the bigger children helped us to dress.

I had no heart in preparing for the day that stretched before me interminably. It taught me that anything is endurable as long as my mother was with me. Without her, I would have been prepared to lie in the cot and suck my thumb until I died. I was a ragged lump you couldn't shake into life. I'd lost interest in my surroundings. I had no appetite. The gong summoned us to breakfast in the hall. Sometimes, it was porridge, and other times bread and margarine with a cup of sweet milky tea. We ate mechanically; slapped if we did not eat. Talking was not allowed at the table.

Afterwards, the older children had to do their chores, making the beds and washing the floor of the dormitory, but the little children were shown how they must dust the chair legs and the banisters and clear away the breakfast tables. Then it was playtime for the young ones. This involved indoor pursuits so there was to be no running or climbing, or anything too strenuous. We could throw rubber rings or quoits at each other or play catch if you had the heart or understood the rules. Others chose to do colouring or drawing or take a slate board and a hard lump of malodorous Plasticine, and mould shapes with it.

I remember making a nest with birds' eggs inside. I had never seen a bird's nest and had no idea birds laid eggs. I simply copied the girl sat next to me. When we had finished, we would squeeze our birds' nests and eggs of various colours, which mixed into a grey ball and begin again. I found the repetition repellent but couldn't break out of the activity. It was as involuntary as blinking, as if my life depended on it.

The desire to see my mother again produced vivid hallucinations that presented obliquely just outside my direct vision. As she peered at me through the classroom window holding her gloved hand to her eyes to shield them from the glare, I saw a golden halo of her hair caught in the muted sun light, but when I turned to look, she vanished… Other times running along the corridor, I sensed her presence in the shadows on the hall landing as I passed by. A glance up the stairs revealed no one.

A gong announced dinnertime, and afterwards there was enforced rest. Camp beds were erected at one end of the dining hall. I lay staring at the wall. Every day I continued to tell staff that my mummy was coming but as the days passed, those words lost their comfort.

In the late afternoon, when the other children had come home from school, permission was sometimes given to go outside and play, but I didn't want to play outside. I wanted to grow smaller and smaller and melt to nothing. There was no freedom in the home; in fact, there were strict rules about where the children were allowed to be. Through fear of punishment, no one dared break the rules. I never witnessed punishment, but the threat of something terrible hung in the motes of the air we breathed. The severe expressions of the staff, and the way the large clock and the gong ruled our time, made us afraid to express our preferences. With mechanical precision every tedious and loveless moment of our existence was determined; when to eat, to drink, to make birds' nests and to sleep, served as a warning that we had to do as we were told.

There was nothing to relieve this heaviness of their intent to control us and nothing to disguise the fact; no suggestion of luxury was permitted, no bright pictures on the walls or colourful crochet blankets to make the home homely. The term *home* was a misnomer. There was instead a sense we had been delegated this place on earth because we were children who had proven unworthy of comfort and love.

The older children were allocated jobs on a strict rota. Baths, basins and toilets had to be cleaned, and the dishes after meals washed and dried. Saturday was Spring Cleaning Day, when the hall, corridors, dormitories and kitchen had to shine before inspection. If something was considered substandard, it would have to be cleaned over again.

On Sundays, we changed our clothes. There were three piles from which to pick our clean clothes: large, medium and small. Then we walked in a crocodile to Church in our ill-fitting outfits.

What was going on in Church was a mystery. First, the foreign words made by the man in a white apron, followed by kneeling and mumbling. Sitting, then standing and singing, and sitting and kneeling, might have been comical if it wasn't for the fact I was lost and confused. The church smelt like a sweet shop and chemist in one, mixed with strong scents of polished wood and incense. We fidgeted in the pews, unable to keep our feet still.

The scar on my leg was raw and red. The church visit was incomprehensible and served no purpose except to make us suffer the man's incantations released like mist from his mouth, but which did nothing to warm the cold air.

In the afternoon, a nap was denied. We had to go to Sunday school shortly after dinnertime and sit in a circle while a girl read us stories that were all a puzzle.

I couldn't fathom the meaning, the latent morality lessons lost on most of us. The stories troubled me since it was impressed upon us that we must learn by them.

At six in the evening, the gong announced tea-time, and afterwards it was bath time. Three children went into the bath at the same time, the dirtiest trio first. Other days we were supposed to strip wash, but the water was often too icy. Then it was into the cot to lie cold and silent in the dark.

As the thin and spectral days slipped away I gave up hope and lost the will to participate. I was abruptly cured of my obsessive egg and nest making by catching a bad cold and put in the quarantine corner of the dormitory to await recovery.

Sometimes, my mind wandered to when my mother wanted me and we were sitting in the park under the pink arch of almond blossom. Or a picture would slide across my eyes of Grandmother's puffed-up Yorkshire puddings, placed next to thin slices of beef and gravy. Other times I remembered our secret bedroom, and my mother singing 'Hoppe Hoppe Reiter' as I pretended to ride on her leg, holding her hands as she bounced me and then let me fall. We laughed and she began the game all over. I heard Opa's loud voice singing: 'Tannenbaum O Tannenbaum, wie grün sind deine Blätter—O Christmas tree, how green are your leaves.' And I remembered a story about a nightingale who tricks a man into appreciating what he has, rather than yearning for more and more riches.

These fragments were treasured, but still the world weighed no more than a shadow. Then as time passed the dreams ceased and I travelled inward. I had not made a single friend. It was beyond my ability.

Frau Lembke, who appeared rarely, the assistants, the other children were of no consequence. They were all nothing to me, just as I was nothing to myself.

Days, or maybe months later, I was standing alone at the washbasin in the toilets, washing my hands under the cold tap with a grey sliver of cracked soap. I remember clearly, the rough wool of a heavy, brown dressing gown chaffing my neck. I was careful not to let icy water trickle down my wide sleeves to my elbows as it was too cold for wool to dry. I was alone, probably left behind as I was slow and apathetic, and knew I would undoubtedly get into trouble, but I don't remember minding much.

Then above the sound of water flushing through the cranky lead pipe, I thought I heard my mother's voice echoing behind me, calling my name. I didn't turn; certain I had imagined her voice. It had happened to me frequently before. Then the voice came again, and I was frightened. This time, I glanced over my shoulder.

A beautiful vision remained clear and remarkably real. In the harsh light of the washroom, my mother stood smiling in the doorway. Solid and substantial. Radiant.

'Heike!' she said, opening her arms to embrace me. She came towards me, her eyes brimming. My heart burst open with love and relief. I couldn't speak for joy.

But I remember I turned my back on her and continued

to soap and rinse my hands under the cold tap. Then, with my eyes cast down, I dried them punctiliously on the towel before I turned and ran towards her. She lifted me up and I put my arms around her neck and buried my face in her hair.

# Carshalton, September 1948

I was sent to school with a mouthful of a name, and a crooked haircut. My cloth satchel had my new identity slotted into its front pouch with a plastic window. Leonard had written *Susanna Saunders*. It seemed my new initials were overlooked. We were living with Ida and Albert as their new lodgers in a cramped council house.

The house was a shamble, but I didn't care because I had been rescued from the children's home by my mother. Later, I understood that finding lodgings for couples with children was a hard task. So how extraordinarily lucky that Ida became the centre of my idyll, despite the fact she obeyed different laws to Grandmother who loved orderliness, obedience, and adherence to domestic ritual. In Ida's tiny house, everything supported the theory of thermodynamics wherein the universe veered towards chaos. Things were hopelessly lost or crammed in corners or jammed down the sides of the sofa. There was no logic to where you might put things or look for them. All surfaces were occupied by rags, clothing, and assortments of chipped, colourful ornaments Ida had won at funfairs, together with Albert's hammers and chisels that he kept on the shelves beside the fireplace. The wireless, often swamped by old newspapers, stoically transmitted *Music While You Work* as Ida toiled over her sewing machine on the dining room table, the needle maliciously glinting, as she stitched zips into piles of men's trousers for a few shillings a week.

In retrospect Ida's philosophical question on the

meaning of her life amounted to nothing more than: 'Now where did that go?' as she rummaged, overturning piles of stuff, dumping one load on the sideboard and replacing it with another from an armchair, so most things got shifted around the room like an archaic conveyer-belt set in a loop without beginning or end.

This anarchy lifted my spirits. I liked the mealy smell of chicken feed wafting throughout the house, mingling with something always boiling up on the stove in the tiny scullery. If it wasn't a large enamel bread bin full of dirty washing frothing up with soap scum, it was the glutinous concoction of over-boiled old potatoes hissing over the pan. Ida kept the wooden spoon for stirring in her apron pocket. It was boiled white as bone. And like Ida, the house stretched towards a round and supple shape. I noted that Ida's coat buttons, hanging from threads, were under considerable stress, as were the misshapen buttonholes stretched to accommodate her.

There was no doubt Ida was like an inversion of both my physical sense of self, and my head. All the indoor rules Grandmother had instilled were in danger of being forgotten. Ida often dispensed with words, lunged at me, pulled me to her side if she wanted to get me ready to go out, or would shove me out of the front door to play in the street and make friends on my own.

When she felt uncontrollably broody, she would grab my arm and pull me up onto her fat lap and press me close to her cushion-chest. 'Let Nana have a kiss!' And she would offer her cheek to be kissed repeatedly. Her rough physicality was new and she often hurt me, but I knew there was no malice in her. She was all flesh and immediacy, and smelt of lavender talc, her short, straight white hair making her look old one minute, and young the next. She lived daily in the same dress under a wrap-over apron like Grandmother's and would huff and puff up the garden to tend the chickens with a bowl of feed on her hip, or waddle along to the High Street wearing her pom-pom slippers to buy me a bun with jam and mock cream oozing from the slashed top.

She liked to comb her fingers through my hair, and afterwards sing to me with sweat on her forehead and shoulders bent over as she worked the sewing machine. Even when she smacked me for going near the main road or hauled me up the garden path to sit on a stool in the hot sunshine by the chicken coop to let my hair dry in the sun, I loved her all the more.

Once I had settled, I remember sitting on the warm front step, surveying my new territory: the street with identical semi-detached houses and their fronts divided by old doors, corrugated iron sheets and rusty bedsteads, and the dusty bomb sites over the way, and not a tree in sight. But I was in paradise. Everything in my new kingdom, the way the sun fell on the stone path, the deep blue sky and clouds like white roses, chickens in the yard burbling a welcome to the new morning, and the musky privet-blossom perfume of the morning air, dovetailed into perfection.

Leonard didn't catch its beauty. He called it 'The Flipping Mad House,' but enjoyed himself. I couldn't understand *flipping* or *mad*, but I knew somehow it was connected to chaos. He and Albert frequently went out to 'the dogs' or they might see how 'the gee gees' were doing, and I thought it was a shame they never offered to take me to see the animals.

Saturday nights they played cards, first for matchsticks and then pennies. Ida joined them, but my mother concentrated on her knitting. She was attempting to knit the precise English way Ida had demonstrated, but soon lapsed into the more elaborate German procedure of dancing fingers. My mother, adverse to anything too domestic, apart from dusting our room and the obsessive washing of clothes, wasn't dedicated to this craft; knitting was her excuse for not joining in the card games.

During the dark Saturday evenings down in the gambling den, the sewing machine relegated to the floor, I was allowed to stay up late and hide under the table to play with plastic farm animals, keeping my eye on Albert's boots that were likely to give me a prod. I never yelped in case I was sent to bed.

Slaving at the iron press in the fetid steam of the local laundry on the morning shift, was not the England of castles, green fields and chintzy teashops my mother had imagined. Most of the working women were hostile, turning their backs to her except for one woman, the poor, deserted Violet McNally who would share a cigarette with my mother in the toilets. But the men gave my mother plenty of attention, smiling lewdly, making cheeky propositions as they passed her in the laundry. Ida called them 'cheeky buggers' when my mother complained to her.

Returning home after the morning shift, hair and clothes smelling sour, my mother washed straight away in the bathroom and dressed herself in fresh clothes. I liked to watch her put on her bright red lipstick and rouge and powder her nose. She was on a mission to save money in her little grey Post Office book to send parcels home to her parents. She liked to send them Marks and Spencer's brand of cardigans, jumpers and vests because my mother said you couldn't get those lovely warm things in Germany. At home, she said there was nothing left. With my new name and an improved command of English, I forgot about the German language. I forgot about my German grandparents, aunts and my mother's friends. Their faces were like the moon or portraits with bodies but faces not yet painted. I was distracted by this new demanding life, the relationships I made with grownups who came into our lives and then disappeared.

Meanwhile, I liked to practise my English with Albert. Leaning on the arm of Albert's chair while he was reading the newspaper, I plied him with questions knowing this was a way I could get attention. Albert was small and compact, whereas Ida was exceptionally large and spread herself everywhere; although her hand was quick to smack, to take as well as give. Even so, Albert had a sense of imminence about him as if he were about to erupt into decisive action, even when he fell into his battered chair by the fire with legs stretched, his scarf always worn indoors, secured by a knot.

Albert was a man of knots. Observing him closely, I noticed his boot laces were double-knotted, the final extravagance of a bow abandoned to make way for yet another knot. I think Albert wore his railway boots in bed because the knots looked old, oily and permanently fused.

Because of this, any knot I came across I knew was Albert's doing. Not least, the knot of hairy string holding together newspaper pages on the inside of the lavatory door, and the knot of wire round the door of the chicken coop, were sure signs of his gifted knotting and such a man I knew must be reliable and wise.

'Who's him?' I pointed to a photograph in the newspaper of a stout fellow.

'That's Winston Churchill,' said Albert. 'He's the finest statesman on earth.'

Albert puffed out his chest.

'Why?' I had learned this was a clever word that helped me save face and disguise my ignorance.

'He won the war for us, did Winston.'

I was unimpressed as I had no notion of what 'the war' was. I felt I should move the conversation along with another. Winston was climbing out of a black car.

'What's he doing?'

'What's it look like!' Albert sucked in his lips.

Albert's question was gritty and not like a question at all. And although Albert was often unanswerable, I continued to annoy him because I wanted a dose of attention from him.

'Who's that one?' I asked, pointing to another man with a little moustache and bald head.

'That bloke's called Attlee,' said Albert, jabbing my arm away with his elbow, 'and he's making a right mess of the country. Now, Nipper, get orf! A man has to have some peace!'

I left him. I said nothing of course, but later thought Albert was making a right mess himself when he ate his dinner in his chair, spilling gravy on his tin tray depicting the King and Queen dressed up in all their finery. On this occasion, I felt dejected and went to look for Ida in the scullery. I begged for some cooking-apple peel with sugar, shaken in a paper bag as a treat. The peel was so tart, it made my eyes water, so I didn't know which were real tears, and which sour apple-tears.

The day before I was sent to school to become properly *Englished*—Ida's word—I was perched on the scullery table to have my hair cut. My mother tried to advise Ida who wielded her dressmaker's scissors a little too freely, 'No, here, Ida,' my mother suggested.

Clunk clunk went Ida's scissors.

'And now zis side is longer.' Clunk-snip.

'Ach, now zis side is long.' Clunk-snip.

'Stop now,' my mother insisted in dismay. 'She is a boy!'

'I've never known hair like it. Straight as bloody pencils. It shifts all over the place. It's a devil to cut.'

'It is very stin,' confessed my mother.

'*Fine*, we say *fine* for hair not *thin*,' Ida corrected.

Ida, her face close to mine, had a severe look, and then she stood back for a moment and lent her head this way and that. Her hand reached out holding the scissors: clunk, clunk, again and again. 'I'd better stop now, or she'll have no hair left.' Ida laughed.

'Oh no hair,' said my mother pulling a long face. Clearly it was no laughing matter.

I puffed up the wooden stairs to look in the mirror at the boy. A fat round face stared back with a cap of cropped blonde hair, one side longer than the other. I mimicked a whole range of adult expressions before smearing my lips with my mother's coral lipstick to improve matters, and when Leonard came home from work, he said, 'Mmm. Who have we got here? It's still Old Pudding Face I see!'

Insulted to the core, I fluttered my eyelids to banish him from sight, and left him laughing in his usual wheezy way. His mocking always diminished me, and my haughty, miserable look increased his pleasure.

My mother took me to school on my first day, but that soon became Ida's responsibility. We walked along the streets and I made a mental note of the way home to Ida's house, just in case I found myself abandoned again. By the school railings my mother bent so her face was level with mine to impress on me a secret, one I must never tell. 'Susie, you must never tell anyone you are a girl from Germany. Forget your old name. You are Susanna Saunders now. You understand?'

I nodded with an impending sense of doom. What might have been a straightforward first day at school, became fearful. Ironically, I had forgotten all about my old name, but now it had been momentarily resurrected, I wondered why it had to be forgotten. And as for confessing I was a girl from Germany, I would never have dreamt of saying such a thing. Grandmother had taught me the danger of that. All the same, the memory of my old name lingered, a spectral presence like a lost twin who lived inside me for shelter. I knew the pain of my former self and had no choice but to become Susanna Saunders with a promise of becoming a worthier, luckier English person. I strode into the schoolyard expecting the rules and regulations of Frau Lembke's children's home without shedding a tear, unlike some of the other little ones bawling and clinging to their mothers. My maternal bond had already been cruelly broken and now renewed. But I did feel for them and understood their misery.

As it turned out, school was not quite as painful as the children's home, although in some respects only marginally different. The missing parts were boarding and having to do chores. But most of the day, apart from playtime, we were made to sit for long hours on hard little chairs or cross-legged on the wooden floor to listen to the teachers. It's a wonder we didn't grow crooked with callouses on our bums, our brains stymied by boredom and chalk dust. As the teacher talked interminably, the children sagged over the tabletops in a stupor. I tried to pick out words I could understand, but having the disadvantage of barely a year's knowledge of English, I had to rely on my wits and copied what the other children did so as to be inconspicuous. Trouble meant a good slap on the hand with a wooden stick. It was always important to register what might trigger this punishment, pitfalls to be avoided, especially when one little mite howled and then received another whack on her forced open palm for making a noise. I could feel my own tears welling. I was learning that there were two forces in life: the turmoil of one's inner life, and the suffering of others we were made to witness daily.

It comes as no surprise. I didn't like school. It was a miserable classroom presided over by a grim-faced lady, a Miss Gibbons, who was likely to strike without warning. I understood why my mother made me promise to keep my past-self hidden. This was a dangerous place. I often daydreamed about staying at The Horseshoe with

Grandmother who always knew the best solution to everything, and I missed dog and Auntie Dolly, her house filled with her piano notes and lovely golden light.

The only escape from the day long tedium was to slink off to the Reading Corner. Lying on the floor, I gazed at extraordinary illustrations of rabbits and geese and hedgehogs in white aprons, although the names of these creatures were unknown to me. Books were like tiny doors you could open and enjoy yourself inside. Like me and my double self, they were both supernatural and concrete. I imagined I was like a dull, pot-bellied book myself; the first few pages of my life filled with homely events in the snow, and the rest disappointingly grey with the secret of my short past in the last pages.

During the playtime frenzy, I hid in the toilets or crouched by the wall, wary of other children swarming the tarmac like angry wasps likely to sting me to death if I mistakenly disclosed my identity. The reality was that no one was interested. Having spent little time with other children, I had no idea how to make friends, or to play properly. I didn't know the games, let alone the complicated rules that governed them. Watching others play at Hopscotch, throwing marbles, race around in chase and *What's the Time Mr. Wolf?* undermined my fragile confidence, having no idea what was going on.

No doubt these early school days were difficult. At home-time I was in a more distressed state than when I arrived at the school gates every morning. I had hoped Englishness would be bestowed upon me as a gift for my diligence, but I felt no more English after the first month at school, than when I first walked through the classroom door. Every day at home-time, waiting at the gates like an orphaned duckling, I attached myself to Ida, my identity crisis in tow, dawdling all the way to Carshalton High Street, never letting her out of my sight as she slippered down the street, her empty maroon oil-skin bag flapping in the wind.

The only time I felt something rewarding stir inside me at infant school was when a Miss Gibbons led us into a narrow anteroom in her flat-footed way and took a scroll from a cupboard, unrolling a coloured picture-poster she hooked over the blackboard resting on an easel.

'This is Jesus,' she said, softening her voice, transmogrifying her former self from a prison warden to a beloved Madonna. Crossed legged on the waxed floor, we were obliged to rest our eyes on the man she called the son of God, the Father, and the Holy Spirit. Her words touched me, but the key word that hit me with force was: *Father*. My mother had recently told me my father was killed in the war. In the dark about such a phenomenon, I understood both the war and killing were responsible for his absence. But here he was at last. The Father. And it seemed my Father, wearing a nightdress and carrying a lantern by an ivy clad door, was to be shared with everyone else. I wondered about the Holy Spirit, although I seemed to remember Albert smacking his lips and commenting on the beneficial attributes of spirits of which he was particularly fond.

My heart pulsated. I believed I had made a remarkable discovery. There, perched on Father's shoulder was a small bird like a brown smudge. I fancied somehow it was linked to me, that there was some unseen connection with the little bird as if it appeared as a sign, but I couldn't put all these feelings into words. Every time Miss Gibbons ushered us into the anteroom and took our Father from the cupboard so we could peruse his holiness while she informed us about heaven and hell, the little bird never failed to excite. In any case, her description of hell fire didn't frighten me. I was made of fire. My scar never fully revealed its secret of how my skin happened to be branded. It looked like a slash with an outer line of tiny pinpricks and an inner fleshier layer of pink crazy paving. It was water that frightened me, and my mother's tears. In any case, the brown bird was going to save me from loneliness and fear.

'And look,' said Miss Gibbons in her softened, holy voice, 'see how all the children in the picture are sitting at His feet just like you are. He's telling the children they must be good. They must follow Him and fight to the death for Him and your country. Then He will always forgive you when you do something wrong. One day, if you serve Him all your life, you will go to heaven.'

Deep in the silence of myself I knew the truth: I didn't want to go to heaven. I wanted to go to Germany.

# Lüneburg, October 1932

When my mother was young, she never had a little brown bird to save her. She grew up like a defenceless mouse under the shadow of the predatory eagle with eyes that could detect the tremolo of fear in the grass as it circled hundreds of feet above. The all-seeing eagle served the new Holy Trinity of *Führer, Volk,* and *Vaterland.* Hands on desks. Straight backs. Upright but not rigid. Tough but not coarse.

The race creed had to be instilled into all the little children malleable as wax, innocent as lambs—they must be taught the superiority of the Aryan race: blonde, and blue-eyed. Clean and fresh. Sophie, wearing her checked dress with a large green bow tied under a white Peter Pan collar, was silenced by the demonic spell. Clean and fresh. Keep the blood pure. It is not yours alone. That's what the teacher said. O pity the poor dark girls with brown eyes. Abhor the browned skinned gypsy girl, the Jewish riffraff, the peasant Poles.

Now the children's backs are straight, unlike the curved cane the teacher uses to beat them, her manly arms exposed, her sleeves rolled like a farm worker, her brow glistening with sweat, a reminder of the pain she can swiftly dispense for any sign of rebellion or deviance. After, when the crooked child is made straight, and the tears are wiped away, the teacher holds up a book called *The Poisonous Mushroom* and then begins her story.

'There are good mushrooms, and there are bad mushrooms. There are good human beings, and there are bad human beings. The bad ones are the Jews. But it is often difficult to tell the good human beings from the bad ones. Be careful. Here is an example:

'A little girl is sent to the dentist by her mother. She sits in the waiting room with another girl who is the first to be called in by the dentist. The dentist has a Jewish face with a hooked nose, protruding lips and big bags under his eyes. Now the girl is sitting alone in the waiting room, and she hears screams from the surgery: "O no Doctor, please don't Doctor!" Then silence. Then the dentist comes out and beckons her in. And at this point she runs away.'

But stories such as these to make the children frightened didn't stop Sophie playing with Maria from the shoe-shop. Maria's father didn't have a hooked nose and big bags under his eyes. Maria and her family were close friends of the Beck family. Not too long in the future Robert Beck, Sophie's father, would help Maria and her family over the border into Holland. But for now, the story she heard at school made Sophie frightened of dentists and anyone who threatened 'treatment' in a white coat behind closed doors. The fact that the dentist in the story was Jewish made no impression.

But unable to shake off the delirium of the New Age, the freedom of singing and marching, the voices chanting, garlands and festivals, commemorations, anniversaries, Labour days, sacred Mother's Day, and the beloved Führer's birthday, Sophie was swept along by their emotional and patriotic fervour. It was impossible to resist the excitement of burning torches, hymns and the clatter of night marches in the cobbled streets to celebrate the nation's achievements, most notably the abandonment of the Versailles Treaty, high employment, building of homes and autobahns and the defeat of Communism. And so much more!

Mesmerised, the girls vowed to serve the Führer selflessly, the black scarf of the BDM tied solemnly, like a military decoration, the voices singing, 'Flames to heaven,' and at last initiated they chanted as one: '*Wir gehören Dir*'—We are yours. We are yours.

The Führer was partial to long blonde plaits on pubescent girls and young women.

Plaits in various formations were the approved hairstyle. Lotte, Tia and Sophie, the close, blue-eyed blonde friends, wound each plait into coils over their ears like headphones, and wore white shirts and their black knotted scarves and blue skirts, and kept themselves fresh and clean, fresh and clean. Blood was not theirs alone. It must be kept pure for the Fatherland.

But one day there was a local scandal like a threatening ripple on the calm water. Sophie's mother, Gustchen, walked into town from the house by the river Ilmenau with her shopping basket on her arm to buy rye flour. Red swastika banners hung from the Town Hall, obscuring the richly decorated façade of sandstone figures decorated in gold. Despite protests and demonstrations in Hamburg, some people wore Yellow Stars stitched to their coats, most because they had to by law, and others in sympathy with the Jews. You barely noticed these ridiculous things anymore. It all seemed pointless, meaningless.

On impulse Gustchen went to the hairdressers and was seen without an appointment. 'Oh madam, are you sure?'

'Ja, I'm ready for a change. I'm determined to have a

different look. I've seen in the films and newspapers what the women in New York are doing. Please go ahead.'

The hairdresser gave a sharp intake of breath. She had read in the local newspaper how the Führer hated all things American. But what is it to the hairdresser if a woman wanted a Hollywood hair style? She was running a beauty business not a Nazi propaganda office. So, after a vigorous shampoo, out came the scissors and Gustchen's long locks, which she had worn coiled into a bun, fell in long wisps to the floor.

Gustchen, the strait-laced, strict Lutheran mother, caused a minor sensation among the gossips when she returned to the street *Vor dem Roten Tore*, her black hair no longer gathered at the nape of her neck but cropped short with a straight fringe like the flappers of London and Paris. She swung her hips, tossed her head feeling lighter, breaking free in her mind's eye from lies, celebrity worship of bigwigs in the town hall, inflation, degrading poverty, and penny-pinching all of which ground body and soul into an early grave.

Oh curse, she had forgotten to buy the rye flour. That's what happens when you go against the scripture: *'But if a woman has long hair, it is a glory for her: for her hair is given for a covering.'* No such modesty or glory for Gustchen, but a barefaced effrontery to the values of the age from a woman thought to be a devout German mother and wife.

How the neighbours gossiped, smirked with pleasure to find weakness in one so strong. When you allow vanity, you are lost, they said, more than ready to cast the first stone. They blamed her husband Robert for putting fanciful ideas in her head with his talk of emigration to America.

Sophie was both shocked and proud of her mother. She ignored the gossips' united condemnation of Frau Beck, a cover in some cases for admiration and envy but also fear.

'*Gott im Himmel!* Have you seen Gustchen Beck! At her age too. What will Herr Beck say when he sets eyes on her? Mine would give me a beating if I came home like that!'

'That hair-do is not a good message to give a daughter. You must be an example to young girls. We can't all go around like those girls in Berlin. Youth today must be obedient.' They folded their arms in unison as if to consolidate their bond of righteousness. Sophie's mother in turn thought the German fashion for grown men, dressing up, posturing in leather boots, and all that theatrical saluting, and women in white with flowers and hair in braids like milk maids, silly 'backward' nonsense. She wanted to look ahead, be in the vanguard.

After the war, Gustchen, my grandmother, like many of her generation, abandoned her aspirations of modernity having lost the strength to uphold it. It was crushed, stamped underfoot, leaving women no choice but to step back from the iron fist that threatened to destroy them. By 1945, Gustchen's hair had grown iron grey and long again from despair and neglect. Everyone had forgotten the day she had hair styled like a flapper. She made a bunch at the nape just the way it was in 1918, when she met Robert from Dresden visiting cousins in Lüneburg, but her hair no longer had the same lustre.

# Carshalton 1949

In the street where we lived with Ida, a girl called Brenda took charge of me. I may have been marginally older, but I was a perfect candidate for her domination. If I refused to obey, she slapped me on the arm, or administered a Chinese Burn, twisting the skin of my arm in opposite directions. The memory of the stinging pain made me compliant: we played hide-and-seek in large gangs; pestered an old man next door to let us see his stack of hutches full of rabbits in his backyard; begged the boys to have rides on their go-carts, and in gentler moments, played Princesses on the bombsite, which exuded a shattered beauty of wild flowers growing in cracks of broken walls.

We galloped to the corner shop pretending to be horses and stole sherbet and gob stoppers from the counter, slipping them into our elasticated knickers. Back in the street again to swing ourselves around the lamppost with a loop of rope.

'We hanged Hitler up there stuffed with straw when we had our street party,' said Brenda. I had no understanding of such practices. I could only imagine Hitler was some undesirable local, like the cruel rag-and-bone man who beat his starved horse in the street.

Brenda, her earnest face, bright little eyes beneath a tangle of brown hair, taught me all I needed to know to be worthy of her illustrious company, but sometimes her own ignorance left me apprehensive and muddled. She said boys had worms with which to piss against the wall, and that babies popped out of the belly button. This she demonstrated with her hands, making explosive noises full of spittle. However, she did teach me practical things like how to pee outside, crouching in the dirt and clutching my skirt high under my chin so as not to wet myself, and when we were hungry, we ate the new leaves of the hawthorn she called the Bread and Cheese Tree. But I was not to pick dandelions for I would wet the bed and be beaten with the laundry stick. I knew to run and hide in the bomb-site when the rag and bone man came on his cart pulled by his bony horse, its head low as if the blinkers were made of lead, and the bone-man's long, woeful calling *'Bone. Bone. Bone'* frightened me to the core.

Although I was afraid of Brenda too, I had faith in her, certain she would *English* me. She taught me stoicism, to suffer with dignity in silence and not to be a cry-baby. She mapped the social boundaries. She taught me that poverty had two faces: the respectable kind, and the other to be remorselessly shunned. The street kids at the top end of the road were scum and smelled nasty. They tortured cats, hunted rats to eat, and trod on snails. Vi McNally, who worked with my mother in the laundry, was mother to the worst kids in the area. They had no father, which for some reason I could not understand made them shameful. I kept the fact that I had no father a secret from Brenda. The official reason given about Mr. McNally's absence was that he had not returned from the war. At this point I decided the war was another country. People gossiped and said he was more likely to be in prison and that his wife was a slut. Prison was clearly another country, but slut was interesting. 'Ida, what is a slut?' I liked the word. It reminded me of rain falling on the tin roof of the chicken coop or splashing against the window. She stopped her work on the sewing machine and thought for a moment, raising her eyes as if the answer would appear on the far wall. 'Well, it's not a nice word. It means a person who doesn't do the washing up.' I felt satisfied. I knew 'slut' would have something to do with water.

In the street, I now freely abandoned Grandmother's manners. I no longer had to say *Please* and *Thank you* and outside the house, no longer had to keep my mouth shut like a clip-purse because I could speak in the English tongue and its variations. I could mimic Brenda's south London dialect, including glottal stops and long wide vowel sounds, and thanks to Ida and Albert, I increased my English vocabulary indoors. I understood: *a cup of char, bums, bugger off, tea's like gnat's piss, farts* and *cor blimey*. These colourful additions flounced brazenly out of my mouth without shame. In the street, with the fearless Brenda as my friend, I thought I was the *bee's knees* and thoroughly *Englished*. But I was not allowed to speak like children in the street in the presence of my mother. I had to talk 'nicely'. *Nicely* was a form of English my mother recognised as distinct from how Albert and Ida and the children in the street spoke. Although to others my mother had a 'broken' English accent, I rarely noticed it. She pronounced every letter with precision but had problems with *th*, which she transformed to *s* or *z* and since the English language had thousands of s's it did not sound unfamiliar at all, but blended well.

Ida too had her standards, like Brenda. The poor could be divided into the *common* folk, and the more superior deserving. Both groups it seemed shared the same version of the English language. I understood *common* to mean the McNally family, or anything unwanted, worthless, doomed to end up on the rag and bone man's creaky cart of horrors. Ida's judgement about who and who was not common reinforced Brenda's class distinctions and my mother picked up on the word and gave it her own meaning for the unreserved, impolite rabble. A woman was singled out as being the guiltiest if she wore too much makeup and showed too much of her body, which I thought was bold and glamorous. There were fine social distinctions I yet had to learn. As far as I was concerned my mother was right. She dressed modestly and wore a little rouge on her cheeks and soft rose lipstick, but not when she went to work the morning shift at the laundry.

Then when everything in the street was going well, my immune system crashed, and I caught whooping cough, chicken pox and mumps throughout the winter, which temporarily put an end to my English education.

At home with Ida, I occupied the sofa under the window wrapped in a grey blanket with red stitching ungathering, and one of Albert's brown woollen socks permanently tied around my neck in a single knot, although no doubt Albert would have attempted another knot given the chance. All the same, I was perfectly content to stay at home with Ida.

'It's the best cure in the world for coughs and sneezes,' Ida informed my mother who thought the idea of the sock absurd, but said nothing in homage to Ida's English expertise and eccentricity. These Islanders were strangely non-conformist, individual and often very funny. My mother allowed Ida to indulge in her folk-remedies and coaxed me to drink warm milk with fragments of yellow skin floating on top, while Ida worked on the sewing machine. Coming home from the laundry a little earlier than usual my mother would ask Ida for the latest prognosis.

'Her temperature's down. I was a bit worried this morning. She was sick all over herself, but kept bread and lard down later. Didn't you, Fanny Adams?'

They would both look at me expecting something I felt unable to give, so I hid my shy face under the blanket, put out by another name given to me.

'Brenda, and the three McNally boys want to come in and mix with her. They haven't had mumps yet and their mums are keen to get it done. I'll ask them in at the weekend. They're rough. You wouldn't mind, would you?'

'They must all come,' said my mother, backing away. 'They will give poor Susie someone to look and play mit.' My mother could never pronounce *with* so she simply substituted the word with its German counterpart. One other word she could not pronounce was *whether*, so again she popped the German equivalent *ob* into her speech, and as far as I know she was never questioned or corrected.

Unknown to my mother I had plenty to look at. I had a secret mission to find out what *German* was precisely. I had the temerity of a fool to consider myself to be well on the way to becoming fully *Englished*, unlike my mother who seemed to be faltering and lagging in spoken conversation. I fancied the answer to *Germanness* lay among a hoard of secrets in the black suitcase under my bed, which I intended to investigate. Meantime, in a feverish sleep, the sound of the sewing machine shuttle betraying the swift, silent action with a rackety-rack, rackety-rack like the sound of the night train faraway, was a comfort to me and I fancied I was being carried home to Oma.

As I grew stronger, I luxuriated even more in not having to attend school. I liked to watch the muffin man with a tray on his head come up the garden path, ringing a small handbell; I liked it when another man collected the trousers Ida had finished, and shouldered piles of them like a dead man out of the door, while Ida stuffed her wages in her apron pocket and waddled to the scullery to put the kettle on for a cup of tea.

Soon Brenda came to catch mumps clutching a red tin box with the beautiful letters OXO printed on it, full of her jewels to show off. Afterwards she taught me how to play Snap, and I loved her astonishment when in stepped the three untouchable McNally boys, looking as if they had dressed in each other's clothes by mistake, the youngest wearing clothes too big, and the eldest in clothes too small and tight over his thighs carrying a jam-jar with a newspaper lid tied over the top. They stood in a row with their big bellies as if rooted to the floor and I felt so sorry for them. Their mother, the 'sluttish' Vi McNally, pushed them towards me. I'm surprised they could find me half buried among blankets, men's trousers and dried washing on the dilapidated sofa.

'Don't talk to them, Susie,' whispered Brenda sidling up to me. 'Remember what I said.'

It was impossible for me to be talkative with such a painful and swollen face, but Brenda seemed not to have noticed. She made the boys watch as we played cards first, and then allowed them to join in, quite forgetting her prejudices. The eldest boy told us the spiders he had caught in the jam jar would eventually eat each other. He very kindly allowed us to observe them as they climbed the slippery glass before their cannibalistic impulses got the better of them. Common diseases brought us together. When I got better and played in the street again, the McNally boys were often included although Brenda still preferred to feed her prejudice against them.

Meanwhile during convalescing, I enjoyed being left to my own devices as Ida continued her industry. She had taken in extra work for Christmas, making crackers and paper hats so the floor was covered in cardboard boxes full of tissue paper and the air was filled with the sweetness of almonds as Ida opened the pot of grainy glue and set about making tissue crowns in bright colours and letting me help fill the crackers with little whistles and yellow plastic rings.

When I recovered from mumps, Ida took the credit, pointing out that her old-fashioned nursing remedies were the best, and finally when the tin bath was carried through from the scullery and hot water from several saucepans melted the Lux soap suds, I was allowed to wallow in the milky pool by the blazing fire and felt special indeed.

One day, by chance, I made an odd discovery. During my whooping cough convalescence, my chest covered in a thick layer of eucalyptus grease and wearing a wet rag around my head to ensure a high temperature would be kept in check, I managed to drop down from the sofa, shuffle over the floor to the fire and pull out a pile of magazines stuffed behind the coal scuttle. In one, *London Illustrated*, I came across a photograph to which I connected, but I couldn't fathom how it was that it held me in its thrall. It was a shot from Eisenstein's film *The Battleship Potemkin*. I hid the magazine under the sofa so I could look at the photograph several times a day, certain the more I looked the more its mysterious significance would unfold itself and be known to me. My eyes often grew tired examining every aspect of the photograph, but it remained a disturbing conundrum: a line of soldiers stand on the Odessa steps with their rifles high, having fired into an innocent crowd come to welcome home a mutinous ship. Below are fallen bodies strewn all over the steps. At first it looks as if people have shed their clothing, until I noticed a hand, a head and an occupied shoe. In the foreground, a woman in black holds a lifeless child in her arms. In the corner of the frame, unaware of its significance, I gaze at a haunting white umbrella, exposed like a tulip blasted open by the sun, balancing two spokes on an empty step. My eyes brimmed with tears and my heart pounded. The cinema-still printed itself on my mind to haunt me. The chiaroscuro of the ever-diminishing shades of black contrasting with the luminous cloud, and the purity of the white umbrella, was unnerving. I tried to stop myself looking at the picture. But I was out of control. With a heavy heart, my scar raised and irritated I tortured myself with the mystery of the picture.

And then one evening, as the dark dallied, and my mother and Leonard had gone to the pictures, I left Ida and Albert eating winkles from hat pins while they listened to Arthur Askey on the wireless, and crept upstairs to drag the black suitcase from under my bed as if the answer to the black figures lying on the steps in the photograph may be secreted in the suitcase. Lifting the lid, I breathed in its strong interior aroma of stale, cut wood. With hot, nervous hands, I removed an elaborately carved, silver sheath, and discovered a sword, the metallic sound of its withdrawal made the backs of my legs weaken. With difficulty I managed to return the blade to its sheath. I had a notion the sword belonged to my father, and my mother kept it because she loved him.

'Your father is dead.' she had said. 'He died in the war.' Those words often repeated themselves inside my head.

Next to the sword was a scrolled hand flag. The finely turned wooden handle felt warm in my hand compared to the chilly steel. When I unfurled the red flag, it became an elongated red triangle with a white circle like the moon, and inside was a four-legged creature not unlike a spider. I was startled by it. I understood the sword and flag belonged to my father when he was in the war, although I had no notion of what the war was since no one talked about it except to refer to the time *before the war, during the war*, and *after the war* as if they were different places or seasons to which we might return.

Under layers of brown paper were photographs of home. There was one of a girl, whom I presumed was my mother as a child with long plaits down to her thighs, standing by a gate with the sun in her eyes beside her older brother, my Uncle Erich. It was Uncle Erich's lederhosen that made him appear different to the boys I knew. In another photo, there was a soldier, his upper lip misshapen and eyes full of sadness and I realised that this was a photograph of Uncle Erich as a grown man and all the light had gone from his eyes. I looked at the photos for an awfully long time until the darkness of the bedroom claimed them. I tried to imagine what happened after the photo had been taken. Did Uncle Erich come to life, rise and stroll outside in the brilliant sunshine? Maybe he took the arm of his *Liebchen*, his darling, to walk along the avenue before he was sent back to the place of war? I found nothing to explain why the disclosure of my German self might result in danger, opprobrium and shame, a sense instilled into me by Grandmother. Keeping the lid of the suitcase open, I curled inside for comfort longing once more for home and then I drifted off to sleep for a while, but on waking, I was cramped and shivering.

The following morning, while I got dressed, I dared ask my mother a question. She was combing her hair at the dressing table with her back to me.

'Mama, do you have photos of my father?' Her back stiffened. She put down her hairbrush and remained still. Silence.

'No, Susie,' she said eventually, with her back to me, 'I had to burn them.'

Our first and last Christmas with Ida began with Albert standing on a chair putting up paper chains from a corner of the room to another and hooking an enormous green paper bell from the central light shade. Ida killed one of her clucking hens by wringing its neck with one deft movement. She plucked its feathers over an empty pillowcase in the scullery. The plucking made tiny tearing noises: pock, pock, and seemed to come from the chicken's mouth, its neck hanging limply down Ida's leg. I turned away, shocked by her barbarity.

Ida's daughter Barbara, who had taken a dislike to me, arrived and had the temerity to pull my thumb out of my mouth, pressing me against the landing wall. It was she who suggested I should have my thumb painted with a bitter brown liquid to stop me sucking it. Barbara's boyfriend, Colin, arrived next. I watched him on the sofa as he cracked walnut shells between his rotting teeth and fed me pieces from his mouth, which I took out of politeness. A man of few words, he winked at everyone. I believed this to be an involuntary tick. The creamy taste of walnut mixed with a metallic taste of the air. Smoke billowed into the room from the damp coals. Albert knelt on the cold linoleum.

'I'll get this blasted fire going, if it's the last thing I blinking do,' he cursed.

I am a bad child. I don't like my Christmas presents. I have a naked plastic doll from Ida and a metal spinning top. First thing, Leonard sits on the floor, showing me how to spin it into a frenzy while I crunch shelled walnut pieces from Colin's mouth. I have no interest in the noisy spinning top, and once Leonard has completed his demonstration, I leave it alone on the floor. I'm disappointed I don't have a picture story book, or pencils and paper.

My mother sits close, wearing her best pinafore dress with the little leather seahorse brooch on the shoulder strap, sewing calmly while Barbara talks about hair-sets and permanent waves, but I know my mother isn't calm. She blinks back tears and when she pricks her finger, I catch sight of a tiny globe of blood swelling into a trickle. She sucks her finger so there's blood on her lip. We are both cast under a spell, unable to speak, watchful as animals.

In the evening, my head is a mass of small explosions. Albert is swaying and drinking; his nose lumpy and red and shiny with sweat, and his hair plastered down with grease. Leonard smokes cigarette after cigarette, beer glass in hand. My mother has gone to lie down. I survive under the table partly hidden by the red chenille tablecloth. The popular song 'Put Another Nickel In' pounds from the wireless. Ida in her new fluffy slippers dances with Albert. The floor reverberates like the skin of a drum. Leonard pulls Barbara from her chair to dance. She has a new permanent wave, and her face looks burnt around the edges where the hairnet dug in. He swings her round and round until she cries out to stop, she feels dizzy, clutching at her white blouse. She falls on Leonard's lap as he reaches out to catch her, and she leans over to kiss Colin. All three tussle and laugh.

Unseen, I crawl up the stairs in need of restitution. I know something isn't right. The day has made me miserable. At school, Miss Gibbons said Christmas is a happy time because it is Baby Jesus's birthday and the Shepherds and Three Kings, guided by a star, come to see him in the stable bearing gifts. But our day bore no relation to the story.

I have a strange feeling something had been stolen from me as I undress. I keep my vest and knickers on under my nightdress and slide in beside my mother. She folds her arm over my waist and lifts the blanket to cover my shoulders. I think about Grandmother at The Horseshoe, who would not like the noise downstairs and would storm into the house, clap her hands and put a stop to it. And then I see my other grandmother, Oma, faraway in another land, sitting at the kitchen table, her hand smoothing the tablecloth over and over. I have never remembered that before.

After leaving Ida and Albert, we became urban nomads, packing our belongings, squashing them in the black suitcase, moving every few months. My mother tried but could not settle. We were like migratory birds; a *Wandervögel* movement of our own. After a few months, she became restless again and searched for an excuse to move on: 'Len. I want to go. I don't like it here. It is too quiet, too dirty, too noisy, too far, too near, too cold; the beds are too soft, too hard...'

Leonard didn't understand that part of the problem was my mother's *Heimweh*—homesickness—so that nowhere gave her peace to stop her heart's longing. The landladies, she said, troubled her. They were convivial until their hospitality wore thin and they decided to revise the house rules: no visitors, pets, use of the garden for drying washing, use of the kitchen, only between 5pm-6pm, and no baths at weekends. It was as if taking in foreign lodgers was a special dispensation but under constant revision.

My mother continued to bear the hostility shown by the women workers at the laundry. It was forbidding, darkened by mucky steam. The hammering of industrial washing machines, the steam presses hissing and spewing hot air that dried and clogged the eye of workers with a grit substance, brought my mother, like many of the women, to her lowest point.

After months on the back-breaking steam press, my mother ran away and wept in the works' lavatory. The postman did not bring letters from home, despite the parcels of warm clothing she had sent to her parents with the few pennies she could save each week.

It was the 'slut' Vi McNally who comforted her, and offered us a bed for the night when Albert decided he didn't want Nazis in his house after all, and Ida skulked in the scullery, sniffing and busying herself with a bag of chicken feathers refilling her depleted pillows.

The row started on a Saturday night after Albert had drunk too much beer and accused Leonard of cheating at cards. Leonard pleaded innocent as a gentleman of honour, and as someone who had seen the war. Albert in frustration vented his anger on me kicking my legs under the table with his knotted boots. I cried out and emerged frightened. 'What's she doing still up?' he shouted. When my mother rose from the table, tut tutted and mumbled something under her breath in German drawing me protectively towards her, Albert rose in retaliation, thumped the table with both fists, and said we had no right living in his house with airs and graces. We should be ashamed of ourselves.

'You! You in particular. Where is your shame?' He stabbed his finger in the air at my mother.

'Please, don't speak to my wife like that.' Leonard rose from the table.

'You call yourself a gentleman and try to cheat me out of my due,' Albert bawled, ignoring the issue of my mother.

'Well, if you must,' said Leonard, 'for the sake of peace and quiet, have the money.' Leonard threw down a ten-shilling note on the table.

'Don't you bloody patronize me. Who do you think you are? We know about things in this house, bringing shame on us. Ida nearly had a heart attack when she saw that stuff.'

'What are you talking about? What's going on?' Leonard looked first at my mother, and then at Albert, his mouth thrust forward, his hands knitted together.

'We've had enough. We don't want people like you in our house. When I think everything Ida's done for you. You can pack your bags and get out.'

I looked to Ida. Ida would save us, but Ida sat slumped, her arms hanging loosely at her sides, her eyes on the fallen cards on the table.

'Take no notice, darling. It's the drink talking,' said Leonard by way of comfort to my mother.

Upstairs my mother packed the black suitcase. I watched her as I knelt on her bed and turned my eyes to the dressing table mirror where I saw her distress doubly reenacted. I braced for another night flight with the accompanying uncertainty and fear. Leonard heaved the black suitcase down the stairs letting it fall on each step with a thud, while my mother firmly took my hand as if she thought I might defect and swung me down so that my feet barely touched the stairs, and we were out of the door. I managed to glance at Albert, his back to the room, his arm resting against the mantlepiece staring into the cold fireplace. His knots should have warned me he was not to be trusted. There were no cuddles or kisses from my loving, adorable Ida. No waves or goodbyes. She busied herself in the kitchen, amber chicken feathers falling on the floor, eyes down. I never saw her again.

Brenda would have been appalled to learn we spent the night down the bad end of the street in the house of the stinky kids. The night of our eviction, I lay with the three McNally boys in a double bed with no bed linen, no pillows, just a filth encrusted army coat flung over us in a room of bare floorboards and bare windows, and two *Tizer* bottles Vi McNally kindly filled with scalding water and placed at the foot of the bed, far too hot to touch with our bare feet. But how I loved the company; the tickling and laughing until we lay fully dressed, exhausted, huddled under the old coat. How I relished the warmth and comfort of their loud, regular breathing and little bodies nestled close to mine as they slept. But guilt pricked, deflating the pleasure of the boys' company. The McNally family had nothing, the children fatherless, and probably hungry, but Vi took us in that night and gave us shelter, welcoming us into her home. I had a strong belief I was to blame for the eviction. It was because I had stayed up late and hid under the table that lead to the quarrel at Ida's. Also, the discovery of the sword and flag inside the black suitcase, and the fallen white umbrella on the Odessa steps, seemed to be inexplicably linked to Albert's determination to send us packing. Ida hurt me. If only she had helped. If only I had been in bed fast asleep, then Albert would not have been cross and kicked me under the table, and we would still be living with Ida. I harboured this guilt for a long time, well into adulthood.

My mother said I must never look at the moon through

glass. But I did several times. The moon commanded it, crackling with a mesmerizing light, but I had to bear the consequences. When we left the McNally's, Leonard advocated a fresh start. We would move from Carshalton to Putney. He told my mother Putney had a Heath and an impressive history. The Heath was once a leisure playground for the rich to race their horses and enjoy the sport of hawking. Queen Elizabeth I frequently progressed to visit friends in Putney village, and Thomas Cromwell, the chief minister to Henry VIII, was born there, as well as Clement Attlee. Mary Shelley, and the poet Swinburne had also resided there. So, we were to live among illustrious ghosts in a town that grew up from a small fishing village a few miles from the city of London. Wouldn't that be amazing? Surely that would make my mother happy again.

If that were not enough to persuade her, Putney Hill had beautiful Victorian houses with splendid trees and double drives with tall gates, and Upper Richmond Road was lined with white-pillared Georgian houses. Down by the river, there were the boathouses, and a park and swans, and pleasure boats, and hunched at the foot of Putney Bridge St. Mary's church where, it was said, Samuel Pepys had visited, dismayed by the lack of pretty schoolgirls to please his eye. So, it is not surprising my mother and I liked the sound of Putney. There were no bomb craters, or laundries, but three cinemas and attractive shops; a library in Boots stacked with romance novels, and a delectable cake and chocolate shop called Zeeta's. My mother also liked the avenues lined with a profusion of cherry trees and the houses had grand fronts and back gardens wide as orchards. Leonard hoped Putney would cure her homesickness, and as luck had it, he found an unfurnished, one-bedroom attic flat in a large Victorian house on Putney Hill next door to a more Gothic mansion with turrets and towers. It was expensive, but he wanted to make my mother happy. Maybe, he thought, it had been a mistake to have left Germany. He could have remained in the army. But it was too late now.

And so it was that we left Surrey, the hunting ground of kings; the-once-upon-a-time-land of flower fields: of peppermint and lavender, poppies and mint and wormwood, long before the houses smothered all the flowers, and disturbed the graves and the elms were felled. We turned our optimistic faces to the most northern aspect of the territory to the ancient fishing settlement of Putney on the Thames, but sadly no longer providing eels and winkles in the polluted waters.

I remember how we climbed the four flights of stairs to the top floor flat and tasted the flavour of its cupboard air and saw the clouds and tops of horse-chestnut trees through the high windows.

'Ah,' says my mother, '*our* front door!' She opens and closes it smiling. Leonard stands back leaning against the kitchen door jamb, smoking. This is the answer he thinks to himself. He looks relieved she is happy at last. But there is something he does not know; the danger he has brought us. But first, unaware, they buy furniture from a second-hand shop in Lower Richmond Road, and I have an iron bed in the corner with a sagging mattress. I curl up in the hole under the slanting ceiling and wait.

Once again there is an air of foreboding because I had disobeyed my mother and couldn't help but stare at the sun-scalded moon through attic window. Early on, I felt the same as before. Then slowly, something happened to me out of my control. While I slept something malignant took root. I suffered badly with headaches. Now as my mother relished her new life, and hope brought light to her blue eyes, I was inflicted with the doldrums. I became morose and irritable, showed only my most mulish face at home and at school, that dark, oppressive Victorian building in Hotham Road. I elected to become mute again. We didn't know anyone in Putney, and I wanted to go back to Ida's house. And even further back to Dolly's and Grandmother's, and then over the sea to a place I had forgotten but rested like sediment in my honey-combed bones. I imagined myself walking backwards and sailing on a boat in retreat, the island of chalk cliffs growing smaller and smaller in the distance as if set in the clouds, and even the train retreating across the slake flatlands to stop at the little town where we'd lived, spitting fire from its turrets. Only then could I walk forwards again into the countryside to find my grandparents' house on the edge of the pine forest.

Luckily, the teacher in my new Putney school with her squinting, suspicious eyes always insisted on silence, so I knew it was what she preferred. She did not notice that I had a wintering dormouse for a tongue. I remained inside my head looking out of its two little windows. In poured the bright sky, the sunshine, the harsh wind, the white snow, the ice-cold air settling on the eyeball, the quiet breath of grass. I became a receptacle for all things and stored them in my treasure house. This was the first stage of my awful transformation.

My mother was upset and worried I might be regressing. 'Talk to me Susie!' she said. We were at odds; dangerously close to becoming enemies. She sent me to bed because I had refused to eat my tea. She coaxed me to drink pints of water. I thought badly of her. I thought she wanted to drown me and douse my fiery spirit. I grew angry. But I couldn't hurt her. I loved her. Still I was stubborn, and wanted to win. I couldn't understand what was happening to me. I refused to do anything my mother commanded. I was outside myself, lost. I paid no attention when Leonard told me to hurry and get dressed for school so he wouldn't miss his train to Fenchurch Street. He was responsible for taking me down Putney Hill and crossing Upper Richmond Road where we parted ways, he to East Putney Station, and I along Upper Richmond Road, until I reached Hotham Road. I held his hand down the hill because he insisted, and we walked together. We never spoke. Day after day our little routine was performed in silence, which suited me. In fact, if Leonard had spoken, I would have probably felt too shocked to answer. But I was getting used to him now and didn't mind that he was locked in his own thoughts. It was understandable. I grew to love his hand. It was soft, like a lady's but broad and stronger. I loved to feel the heat inside it.

But one morning as Leonard prepared for work, I found myself in a mental loop, trapped inside a rogue circuitry. My school beret was the problem. It refused to sit on my head the right way. I put it on, took it off. I couldn't stop this repeated action, determined to acquire perfection, becoming more and more distressed, not so much with failure but with my ridiculous need for perfection. In my anxiety to perch it perfectly, although I wasn't quite sure what the perfect way was, I toppled from a chair, and saving myself, knocked down a mirror I had propped up on the windowsill. It fell to the bare floor with a crash and broke.

Leonard lost his patience. He picked me up, threw me down on the sofa and gave me a good hiding. Because my mother had already set off for work, and I had taken a vow of silence, I didn't utter a sound. My thigh hurt and my bottom burned, but what hurt more was the act—not the pain but the humiliation and shock that Leonard had exercised force as an unfair advantage. Afterwards he took up the beret from the floor, gave a good shake to free it from glass, and stretched it over my head, and virtually over my eyes so I could barely see. He dragged me down Putney Hill, my feet deliberately stumbling in shock and defiance. His silence, once mysterious and full of integrity, I took as a weapon against me. I lost trust in him, and it was never restored.

Unaware of the reasons for the morning drama, my mother mourned the mirror. 'Seven years of bad luck, Susie!' she said, when I had to confess after school. Something hard in me abjured sentiment because the mirror itself had no other significance except as an object of my own badness. Not surprising then, that my mother became afraid of everything that might compound our misfortune. To ward off evil, counteracting the curse of the broken mirror, I was subjected to a different set of rules. No new shoes on the table. No open umbrella inside the flat. She pulled me away from the window to stop me looking at the thin curl of moon through glass. She cried because she didn't know how to make me better and then I cried, but I couldn't explain what I felt. There was a malevolent presence among us. It was cold-blooded and savage. Invisible, it mocked and flaunted its power. It squeezed out kindness and understanding so all that was left were bitter seeds planted by the light of the moon in my fertile imagination. And it all got worse.

In the evenings I could hear my mother and Leonard quarrelling. She raised her voice, and he mumbled low and deep. On and on and on. I tiptoed to the bedroom door and listened hoping I could find out what was happening to us.

'There's no need for you to do that kind of work. I've told you before. I don't want you to work in a place like that laundry.'

'I clean Len. The job's not far, near Putney Heath. Just for the morning. Susie is at school. Mary in the flat downstairs told me the lady needs someone. It is easy. Just a little work in the house.'

'They want a charlady. They will be pleasant at first and then make you work like a slave. No. No. There's no need.' Leonard sounded exasperated and resolute. I heard a chair scraping the floor. Then silence. The silence was more unsettling than the evening arguments. Leonard was unable to persuade my mother to give up her cleaning job.

Night after night, an incubus took possession of my mother. Across the room I could see its heavy shape covering her body, weighing her down. I heard her quiet groan of protest. She wanted to be left alone. She struggled, making little noises in her throat, but the incubus sat on her like a heavy black rock.

The nocturnal visitations played havoc with our health. I put my hands over my ears so I couldn't hear the unearthly sounds in the dark. During the weekend mornings my mother stayed late in bed with hollow pools under her eyes. During the week, I fell asleep at school. I often dreamt of Ida. The softness of her lap. Her firm grip pulling me towards her. Ida going up the path to the chickens. Ida at the sewing machine. Ida singing along with the wireless. I heard Leonard say it was all Ida's fault for snooping in our bedroom when we lodged with her. It was none of her business to rummage in my mother's black suitcase. I tried to think of its contents and what Ida might have found that made us bad. Maybe it was the sword of God the Father because only recently my mother was forced to part with it. Leonard said it was too dangerous.

'And you must throw the flag onto the fire together with the photos. It's the uniforms which upset people. You'll be asking for trouble if you don't.'

But my mother could not throw the photograph of her brother into the flames even though he's wearing a soldier's uniform. She could not throw the flag on the fire either and locked everything up in the black suitcase with a few remaining photos. But she did hand over my Father's sword to Leonard; he never said what he intended to do with it.

Then my mother slipped out into the pouring rain. From the attic bedroom window, I watched the rain make lace patterns on the window, and felt sad for my mother walking out alone. I wanted to be with her, to hold her hand. But I knew she would come back. I saw the black suitcase on top of the wardrobe, so I knew I was safe. She would never leave without it.

In Hotham Road Infants' School, I was *aus in der Fremde*—in a foreign land—unable to engage with classroom life, I was a lonely outsider. I had one ambition, which kept me breathing. That was to learn to read, but day after day, the means eluded me. Shortly after my arrival I was assessed as a 'backward' child and joined others in the same predicament forming a 'retarded' group left to amuse itself silently with crayons, while the clever girls flaunted their reading and writing abilities, and looked down on us, some with pity and some with contempt. In the playground they tormented us with jibes: *stinky, bum-face, stupid, bogies* and excluded us from their games, left to huddle close outside the toilets.

The boys didn't care about us. They mechanised their bodies at every given opportunity, zooming around the playground pretending to be aeroplanes, armoured cars, tanks, arms outstretched or in appropriate shapes for attack. They liked to hi-jack an unsuspecting girl, and help themselves to a piggyback ride, their forearm pressing down on her windpipe, legs gripped at the waist, the other arm whipping down on her backside to urge the beast on. Mostly the girls took sanctuary on a long bench in the covered way grooming each other's hair, swapping butterfly hairgrips and satin-coloured ribbons I longed to own. They stared away intruders and undesirables while they played cat's cradle and sometimes a game called Shows with avid performers singing and dancing along the wooden bench. I had no strategy for acceptance, but I stubbornly hovered on the edge of their group for protection from the savage boys.

By far the most popular sport was called *War*. At last, I discovered the meaning of the word. It was all a game. The Germans and the English lined up on opposite sides of the playground and on the command of 'Charge!' their battle cries rent the air and the English rushed forth to engage with the enemy and fight to their deaths. Any means of inflicting death was acceptable. They kicked, stabbed, punched, shot with two fingers, tripped and slapped and pulled hair. But all manner of deaths was invalid without the pronouncement, 'You're dead!' Some of the dead miraculously regained life, 'No, I'm not dead. I'm just wounded,' when a real fight ensued to the bitter end.

I watched apprehensively but never took part until one day the Commander, a sturdy cumbersome boy with a gravelly voice noticed the severe shortage of Germans and pointed at me. 'You've gotta be a German,' he ordered, grabbing me by the arm. 'Cus we ain't got enough.' He dragged me to the wall where a line of skinny children stood dejectedly, cursed to have been chosen, but without the will to oppose him.

But I had to find my voice. I had to break my silence. I could not be a German. I had promised my mother to deny any suggestion of being German. First I screamed to test out my rusty vocal cords.

'No,' I said croaking afterwards, 'No! Leave me alone. Get off me!' I wrestled with him, but he was strong.

Then I spat out: 'No, I'm not a German. I don't want to be. Never!' It was the only way. I disguised the truth with lies. I wriggled from his hold and ran off to join the English. I was surprised by my own daring and passion.

But I had defied the bully who had wanted to relegate me to the defeated tribe. I felt the hot surge of triumph and indignation, mingled with a confusing consternation. I was not myself. I was an interloper, a fraud. I would be punished sooner or later. Suddenly, it came to me. I was not truly *Englished*. I was homesick but wanted to be like everyone else. But I didn't belong. I couldn't understand why my efforts didn't work. Minutes later, I tried to enjoy the defiant song the waiting English sang with gusto feeling sorry for the deathly enemy without balls: '*Hitler has only got one ball. Goring has two but very small. Himmler is somewhat similar. But poor old Goebbels has no balls at all.*' I obeyed the order to charge and joined in with the long battle cry. From then on, in a fierce attempt to hide my true origins, every playtime I killed as many Germans as I could lay my hands on, believing this was one sure way of receiving acceptance, afraid what might happen to me if anyone found out who I really was.

On Sunday evenings, in desperation my mother took me with her to the Methodist Church Hall where blue cloth pockets for the hymn books sagged on the backs of wooden chairs. She sang hymns and prayed to God that she would receive letters from Germany. She continued to send my Oma and Opa new clothes and ground coffee from the little narrow coffee shop squeezed between Zeeta's and Putney Station. But on the cold nights when we left the hall and braced ourselves to breathe in and swallow the bitter, swirling fog, I sensed the futility of our attendance. I had an idea that people from yesterday were gone forever and survived only in our memory. I squeezed my mother's hand to comfort her. In recognition of my sign, she squeezed mine in return, and we walked heads down, into the sulphureous fog.

After months, and still no letters from Germany, my mother saw sense. She became impatient and abandoned her visits to the unheated Methodist Hall, turning to Hollywood for respite. Saturday afternoon became taken up with cinema visits. I remember beggars wearing threadbare overcoats crouched on the pavements in Putney High Street, the strong fishy smell mingling with the earthy, fetid wafts rising up from the Thames. Outside the Regal, we stopped to fathom the narrative created by a strip of stills of films showing that afternoon. Inside we snuggled in our black shiny seats, their red, velvet patina long worn away. We basked in the dark pleasure of forgetting and seeing. Leonard rarely came to the cinema with us. On Saturdays he watched live football or cricket and spent late afternoons dutifully visiting his parents at The Horseshoe, where my mother and I were not welcome.

My mother liked films depicting couples thwarted in love, but who ended with their final union. This usually entailed singing and dancing right through the credits. My mother's favourite films stars were Doris Day, Margaret Lockwood, Humphrey Bogart, Cary Grant, Richard Widmark, and Ingrid Bergman.

Pathe News was heralded by a crowing cockerel and followed by a cultivated voice-over, while black and white images flashed up on the screen: soldiers marching in a land called Korea; soldiers with fixed bayonets aimed at men huddled in a ditch. Flick to men carrying wounded men over their shoulders. Flick to submarines surfacing and warships steaming towards land, guns swivelling. I heard the words: *Communists, American Marines*, and *Our Chaps*, but I was never entirely sure who the good men were, and who the bad. The B film was invariably in black and white, too, with frequent gun battles in dark alleys, and blondes standing at bars, alluring, lonely and dangerous. Sometimes, we watched the endless slaughter of Red Indians, or a war film might be showing with clean-cut soldiers stabbing slow-witted Germans in the neck.

I learned to hate the *Dummkopf* (slow witted, stupid) German soldiers when I watched these films. They never played fair and did nasty things such as locking people in barns and setting them on fire, ignoring their pleas and screams, or spiking puppies on the end of their bayonets. Someone ought to have been shouting in protest through the thick haze of cigarette smoke, or pelting the screen with ice-cream spoons, shaking their fists at the brutes on screen. But the audience puffed on cigarettes or watched impassively, waiting for the main film. But the Germans made me angry. My mother invariably left the cinema in a dark mood after seeing the war films she hadn't intended to watch. I wanted to ask what made the Germans so different to the fair-minded English fighters. But my mother marched along, her eyes fixed in the distance while I skipped, ran and leapt in varying degrees to keep up with her.

Deeply unsettled by these post-war propaganda films and the kitsch American musicals, their garish technicolour depicting a surfeit of wealth and luxury followed by schmaltz endings and shrimp-coloured sunsets, we left the Regal, dissatisfied and hollow. I was beginning to understand that we were members of a barbaric race, the image of which conflicted with the knowledge I had of my gentle, patient mother. It was becoming all too clear why I must always denounce the German people. We would shuffle our way out of the cinema aisle often drained, squinting into the diffused light of the cloudy summer evenings, making our silent way up Putney Hill as the Thames coursed its way to the sea, and coal tugs chugged upstream on tides of black slime towards Battersea power station.

Towards the end of my sixth year, we moved out of the perniciously haunted flat and to Mrs. Bailey's lodging house, next to a row of noisy boathouses on the banks of the river Thames. It was a dank, terraced house presiding over both the river and leafy Bishop's Park adjacent to the Fulham bankside.

Mrs. Bailey liked to live in the dark. The curtains were rarely opened, and the windows were draped in thick nets yellowing with age and acrid coal smog. Our eyes soon grew accustomed to the darkness, but when we came into the hall from a bright day outside, we were rendered sightless for some seconds and had to grope along the wall to reach the parlour, already made dark by a permanently wet wall of the boathouse next door directly opposite the grimy window. And leaving the house had the reverse effect; the light stabbed our eyes and made us squint all along the embankment. Even the oily, multicoloured river rolling by in the sunshine, could send your head into a spin of whizzing stars.

The house, as far as I could tell, was steeped in various magics for, as luck would have it, Mrs. Bailey dabbled in the occult. Fortunately, with Mrs. Bailey in control, my experiences here were different to the evil spirits causing havoc in the attic flat. Since neither the Church nor Hollywood could ease our troubles, maybe our new landlady's talents put to good use might enable my mother and I to exorcise our demons.

Mrs. Bailey was tall, erect and stately. During her waking hours, she wore a dark brown hat like an upturned flowerpot. Consequently, you were never sure if she were about to go *out*, or she had just come *in*. Her old-fashioned outfits, more suited to a country lady—her buttoned-up-to-the-neck blouses, dark brown cardigan, knife-pleated skirts and 1920s brogues, belied her covert powers. Without her hat, she looked incomplete, her hair cut in a short bob, with a wispy fringe. The hat gave her, in my eyes, a certain authorial dignity and gravitas as a wise woman to replace Grandmother, although as it turned out her powers were different to Grandmother's who had insisted on obedience. The reason I took to Mrs. Bailey may have been partly intuition and partly because she never made an issue of the fact I was a self-elected mute, reassuring my mother I would speak by the time she had finished with me. I didn't receive this as a threat, but as an act of confidence in her power to fulfil her ambition. I sensed she was curative and her graceful manner earned her trust reminding me so much of Auntie Dolly. I later overheard Leonard say Mrs. Bailey was with the fairies. This increased my admiration; we were in the presence of a remarkable lady who could converse with a whole population of tiny, winged invisibles and I couldn't wait to make their acquaintance. Above all, Mrs. Bailey had impeccable manners, and treated me with the same respect and regard as she would adults. My admiration for her meant I barely noticed in the gloaming of her house that most surfaces were caked in layers of dust mixed with soot from decades of lighting fires and clogged up chimneys and that downstairs was vermin infested. The upstairs rooms were rented out to a married couple whom I never set eyes upon. Only occasionally one might hear a soft footfall across the ceiling.

Downstairs, where we lodged with Mrs. Bailey, the rooms were often damp and cold having been subjected to numerous floods. The cunning old Thames frequently seeped underneath the front door, and at times when the tide was in and gathering momentum, it swilled and sloshed along the hallway in search of escape into the backyard. Mrs. Bailey, unperturbed, and even less that rats elected to remain in the house after the flood, reassured my mother there was nothing to worry about.

'The river rats are quite different to the awful sewer rats. I can certainly tell the difference. I would never endure the sewer rats in the house, believe you me. But the water rats seem more blessed by nature and always return to the river when the tide goes out.'

Mrs. Bailey, speaking in a cut-glass accent, relishing the letter 't', had such certainty in her tone no one would dare contradict, despite the fact we might have some serious misgivings.

'Ach, so...' said my mother looking around the floor when she and Mrs. Bailey convened in the parlour. I mused that an English person would have been more likely to have responded with a doubtful: 'Oh, I see…' Because I *knew* for sure the water rats did *not* always return to the river. For a start, you could smell them. The smell is distinctive but hard to describe. If mud could go sour, that's how rats smell. I often felt rats run across my back at night and could hear scurrying and scratching in the scullery. I remember Mrs. Bailey picking out droppings from the sugar bowl and cupping them in her hand like seeds, examining them individually.

'Mmm. I think these are without doubt mice droppings because they are rather small and varied in shape.' She would then pour a few into my palm to observe and share her findings with me. I would look suitably experienced and pretend to examine the dark matter but was unable to confirm or dispute her conclusion.

Untroubled by animal invaders, she was most caring and considerate towards my mother whom she knew intuitively was both vulnerable and stricken by depression and homesickness. At the parlour table with her hat on, of course, increasing her wizardry, she would read my mother's palm as well as the teacups, and soothe my mother with predictions of prosperity and joy affirmed by the Ouija board, the glass tumbler gliding under my mother's touch to spell out replies to her enquiries about her parents. A spirit called Master spelled out that her parents were well and had received all her parcels. This brought much relief to my mother. You could see her face relax. When I held out my small palm to be read, Mrs. Bailey squinted at the feint lines and said, 'Your life will be cut short but there's plenty of time for you to make your mark.' I believed the lines in one's palm were scored into the skin by experience so my foreshortened life was no bother to me; I could add years to a life by using my hands. The tea-leaf readings were Mrs. Bailey's daytime favourites, staring down the narrow cups to search for a narrative.

'There is a man far away who calls for you,' said Mrs. Bailey, lifting her head to catch my mother's expression for clues. I leant on the table with my head in my hands hoping this would be the beginning of a story.

My mother sat bolt upright, and Mrs. Bailey sucked in the gloom and returned to peer into the cup for a more prolonged reading of the tea leaves. 'The more you look, the more you see,' said Mrs. Bailey, a piece of wisdom I tucked away for future use.

After a while she continued with renewed interest. 'One day you might meet this man again. Maybe... ah yes... maybe you will hear from him. But not yet. He is so distant. When you meet again, he will be almost a stranger to you. Look, see here. See that stick-like piece. That means a stranger.'

'Is that my father? Is it an old man you see?' My mother tilted her head to try to catch a glimpse of the tea leaves in the bottom of her cup.

'Ah now, let me see,' said Mrs. Bailey turning the cup this way and then the other. 'I'm uncertain. Maybe later we could contact the spirit Master and find out more.'

'Ah,' sighed my mother, looking wistful and longing for news from home.

I offered Mrs. Bailey my teacup, hoping she would read my good fortune in the dregs.

'No, dear. You are too young. You haven't any history yet.' I stared into my cup and thought the clumps of tea leaves at the bottom looked just as plentiful as my mother's and puzzled over the meaning of history and wondered where or when I could get some.

After the tea readings, I was often allowed to enter Mrs. Bailey's dusky bedroom where I was tempted by crystallised sugar mice from a stash of confectionery in her capacious chest of drawers. The white sugar mice lay row upon row on trays lined with tissue paper, and they glowed with a disturbing transparency emphasizing their black eyes, like fragments of mutilated bits of houseflies locked in their sockets. I withdrew my hand and focussed my attention on another tray.

'Mmm. I thought you would choose a pink one again,' Mrs. Bailey would say knowingly. 'Now you have to kiss my hand to say thank you. Then curtsey.'

Dutifully, I would do as she commanded. It was a fair exchange. I owed it to her. I would have kissed her feet if asked. But the mice feast did not entice me to speak if that was her plan. In her light-starved bedroom, I entered her private world, at ease on her soft, unmade bed, where conspiratorially we tore off the heads of sugar mice with one bite.

The pleasure of these afternoon soirées, unfortunately, was sullied by a large wooden crucifix on the wall, with a man nailed to it. I kept my eyes down to bed level. Eventually, I suffered toothache in one of my molars, which I had to have extracted by gas, taking the edge off my craving for sweetness. However, Mrs. Bailey's thoughtfulness and willingness to help us, were sweet enough for me.

On Saturday nights, when the séance session was over

in the parlour where I slept on an old horsehair chaise longue in the corner, Leonard or my mother would light the little paraffin lamp, its single flame releasing a thin wisp of pungent smoke before it swelled and steadied. If by chance I woke scared in the night by the scavenging rats, the ashes in the grate grown cold, it was my little oasis of light and comfort in the dark swamp.

That summer, I was let loose on the river slipways, the mud-banks, and in the park. Sometimes I curled up in the moored fishing boats beside coils of warm rope, the sun pouring onto my head, and I sailed away with the clouds, taking with me everything I claimed as my own for a new kingdom much as I had done in Auntie Dolly's garden.

The gliding swans, the quarrelsome mallards, the tugboats loaded with coal and timber, the steamers, the river police patrols, and the pleasure boats on their way to Barnes; the fallen moon, the sun and stars, shattered to smithereens of sparkling gold and silver, all mine to scoop up like the wood shavings ankle deep in the boat houses and the almond blossom in the park.

And I was happy, free to wander, free to swing in the park with other children, to beg rides on bikes, to explore the mud flats and look at picture books I took with me to study in the belly of a moored boat, nestling down under the unchanging sky.

Then once a year, on Boat Race Day, curtains were swept aside, up would go the sash windows in the front room, kept locked for best occasions, the net curtains tied back with ribbon and the stale, fusty air ousted by the crisp breeze wafting up from the river. Bright light poured in, startling the furniture; the table, laid with best china, cupcakes and Chelsea buns, looked proud with its white lace tablecloth. And from the privileged window, we watched the throng pass by and waved our paper flags, invariably dark blue, as the world poured inside; the chattering and cheering, the tooting of horns, the clug-clug-clug of the oars grinding in their sockets and the cries of street sellers filled the room.

And sometimes in the evenings, after a hard day in the park on the swing or on the riverbank, my arms entwined around the embankment railings, my legs dangling almost touching the water, I gazed into Lethe's murk, flotsam gathering in a stream of scum: rags, swirls of sawdust, splintered planks of wood, brown paper bags, carrion and a baby's shoe bobbing downstream. And I took possession of everything that leapt into my eyes like a hoarder with a deluded entitlement.

One morning, I achieved my one ambition. It was a cataclysmic revelation that occurred unexpectedly in the classroom. I opened the page of my reading book ready to face the indecipherable marks on the page and skim the cryptic lines of print in despair and frustration. But on this day, when the sun banged hotly against the high window, and the smell of sour milk clung to our clothes, and our empty, acidic stomachs gurgled, I found by chance the decoding key. I had an idea Mrs. Bailey's magic might have had something to do with its arrival.

It slipped easily into the lock and turned with a pregnant flourish, that exhilarating shot of a bolt springing back and the door opening into another world.

I read the story of *Chicken Lichen* silently in my head. The code had been cracked miraculously without forewarning. An acorn had fallen on my head just as it had on Chicken Lichen's, but mine was a golden acorn. All my straining efforts had paid off. My tongue itched at its root, wagged to be free.

No longer would I be beaten on my hands with a wooden ruler for failing to sing the verses of *O little town of Bethlehem* written on the board, and no longer would I have to pretend I could read, pacing my finger in the book and rocking in my chair; no longer would my tongue lie idle and waste away.

I trembled with excitement. My scar itched. I skipped home along Lower Richmond Road bursting to tell my mother and Mrs. Bailey the astonishing news. Praying all the way home, across Lower Richmond Road, down into Bendemere Road running my hand along the wooden fence, praying my mother would be home. I pulled the string with the key through the letter box and let myself in.

I found my mother in the shadowy bedroom. I peeped round the door. She was sitting on the bed, her shoulders hunched, staring at the floor. Her eyes looked small from crying. The black suitcase was on the bed. She lifted up the lid. 'We are going to another place, Susie. We can't stay here anymore.' My heart sank. I wanted to stay with Mrs. Bailey and her fairies and benevolent spirits.

I was unable to tell my mother the exhilarating news. I held back. My mother looked stricken. She lay on the bed and closed her eyes. I tiptoed out and knocked on Mrs. Bailey's door.

'Dearest, come right in. I've been expecting you,' she

said, leaning over to pull out her confectionery drawer. 'A pink one again, is it?'

'Mmm. Yes please, Mrs. Bailey. Maybe I can try a white mouse instead of a pink one for a change.'

Mrs. Bailey showed no recognition that I was talking. It was the first time I had spoken since she had known me.

'I'll let you into a secret,' she confided, 'the pink and white mice in my opinion, taste the same. The colour has no bearing on the taste. The truth of the matter is one's preference is only determined by appearance. Here take one of each. Soon I'll have no one to share them with Susie. I will wrap one or two in this paper tissue to take with you to your new place. Remember to kiss my hand and make your usual curtsey.'

I obeyed and bowed my head in reverence. Then we laughed quietly in secret, sitting close together on the bed. I cuddled up to her. We sucked silently on our sugar globules. Then with the sugar melting in my mouth, I told her.

'Mrs. Bailey,' I began.

'Yes, what is it?'

She smiled as she sucked on her mouse's rump.

'Mrs. Bailey,' I persisted tucking the remains of the sugar mouse into my cheek-pouch. 'I can read.'

'I know dear.' She patted me gently on my back. 'Well done.'

Miss Joyce at Hotham Road School, the spokesperson for the Lord, told us that angels were God's messengers. How long it would take them to get my message up to Him was debatable considering their tiny, unformed wings and the vast distances of the black void they had to traverse. I prayed every night to ask God to make my mother settle and stop searching for something she held secret so we could have a home of our own.

But God had other ideas. He had a plan to help Dora's soldier son who had just come home from the army, to settle down in the very bed I lay in under the framed picture of the cherubs who had promised to represent me, and so we were once again *mis*-placed and had to say goodbye once more to the lady of the house in Bendemere Road. So after only a few months, we were on the move again.

This was a shame as Leonard and Dora seemed to be exceptionally good friends. I knew this because when my mother was out shopping, I often saw them huddled in the corner of the drip-drip conservatory, the rain hammering on the rackety roof when I was supposed to be watching *Muffin the Mule* on Dora's television the size of a book so that you had to get up really close to the screen.

A good thing Leonard managed to find new lodgings in Chelverton Road, just off Putney High Street. This was Margery's house, a spacious Victorian villa with most rooms let out to lodgers. We had the one at the back on the first floor. We had to be quiet and live like fugitives. We never saw the other lodgers padding softly in the evenings getting ready for the night shift. Margery and her three children lived on the top floor, and the house vibrated and trembled with their wild antics once the night shift had gone to work.

Although, I no longer had Dora's angel picture above my bed, I prayed to the angels every bedtime. I imagined them looking down on Dora's soldier son as he lay dreaming of his new life and I wondered if he noticed the pink blossomed wallpaper I picked at during the lonely evenings when I listened to children playing tag in the street.

It was a shame we'd come here to Margery's house. It was a shame to leave the river residence and the spiritual guidance of Mrs. Bailey and her stash of sugar mice. Sometimes, out of the window from behind the net curtains I would catch a glimpse of Mrs. Bailey in her old cloche hat making her way home from the shops with her wicker basket in one hand and a string bag of potatoes in another. I knocked on the window, knowing that wasn't a very polite thing to do, but desperately hoping she might hear and invite me into her room, where I would happily curtsey and kiss her hand. But she just glided her way home.

I wouldn't have minded staying with Dora either, impressed with her pink fluffy slippers and kindness. She showed me how to sow nasturtium seeds in a little plot of mud outside her back door. I was looking forward to seeing how beautiful orange flowers shown on the seed packet could sprout from tiny black seeds.

Now we were in this house in Chelverton Road, and it was another dreadful mistake, but Leonard wasn't to know. My mother wasn't to know either. The room was small. There was barely space between the furniture, so you had to squeeze past the beds and arch your back, and inch sideways to pass the two bald armchairs hugging the small fireplace and shift the chair under the table to pass to the door. Leonard kept a sack of coal under my bed because if it was kept in the yard someone would steal it. I hated it there. It had the coldness and eerie sounds of anonymity, of others hidden, moving as if inside the walls but with no knowledge or reassurance who the strangers were. I was anxious about opening the door to the landing on the first floor in case a monster, murderer or fiend appeared out of the darkness, invading our space to destroy us. But neither my imagination or presentiment saved us from an assault.

I didn't see the devastation with my own eyes because I was at school, but my mother said she came back from work one day, unlocked the door to our room to find that very little of its contents had been saved from the anonymous hand of destruction. Ink had been poured onto the white bed linen, crockery smashed against the walls, so shards of shattered china littered the floor and table. Baking flour taken from the kitchen cabinet coated the chairs, and the slashed pillows spilled feathers and snowed down everywhere on the windowsill and on top of our black suitcase above the wardrobe. The dead coals and ash from the fireplace were scattered over the beds, table and floor. We stepped on sugar for weeks. It seemed to propagate itself, lived between our toes, and inside our socks and shoes. My mother didn't need to speculate who had perpetrated this awful act against us. There was only one person who held a spare key and there was no sign of a break-in. Margery the landlady was the culprit. I never thought to wonder why. As a child I accepted cruel actions as natural, not necessarily motivated by overwhelming feelings, but happened because it was possible. Unable to ascertain the meanings of subtle signs from those that appeared harmless and kind, I believed witches, dragons, wolves were the very embodiment of evil, just like the devil, just as the laburnum was poisonous. Evil didn't have to have an excuse, or motive. It made the world precarious and infinitely mysterious. It was only much later with the pieces of the puzzle in my memory placed to fit and make an explanatory picture, that the whole sorry business came to light.

Once I arrived home from school, a certain order had been put in place, and if I hadn't overheard my distressed mother tell Leonard, I might have simply wondered why a woman like Margery decided to vandalize our room. After all it was really her room, in her house. However, the day of our departure from Margery's miserable lodgings was repeatedly delayed because everything rested on Leonard's decision, about what I was kept in the dark. It was at this time I wet the bed. I couldn't fathom what was going on, and could only speculate that in the absence of Mrs. Bailey's protection from malevolent spirits, Margery being one in disguise, we were in the doldrums again, just as we were in the attic flat.

For a while, we led a separate and cloistered life. Waiting. Every day, when I returned from school, I would find my mother sitting in the fireside chair with the repose and stillness of a marble sculpture. Both my mother and Leonard were deeply distracted by a secret, and it was therefore unsurprising they had not noticed I was making full use of my English tongue.

'Mummy, can I get you something from the shops?' I would dare ask.

'No please, Susie. Leave me. Nothing.'

'Are you sick? Do you need to see a doctor?'

'No. No. I'm tired. Let me sleep. Read your books, Susie. Be a good girl.'

During this time of untold torment, I would retreat into the corner of my room like a dog in its basket, and crouch there on my bed against the wall, reading or writing stories in a little notebook in a simple style, linking my ideas with that wonderful little word 'and' which best described our lives in limbo as we existed between one strange calamity followed by another.

And so it was that for some months nothing was resolved; no one was brought to justice for the vandalism; Margery clonk-clonked up and down the stairs, and my mother continued to sit still as a doll with all the life punched out of her. Her homesickness was back again. And I waited with the word 'and' bouncing about in my head, powerless to navigate the narrative towards home, now a distant land of apple orchards clothed in the mind's mist. In the evenings Leonard sat hunched by the fire. One night, when I was supposed to be asleep, I lay worrying about wetting the bed again, and I heard him tell my mother she was the one he really wanted. There was no one else that mattered. He told her over and over again. She remained unresponsive. I felt sorry for Leonard. After all I never expected him to want me, not for a moment, but he wanted my mother for his very own. He and I seemed to have reached an understanding of mutual indifference. Clearly, my claim on my mother was not perceived by him as a threat. My mother was the one in his heart. I was like an adjunct, damp and dank and of no use. Now and again, we might try and find some joy or comfort in each other's company, but it didn't work. He'd try the old magic trick of finding a sixpence in my ear, but I remained unimpressed. There were no sparks of warmth or pleasure. He remained for me a necessary presence. If he were a thing, he was a closed door. We were propped against him and yet I imagined he felt very much alone at times. He never shared our language, instead seemed afraid of it, and didn't allow us to speak it. No wonder he let himself to be taken in by Margery's charms with her winged spectacles over those hugely magnified adoring brown eyes and her bright pink lips. Here was a woman who might understand his difficulties, who might comfort him. She would come down the stairs in her high heels, holding the banisters with a gloved hand and tight dress ruckled over her broad hips, humming a popular tune with a cigarette between her lips, smelling of peppermints and nicotine. Her masculine smell, reminding me of Ida's husband Albert, belied her essential femininity. Screwing up her big eyes as blue smoke snaked under her glasses, she would view me slyly.

'Hello, love. When ya going to come upstairs and play with my Billy?'

'Can I come tomorrow, Mrs. Yeats, please?' I answered as way of an excuse because I was afraid of Billy. I saw flash-images of Billy repeatedly thrusting his fist into the face of a pale, underfed boy in the playground and drawing blood from the ear of another weakling who dared defy him. My own deference to his mother caused me to cringe and despise myself, but the truth was she made me exceptionally uneasy and the prospect of having to wrestle and grapple with Billy upstairs made me want to wet my knickers.

'Come whenever you like. Just go up and knock at the

door. You're welcome any time pet.'

'Thank you, Mrs. Yeats, and could you ask him please if he still has my ball? It's white with red spots on it.'

She beamed down at me and nodded, narrowing her eyes. 'Don't you worry. I'll have word with our Billy about your ball to be sure, I will.'

I never saw the ball again. Clonk, clonk, clonk—down the bare stairs she went in her heavy high heels. It was her signature sound, one that always made me stop reading in our room or stop eating at the table. Only when the clonking had passed by our door did I breathe again.

Then just after the Christmas holidays, Leonard told us Grandfather had died of a heart attack clearing snow from the drive at The Horseshoe. Grandmother had found him lying face down in the blackened snow, his scarf twisted round to the back of his neck instead of the front. Somehow the spade had spun out of control when he fell. Grandmother eventually found it in the middle of the flowerbed under the dining room window.

When Leonard told us at the dinner table, I lost my appetite. The black snow and his death and his clothes in disarray were disturbing details. I wondered if Grandmother needed someone to comfort and kiss her. I pictured her shivering in her corner of the sofa, trying to knit under the dim light of the standard lamp, alone in front of a struggling fire in the grate. I prayed grandfather would arrive safely in heaven, the place where all the dead gather. I prayed he would be tending the roses in a garden, a replica of the one at The Horseshoe. I hoped he would have someone to play hide-and-seek with and wondered if heaven had long dining tables and dark cupboards where he might find a small child hiding from him.

My mother was not invited to the funeral. Afterwards, Leonard wore a black armband on his threadbare winter coat for many months, and when summer  arrived he transferred it to the sleeve of his raincoat, and he became so used to it, he forgot to take it off, so I believed that's what you had to do when your father died. I believed it was the English custom to wear the black armband forever. I did not have a black armband on my coat to show the world the loss of my father because he was like me, shameful and a secret German.

There were fewer trees in Wandsworth; no blossom or canopies of green to rest the eye from rows of back-to-back houses like black bats with their wings closed hanging upside down on pockmarked walls of dank caves. If you were to chance on a tree in full bloom, its branches tipping over a garden wall at the end of Alma Road, it would come as an aberration of nature to be admired and wondered at.

Wandsworth smelled sweet and sour. Sweetness oozed from the breweries and settled above the town like gauze until it dissolved into a sickly mist. Sourness rose from smothered tributaries and the rank River Wandle, driven underground like sewers, but erupting and emptying itself further upstream with ferocious force near Wandsworth Bridge, its sour froth of effluence from the local industries gushed into the brown, murky Thames. It would take at least fifty years or more for frogs, shoals of fish and colonies of eels to return.

First, we lived in a spacious bed-sit in Birdhurst Road on the first floor, but a baby kept us awake all night squalling through the shared wall, which upset us since no one attended to it. On several nights, my mother would go out into the landing and knock on the door and try the doorknob to no avail.

'Len, what can we do? The door is locked. Where is the mother? Maybe something has happened to her. The baby is hungry.'

But Len urged her back to bed, 'Don't get involved, girl.' We all tried to sleep with our fingers pressed on our ears until the baby fell into an exhausted silence.

One day, I overheard Gertie, the next-door neighbour, tell my mother that the baby was taken away by the social while the girl was out on the game.

'We heard nothing. What was the game?' asked my mother.

'You know!' said Gertie thrusting her hip backwards and forwards and laughing.

'No, I do not know,' said my mother, and neither did I. The prospect of a baby being taken away haunted me. Who was the social that took the baby, and where had they put it? Gertie said we would be better off moving in with her. 'That house isn't the sort of house you would want to bring up a kid in. We're decent folk Sid and me. You can have a room at ours for a much cheaper rate, I promise you, deary.'

I was happy to move next door to the safer house. We occupied the front room, which had been converted into a bed-sit by Gertie who lived with her son Mick and husband Sid, a garage mechanic.

'Sid makes cakes as a side-line,' she told us, which made perfect sense when I spied two magnificent wedding cakes lined on the sideboard. The mouth-watering smell of fruit cake came wafting in from the tiny scullery.

Although it was much quieter than the house of disrepute, it was far less wholesome in some respects. There was sometimes an overpowering smell of urine in the hallway to which I may have contributed, mingling with the delicate perfume of royal icing and vanilla, and in time my mother's Mansion lavender polish added to the unpalatable mix that hit you as you opened the front door. Also, there was no bathroom, so I had to wash myself down at the scullery sink with one cold water tap and a greasy curtain at the base tied across with string. Standing in my bare feet, I imagined small monsters lurked behind the curtain, sucking at a primeval sludge ready to loop themselves round my ankles. There was an outside toilet inhabited by a swarm of flies in the summer and in the winter the frozen water made your pee steam on the bowl's little ice-cap.

But whereas in the house next door we were confined to our rooms, at Gertie's I was free to go where I pleased downstairs and took pleasure in sidling down the corridor to the parlour where Gertie would be smoking in a chair by the fire, listening to a Dick Barton episode on the wireless and Sid would be mixing his next cake wearing his vest tucked into his wide leather belt. I loved to watch him ice and decorate a cake; with his huge hands he picked out the right nozzles, filled the piping bags with sweet icing, engine oil thick under his fingernails, and with a delicacy of movement he created a snow garden while I stole tiny pieces of marzipan, rolling then into a ball to pop into my mouth later. Both would barely acknowledge me, but if

Mick, their son, came down from his attic hideout to mock me, making me squirm with self-consciousness about my freckled nose, straight hair or long spidery legs, I was grateful to Gertie for defending me. 'Mick, leave her alone. She's only a kid. Not an ugly waste of space like you.'

'Oh, shut up, you old cow,' he'd say and sulk away. I was shocked anyone would dare speak to a mother like that, but Gertie didn't seem to mind. Maybe they were his special words of endearment. Sid just carried on stirring his cake mixture or attending to his miniature plastic bride and groom he placed on the top tier of his magnificent cake.

Sometimes in the backyard, I would help Gertie feed the giant ringer with heavy wet sheets. 'I like it,' she would say, 'when I can hear all the squeezed water tinkle into the tin tub, don't ya?' Then she would wind down the washing line and when it was all pegged up with washing, wind it up again and stick a prop in the centre of the line so the sheets didn't sweep the dirt. Then we'd stand back in pleasure to see the whites rippling in the wind.

When we first came to Gertie and Sid's, I wondered if Leonard would still be living with us since his friendship with Billy's mother Margery in Chelverton Road had caused my mother pain and depression. He persisted in showing his concern for our welfare, and brought with him his leather suitcase, and put it on top of our black suitcase high on the wardrobe and promised he would do anything to make my mother happy from now on; he would save to buy a house; he would work overtime twice a week at the office to get a deposit; he would stop betting on the horses; he would always be faithful to her. She was the only one he truly, truly loved. He sweet-talked her round to loving him again.

He tried with me too, bringing me presents—pencils and pads from the office and sometimes he gave me sixpence on Saturday mornings so I could go to the pictures down the High Street to watch Laurel and Hardy struggle to get a piano up a staircase. It kept sliding back down which made all the children laugh but I cried in frustration. And for my eighth birthday Leonard came home with a flashy chrome and maroon doll's pram, which I pushed up and down the street with the bald doll inside Ida gave me, enjoying my new status as the girls down the road begged to take turns on leave from their hop-scotch game chalked out on the pavement. But what I liked best were books.

I took solace in reading Rudyard Kipling's *Just So Stories*, savouring the pleasure of his warm address to the reader: *Best Beloved*, hoping that sooner or later he would tell me, his *best beloved* reader, how girls came into the world so I could discover the secrets of my beginnings and the mysteries of Englishness.

But Kipling disappointed me. I had a notion, confirmed by Brenda when we lived at Ida's, that we sprang out of our mothers through their belly buttons. And as far as Englishness went, I would often stare at the children at school who appeared so effortlessly English, and I became poisoned with envy.

When my mother bought me *Alice in Wonderland*, I was hopeful that Alice might have the answer. Her world, filled with absurd elements, and riddled with injustices, seemed familiar. Unlike her, I lay on my bed reading, shutting out the absurdities and pitfalls of our lives, whereas she bravely stood for truth and justice. Like her, I lived with a sense of alienation and loneliness, but whereas she confronted it, I was debilitated by it. I drove myself inwards and buried my head in books. Although I disliked Alice for being heartless sometimes, I admired her attitude, her self-possession, and intelligence. And above all her Englishness, which I couldn't unpick and grab for myself.

It was at this time, when I was relieved to see my mother and Leonard showing affection for each other again, I left my mother notes telling her how much I loved her. This was because I had it in mind that it was not the done thing to tell people openly you loved them. Love must always be kept secret, so I slipped scrappy notes into her shoe in the wardrobe, or in her purse or makeup bag. A little wave of happiness would wash over me when I imagined how she might unfold the little piece of paper and learn that she was indisputably my best beloved.

# Lüneburg 1936

Sophie, my mother, once had a secret love, too, which was a blessing or a curse, depending on how you looked at it. Laid out on her bed was her freshly laundered uniform. It made her heart race. It was the uniform of the Bund Deutscher Mädel, or the BDM, the League of German Lasses. The kind Führer, like the Pied Piper, freed repressed children from their authoritarian parents who repeatedly imposed domestic chores on their charges, treated them like slaves, beat them, locked them in cellars and starved them into submission. The Führer took all the German children, abused and un-abused, into his care. Children throughout the land were emancipated, free to roam the forests and hills, marching and singing, filling their lungs with sweet country air, their hearts bursting with pride and their heads stuffed with National Socialist ideals. Their bodies and minds were liberated from domestic and parental tyranny and grew healthy and strong under the paternal eagle eye of the Führer.

But not all children were included. You had to be a full-blooded German to join the exclusive youth club. All the rest, let's face it, were riffraff. The creed crudely inculcated was the superiority of the Aryan race. 'Young Germans must be lean and lithe,' said the Führer, 'as fleet as a greyhound, as tough as leather, as hard as steel. And nothing is possible unless there is one will commanding, and one will everyone must obey.'

Despite the fervent Führer's words and his benevolent attention, at the back of children's minds lurked a fear, tiny and imperceptible as an incipient tumour; the fear of the predatory eye, an eye that could detect a flicker of dissension from hundreds of feet above. The black all-seeing eagle served the Führer who imposed his will on the young—pliable, soft and warm as wax. And the procession of torches, maidens with garlands in their hair, dancing in woodland groves and voices chanting: 'Today we're lords of Germany. Tomorrow of all the world...' was spellbinding, alluring and hypnotic for little girls who thought they were in fairyland instead of gripped by diabolical artistry.

In sisterhood, the older Jungmädel marched with the lads, blew whistles, sewed and mended brown shirts, bandaged the injured after brawls, inspected the younger ones, spied on them and corrected subversive traits, checked their hands, their heads, their beds, their shoes, their scrubbed faces. In their leader's dark eyes, they discerned his charisma, his charm and offered themselves in love letters to him. The children, whipped into delirium, lost the little sense they possessed and like their parents, many became seduced by a sense of bonding.

Sophie looked down at the new uniform her father had bought her. How fortunate she and her friends were to be among the chosen. She sighed. Only to herself would she admit that the Führer's looks were not very appealing and yet his adoration was infectious to many. She knew in her heart she would always love Erich her older brother the best. He was *Der Herrlichste von Allen*, the most loveable: tall, heroic in his youth outfit, an accomplished sportsman. Above all he had a generosity of nature and was always sensitive to her feelings. He would always look out for her, defend her when she was under attack from her mother's sharp words. Sometimes, though, he led her astray. There was a time he told his friend Gunther that Sophie fancied him, driving Gunther into an uncontrollable passion for Sophie leading to an assault in the park when she had to fight Gunther off. She returned home with stockings torn and her hair undone. Admonished by her mother, it was Erich, his guilty secret undetected, who comforted her. When Erich began smoking secretly at the bottom of the apple orchard, jumping down into the dry ditch, Sophie would follow and beg, 'Please let me have a puff.' At first he would tease her telling her the Führer wouldn't like it. Then when she tried to make a grab for the cigarette, he'd relent. 'All right, all right. Don't set the world on fire! Here. Just one puff though.'

The first time Sophie sucked on the cigarette she coughed violently.

Erich laughed. 'You girls think you are like us men, but you cannot do the same things. Ach, you've made the end all soggy!'

'Call yourself a man? I don't think so. Not with that hairless chin!' Sophie pinched his handsome face on the cheek. A mock fight would ensue, Erich leaning back with the cigarette hanging in the corner of his mouth, until they heard their mother calling them to dinner.

She had no doubt that she loved him the best. He was good looking and strong and her best friend. As a young child she had idolized her big brother and idolized him still. When he vowed to shed his blood for the Fatherland, he and his friend Gunter cut their wrists and mingled their blood  she stood witness. Pearls of blood drilled into the snow; Sophie was overcome with pride. But that was before the future arrived, carrying with it a false innocence and nostalgia for a golden time; the inevitable wisdom of hindsight changed the past into a period of legitimized defilement and degradation. Even towards the end of her life, the memory of Erich, her best beloved, made her cry.

# Birdhurst Road, Wandsworth 1952

In Gertie's backyard, I practised two balls between the giant mangle and a diminished pile of wet coal, the remnant of last winter's store gleaming softly in the evening sunshine after the rain. I practised as if my identity depended on it. I wore one of my shabby summer dresses; it was full skirted with puffed sleeves and sagging pockets in faded red gingham. I wore black plimsolls without socks.

I looked and sounded as South London as you can get, but I was hollow with awful inner failings. The whole time I felt an imposter. Caged, trapped. Un-English. Outwardly, my inclusion seemed confirmed by the RSPCA, who awarded me a prize for a short story about a lost dog. I received a five-pound book voucher and bought several of Richmal Crompton's hilarious *William* books from Smiths, and Palgrave's *Golden Treasury* of poetry.

Mr. Newman, the headmaster of my new Church of England School, St. Catherine's, felt it was his duty to ensure we were educated about the world and gave us a summary of world news when few of the pupils had a television. One morning he informed us of a new invention.

'It is called an Atomic bomb, and it can destroy the entire world,' he said, his eyes growing wide in awe. The little mouths before him gasped and bodies twitched. And if that wasn't enough, he continued with news of the appalling Mau Mau atrocities in British controlled Kenya, which did not help my bed-wetting. It was about this time

I began another nightly activity, sleepwalking. Apparently, I never went far, just out of the room and down Gertie's hallway and back again.

In the waking, nightmare world, Mr. Newman announced that an Iron Curtain had just dropped down onto Europe so that millions were divided by it. I never thought to question how such a strange thing could happen, but I thought I heard him say 'coming mists' were responsible. I worried about millions of sad people imprisoned behind its massive bulk and prayed earnestly for the mists to be lifted and the people reunited. We bowed out heads to the command: 'Hands together. Eyes closed.' And we prayed earnestly for God to save the suffering world.

Our young teacher, on the other hand, the petite and pretty Miss Lovejoy, was less concerned with our *Weltanschauung*, and more with saving our souls. She was sprightly, with dark curly hair and lively brown eyes and could play the piano beautifully. Aware she was unable to lift us out of poverty, she concentrated on our mental darkness. With the aim of bringing enlightenment to our primitive heads, she read tales from the Bible every morning and other such myths daily transporting us to an exotic and ancient past.

'It won't be long,' she warned on her way to the piano when we were restless and inattentive, 'when I shall be hundreds of miles away from you in Sarawak.' This made us feel guilty and insecure. We did not want to be responsible for her dangerous departure to a land many miles from our neediness, a need we expressed in a roar of disapproval.

She calmed us, playing Schumann's *Kinderszenen*, her body swaying to the dreamlike music, her fingers barely touching the keys. I soon adored her so that the continued threats of departure to Sarawak alarmed me and were not mitigated by afternoons, when the handsome Father Clifton in his long skirt, bringing the sweetest smile to Miss Lovejoy's face, would sweep into the classroom to instruct us about the Word of God.

I waited patiently for him to reveal *the* Word, but he refrained from imparting his knowledge. Instead, he read opaque aphorisms from the Bible and other more disturbing sayings that he fished out of his black book. One told of how the stroke of the whip marks the flesh, but the stroke of the tongue breaks bones.

Maybe that's what gave some of the pupils in my class the idea to break my bones with the lashing of their tongues. The names they called me sounded hateful without my understanding what they meant. I was a *Kraut*. I admitted to being a Kraut (German for cabbage) with a whimsical smile, which caused a further whipping by their infuriated tongues. At playtime I found a niche near the main gate to hide in, facing the wall, waiting for the going-in bell to summon us back into the classroom.

A tense time was early in the morning when the classroom was locked and a small gaggle of early birds clustered around the door, waiting in the freezing corridor for the caretaker to open it. We were morning orphans pushed off to school as parents hurried to work. Hungry and cold, and with nothing better to do, they eyed me with menacing looks, sniffing and coughing. Invariably I was saved from attack by Mr. Hicks, the caretaker, heaving an enormous coal scuttle before him with a contorted face.

'Now then, mind out, you little 'uns. Out of the way. You can't come in yet till I've seen to the fire.' His massive bunch of keys jangled on his belt. We could see the bright flames in the fireplace and longed to rush to it to warm our numb bodies, but we were not allowed in the classroom until, to our dismay, Mr. Hicks would smother the flames with coal before he beckoned us in. We would run towards the fender to warm our blue hands on it, watching black smoke stream up the chimney, the acrid smell thick in our nostrils.

'Not you!' said Pat Faulks digging her nails into my wrist. 'You're bad!'

'No, yes!' the rest of them chorused. But I edged my way nearer to the fender and grasped one of its hot bars. Her spite angered me, made me strong.

Johnny Wright also sought me out for special treatment. He didn't think breaking my bones by tongue lashing was sufficiently satisfying, so he undertook the singular task of dragging me from the street by my hair and pummelling my soft parts with his fist down the dead-end alley after school. I took blow after blow without a squeal because I was ashamed and wanted to keep the punishment for being a kraut secret.

The girls though, led by Pat Faulks, were bent on a serious mission to exclude me from their games. They chose the silent treatment but had the consideration to inform me of their reasons.

'We're sending you to Coventry,' said Faulks narrowing her eyes, so she looked like a stoat, 'cos of all the bombing you did in Coventry and London, and what the Germans did in the war.'

'Yeah, and my mum said I mustn't have anything to do with you, cos you did dreadful things to Uncle Bill and all the other people,' said Pamela Price.

'Yeah,' said one. 'Yeah,' echoed another. Yeah. Yeah. Yeah...

Other times, when they felt my isolation was insufficient, I was made to listen to their verbal abuse. Their eyes blazed like wild animals in the night encircling me in their hatred. There were so many accusations I lost count. I was without doubt informed that the Germans were thoroughly wicked and could never redeem themselves. No wonder my poor mother was in such misery. I now doubted I would ever be Englished.

And I was beginning to understand what being German meant and how it became a serious setback to my aspirations to be just like the other children. In the playground I found a new means of safety. I galloped and raced like a demented horse so that no one could catch up with me and bring upon me the terrible shame of what happened to Uncle Bill and the bombing of cities. Finally, suffering fatigue but not wholly desensitized to abuse, I tried not to care what they called me as long as they left my mother alone with their tongue lashings.

One day, after school, I ran as fast as I could up East Hill, followed by a small gang of boys calling out 'Nazi!' above the roar of lorries grinding up the hill. Nazi, I thought meant *nasty* delivered in their particular south London dialect. Turning to see if they were gaining ground, I recognized Johnny Wright with a couple of hangers-on. I had already received a bashing from him the day before and was not prepared to take any more. I sprinted up the hill to escape them. Halfway, I started to get the stitch and my rib cage was sore from Johnny Wright's fist, so I couldn't run as fast.

I had just reached the fishmonger's and planned to run into the shop and stand among the buckets of live eels and spider crabs, when I crashed into the softness of a woman's body. About to apologise and feeling doomed I heard the gang closing in. I looked up into the face of my mother. With her shopping basket on her arm, wearing a blue and white floral summer dress she took my breath. I tucked my face into her the folds of her skirt taking in her smell of Eau de Cologne, weak as a baby.

'Ach Susie, these are all your friends?' she enquired looking at the motley group of boys, out of breath, gathered by the fish stall. 'Hello. Come we must move on away from the fish. The smell is so sickly.' She flashed the boys a smile. Meekly they followed, their demeanour now boyish and innocent.

'Here, let me give you some chocolate.' She took a bar from her basket as my tormentors grinned with pleasure.

My mother broke up a slab of milk chocolate and handed out several pieces to each. 'Fank you, fank you, fank you…' And off they went, turning as they walked, grinning.

I was mortified by my mother's mistaken friendliness and deeply hurt she had unwittingly sided with my tormentors while the rule never to be a tell-tale-tit went unappreciated. Not only that, I had been denied a piece of milk chocolate. I hated her for a moment, hated her stupidity, her kindness to others, excluding her daughter. I locked up my anger in a fierce sulk and dreaded the following day at school when I would be further tormented

146

for my mother's weakness, her unreserved generosity.

That dreaded morning, Johnny Wright who sat in the front row bent over his desk, turned in his seat, and leaning on one crooked arm, shot me a smile. I averted my eyes, dreading as usual the going-home-bell, knowing the torture he could mete out. The scar on my leg itched and prickled. Outside the gates at the end of the school day, I braced for punishment, my heart hammering as I looked about but Wright was nowhere to be seen. I furtively looked this way and that, my eyes darting up the hill expecting him to pounce from a new vantage point. The alley where he normally lurked to ambush was empty.

I wanted to thank him from the bottom of my heart and hug him for not hurting me again, but I kept my distance. I couldn't believe for a moment a small piece of chocolate could sweeten him and his gang. Can cruelty be cured by kindness? It may have not been my mother's intention. She had no idea Johnny Wright was my tormentor. I forgave her. But because of my mistrust, I remained watchful until Johnny Wright and his followers disappeared to secondary school.

And as for Madam Faulks and her followers, the campaign of discrimination against me became unsustainable, especially when she needed someone to find her lost marbles, or a minion to hold one end of the rope so they could play skipping or be *It* constantly in the game of chase. My crimes were put aside as long as I was compliant and demure, and made myself a slave to the whims of others.

Soon afterwards another enemy reared his ugly head. He was the school dentist who threatened my very bones.

He drilled into my rotting molar. The drill bore down into the centre of my tooth searching for the nerve. I leapt up in anticipation of pain.

'If you don't keep still, this drill will go right through your cheek, young lady,' he said with relish. Then he pulled my lips around stretching my mouth all ways and filled my tooth with grit before pressing a white paste against my palette. I thought I was going to be sick. I jumped from the chair as soon as I was allowed and ran home with a sore mouth. My mother felt for me when she saw my lips were puffy and my cheek swollen.

'Susie, it must be done. You are nine years old and no child sucks a thumb. The wire will make your teeth straight.'

Once the brace was fitted, and screwed in tightly, I discovered not only did it hurt, but made me lisp and it was impossible not to spray spit when I spoke. The English language is too sibilant for a brace. My tongue felt heavy, like a trapped limb, and chafed against the wire in my mouth. It was difficult to get off to sleep without the comfort of thumb sucking and I worried about wetting the bed.

I also tried to reconcile my mother's gentle demeanour with what I had heard about the evil Germans. It disturbed me to think beneath her reserve, a monster mother lurked, and I feared for both of us like something weighing on my chest. I became anxious. I could find little evidence of an evil German witch behind her flawless face, and yet at the back of my mind was the memory of being abandoned, and although I was rescued, the silent scream lay at my core like a dying star, intense as a black hole so love and light could not be set free and I must only allow my memory to tiptoe around it, should I be sucked into destruction.

Once more, in despair and discomfort, I elected to stop talking, although I continued conversations with myself in my head. I no longer had the affection and confection of Mrs. Bailey in her boudoir of sweet darkness to coax my tongue back to life. Help came from a surprising quarter. It was neither my mother nor Leonard who drew me back into the community of the English language again, but Mick.

At fifteen, Mick was a young, grown-up man in my nine-year-old eyes. Gangly and loping in his long black jacket and skin-tight black trousers he called 'drain-pipes.' He could never keep still. His pinched face was often obscured by black strands of greased hair, which he never touched but would flip back with a toss of his head. I met him sometimes outside in the backyard when I went out to play two balls against the scullery wall.

'Watcha,' he said. I flashed him a half smile. I didn't reply, feeling too shy to speak wearing my brace, and in any case, I was in mute mode.

'I'm just having a quiet smoke,' he said as an apology. He would watch me closely with an amused expression, so I'd lose concentration and drop a ball. He often stood beside a mattress Gertie had put out to dry in the sun. The yellow uneven rings of dried pee were the unmistakable signs of a bed-wetter. I'd overheard my mother sympathizing with Gertie about Mike's 'accidents,' so I knew the mattress belonged to his bed. It didn't bother him, this openness about his incontinence. I stored up sympathy for him as I was a bed wetter myself and had to lie on a sweaty rubber mat slipped under the bed sheet.

One evening, during my two-ball craze, I met him in the yard and my heart sank. I hated the way he watched me with his mocking eyes.

'Do you know what?' he asked, waiting for me to respond. I was trying to master a tricky overarm throw against the wall, followed by a bounce. 'Well, do you wanna know or not?' He persisted.

'What do I want to know?' I asked, equally exasperated, spitting the words through my brace, angry with myself for breaking my vow of silence.

'For crying out loud. How do I know what you want to know? The King is dead!' he shouted.

My cheeks burned. I felt both foolish and insulted. I didn't know the King or what he looked like, but this outburst told me this was terrible for England.

'If the King is dead, have we got another one?' I asked, troubled. I stopped playing two balls now.

'No stupid. How stupid are you? We've got a queen.'

'From where?'

'You're unbelievable you are. You don't know anything. How old are you?'

I turned my back on Mike for shouting at me. He started singing and I turned to have a quick look at him hamming it up.

*If your heartaches seem to hang around too long,*
*And your blues keep getting bluer with each song,*
*Remember sunshine can be found behind a cloudy sky*
*So let your hair down and go on, cry.*

On the verge of silly tears, I wanted to laugh outright, but I was still cross, and to show him I wasn't a walk over, chanted the accompanying prayer: *Matthew Mark Luke and John. Bless this bed that I lie on*, as the balls bounced back off the walls and I caught them. Then we both giggled. I hid my mouth with my hand because of my ugly brace.

In time, practising in the yard with my precious tennis balls, I grew confident enough to try uppers interspersed with a few overs. One summer evening Mike said he wanted a go of two balls and helped himself. He wasn't very good. His coordination was terrible, and I wanted to laugh. I told him all about the game. 'Overs is when you throw the ball over-arm like a bowler against the wall. But that's hard to catch. Some girls at school can do all kinds of uppers and overs, and bouncers too.'

'Bloody heck. What's a bouncer when it's at home?'

'When you let the ball fall to the ground and you have to catch it again, but I never manage all the different ways the other girls can do it.'

'Well, you gotta try harder,' said Mike bursting into song again.

I couldn't stop myself laughing at him gyrating and holding a fist forward like a microphone.

'You're a right little flirt, aren't cha?' He tickled me under my arms, another cigarette between his lips.

I liked his strong hands on me but didn't feel it was right, so I wriggled free, carrying on with my game: *Matthew, Mark, Luke, and John. Bless this bed that I lie on.* And then Mike stubbed out his fag end and went indoors but I could smell the lingering odour of his strong

Woodbines tobacco as if he were still leaning against the wall watching me play.

Once he asked me to dance. The only kind of dance I knew was Scottish dancing we practised at school. Mike held my hand and swung me round as he sang. He showed me how to go under his arm without letting go of his hand.

'This is jiving,' he called out pulling me towards him and then pushing me away as we jigged about. But with his grip tightening round my wrist, I could contain myself no longer and collapsed into spasms of uncontrollable giggles. I wanted to ask him if he thought I was an English girl, but I was too shy and afraid he might say I wasn't like an English girl at all. I was so grateful he spoke to me and didn't go on and on about the disgusting things the Germans did in the war.

Then one evening he didn't turn up in the yard. I saw him staring down from his bedroom window and he shot back out of view. I waited and he didn't come. The following afternoon he appeared with a sneer and seemed different. I wasn't sure I liked him. He watched me as he smoked, crouched on his haunches by the wall. Then I hurt my hand. I scraped it against the fence trying to catch the ball and a splinter drove deep into my thumb. Mike got up and with a cigarette in the corner of his mouth, just like his Dad, tried to pinch it out. Our heads touched and he lost interest in my splinter. He spat out the dog-end.

'Do you know how to kiss?'

'Of course, I do.' I had my pride.

'Go on then, show me.' He pulled me towards the outside lavatory.

'Not in there!' I went round the side by the fence.

He followed. 'C'mon show me.'

I planted a big kiss on his cheek.

'Not like that silly. Like this!' His lips were hot and wet and pressed hard onto mine. I could feel his teeth jarring against my brace; a gruesome clash of bone, metal and nicotine-spit. I was aware of something hard pressed into my groin and his hand wormed its way up my skirt. I thought it was disgusting and pulled back and wiped my mouth with the back of my hand.

'I forgot you wear a brace,' he said agitated, 'it don' arf hurt!'

I held a snigger inside, and wanted to escape. He turned his back and walked away with his usual bow-legged gait towards the house. He left me bewildered and upset. Tears welled but I forced them back. I wasn't going to let him know I was sad that I had failed to please him, so I took up my skipping rope and worked out for a while.

Mike didn't come out again in the evenings. I grew disappointed but never gave up hope. At bedtime I would face the wall to hide my misery. I wanted to tell him we could forget about the kissing. The kissing had never been the best part. I missed his antics, singing and jiving. I missed his company. He was my friend who made me feel like an English girl.

Evening after evening, my bed was blessed as the balls bounced against the outside scullery wall and I expected Gertie to rush out and shout: 'Stop that blessed racket!' But she never did. She and my mother were too busy engaged in the sardonic mockery of men as they drank cups of tea and dunked squashed-fly biscuits.

But life was once again rekindled in Miss Lovejoy's class. I tried to forget about Mick's groping and painful kiss and allow my true romantic inclinations to surface. Miss Lovejoy, as you know, had an enchanting gift for storytelling, so that by the end of the summer term, her pupils had lived through the Fall, the Flood, the Plague of Boils and Locusts, the parting of the Red Sea, Joseph thrown into a pit, David and Goliath, Daniel in the lion's den and the Prodigal son. Afterwards, giving the Bible a rest, we learned how King Alfred burnt his cakes, about the beheading of Queens, and all the goings on along the riverbank, as the wind whispered through the willows as a backdrop to Mole and Ratty's journey in their little boat.

Miss Lovejoy's zest for time-travel fired our imaginations to such a pitch, that when small hands passed a note to the back of the class, unseen by Miss Lovejoy's sharp yet trusting eye, it was difficult not to believe all the children, belonging to Wandle's tribe were willing advocates of an heroic conspiracy. The folded note took time to pass over the classroom swamp and landed in my lap like a limp, wildflower. My heart jolted, and then contracted. Unfolding the tiny square of paper, I read the pencilled declaration of love and part of me flew off. The word *love* burned the skin of my eye to white mists. A moment of vertigo.

Love, I discovered, multiplies love. Instantly, I loved the boy who had taken the dangerous and daring chance to write the note under the nose of the watchful eye of the teacher. I realised you don't need someone's permission to love them. You just can. And they can just love you. This was a liberating and wonderful revelation. I swooned with the thought of loving almost everyone, the whole world, the stars and the universe. It gave me a sense of power, but it was false. Most of the time I had no power at all.

I lifted my flushed face shyly facing the arena of bowed heads and met the wide, knowing grin of Bobby Brand, with his straight hair, red as the feathers of a corncrake, some strands sun-bleached like summer grass falling across his forehead. We both had orange freckles printed on our noses and cheeks. His blue eyes gleamed, a sign. My head swam. I felt a hot lingering flush rise to my face, and I met his gaze.

In the playground, Bobby Brand took my hand and led me into the coal-shed and we swung on one of the rafters, our hair flouncing, arms raw with the necessary pain of stretching and swinging. At first, we were out of sync, hot and panting. Then shifting closer to me along the beam, Bobby stalled so we swung in time, and then he reached over his face close to mine, and our lips brushed, like butterflies mating on the wing, and his mouth tasted hot and sweet like Toffee Creams, and in no time our presence was discovered by others and they joined us on the coal shed beams to swing to our hearts content. There was Valerie, Pamela, Maureen, Wendy and Patricia, Paul and David and Johnny who forgot I was supposed to be in Coventry. Who cared if I was ostracized, and called names now that my cup was brimming over? Bobby Brand was my lover and protector and because of him, I defied the dentist and wrapped the brace in one of Leonard's large white handkerchiefs with the blue L monogram and secreted the bundle in my satchel for home-time and only wore the brace in bed at night.

When Miss Lovejoy chose to present *The Pied Piper of Hamlyn* for the summer show, Bobby Brand was chosen for the Mayor and I was given the part of a rat, a pack of which had to recite several verses in unison to keep the narrative going, while Pat Faulks was chosen to be one of the bands of innocent children the Piper lured, not without giving me the occasional poke up the backside with her black patent leather shoe. As I scurried away across the boards on all fours, hoping to prevent my tail being stepped on, she skipped off happily into the cave under the stage and in my mind, true to the story, never to return.

The dentist did not discover my treachery; I thought he might guess I was only wearing the brace at night. He simply tightened it regularly, and after a year released me from the metal contraption. I shot out of the chair mumbling a thank you and without a second look, left the surgery as fast as possible. I was fortunate in other ways, too, because my mother was happier especially as Gertie didn't mind having Germans in the house. When her friend said, 'Blimey, Gert. Bit of a risk that!' She replied calmly that she found us exceptionally clean and very quiet. Not only did she defend us from spiteful gossips but during the first few months of our stay, she lifted my mother out of her depression, something I aspired to do but never managed.

'All right if I come in?' asked Gertie when she was already in the middle of the room. They soon forgot I was on my bed reading, so I listened and learned as much as I could about adults and their unfathomable ways. Gertie was sometimes a lost cause of self-deprecation. She believed in fate, and yet liked to slyly dodge it. She believed life was a lottery. You either won a prize or didn't. You had to make the best of what you got. That made you tough. She liked a mission and took it upon herself to make my mother happy as one of her projects. Another of her projects was Sid's cake sideline, hoping it would make a substantial profit. 'He practically gives the cakes away,' she told my mother. 'I keep telling him, sugar's no longer rationed, you know. He should charge, but he just says I nag.' She also had a project to launch her son Mick into the world of apprenticeship, but certainly not the kind he had in mind.

'I wish I could get him off his backside and learn a trade,' she complained. 'Instead, he lives like a hermit in his bedroom with his motorbike magazines. Sophie, he's a lost cause. I despair. I really do.'

'He is young,' my mother offered gently but not too enthusiastically.

'That's what I tell Sid. Sid says I've made a pansy out of him. Sid forgets I nearly lost Mick as a baby to pneumonia. We had to make a steam tent out of an old sheet in the bathroom. It was awful, you know, seeing his little bony chest trying to suck in air and breath. Such a little mite he was. I kept thinking we could put him in a shoe-box and not a coffin.' I looked up from my book to see tears in Gertie's eyes.

'Ach,' was all my mother could say, reaching out to touch Gertie.

'Course, he'll be called up. Sid threatens to give Mick a good hiding, to make a man of him. I said don't you dare.

He'll have all that in the army, poor little sod. That's why I want him to get out into the world a bit more, you know. But he just wants to hide away. Still, you can't wash your hands of your own kids, can you? Some do. But I won't. No never. Not my own flesh and blood.'

'My own flesh and blood,' repeated my mother to practise English phrases, which Gertie would acknowledge with a nod if no correction were required. Sometimes, Gertie gave my mother *True Romance* magazines to help with her English, but my mother, despite her burgeoning vocabulary of romantic love and Gertie's cockney idioms such as *having it off, good riddance, getting your knickers in a twist*, my mother never had the confidence to use these strange sayings. She feared the situation might not be correct. Despite all this attention from Gertie, my mother grew restless again. As Gertie's protégée she betrayed her friend and mentor when she confided in Leonard that she could never be happy in this house and could no longer live in its squalor—only she didn't use the word *squalor*, she used a German word. The scullery was filthy, and the outside toilet was *furchtbar*—disgusting. That's not to say she was ungrateful to kind Gertie. But everything my mother said about the place was true. There were whispered evenings of tears and quarrelling between my mother and Leonard. Couldn't Grandmother give us a loan? Couldn't Grandmother release capital from Leonard's inheritance held back until Grandmother died, my mother asked. The housekeeping money was too little.

Susie needs this, Susie needs new shoes. I think she meant plimsolls, but I didn't like to interfere. Despite Leonard working overtime we seemed as impoverished as ever. He became intractable.

'I just haven't got it, girl,' he would say to console her. 'Don't fret, now. I'll try and find another place.' Although I had little sympathy for him since he was slow to fulfil his promises, I did admire his patience and his words calmed my mother and me.

Then my parents stopped talking to each other. They stopped talking to me. The game is the familiar one they played from time to time. Sometimes my mother is too unhappy to remind me what time it is, to get washed and ready for bed, but I know the routine and wander into the scullery to wash my face and hands in cold water at the sink afraid of the blood sucking snakes behind the curtain. The dark festering space under the cooker stinking of rancid lard and decaying food was another place to avoid putting my feet. On my way to the hellhole, towel and soap in hand, I passed through the parlour and it was there I liked to postpone my visit to the scullery, especially if Sid was home from work and icing a cake. I learned from Mrs Bailey that if you looked carefully there was always something marvellous to see.

All the same hating to see my mother distressed again, I made an extra effort and instead of hiding away like Mick upstairs, I tried a different tactic. While Leonard worked overtime in the office, I made the beds, tidied the room, swept the floor, and took the dirty dinner plates to wash in the scullery while she stared fixedly into the flames of a moribund fire. Sometimes she would rise, sleepwalk to the wardrobe and go through Leonard's pockets. Other times she would pull out his leather suitcase from under her bed and rifle through his papers. Then she returned to her chair, defeated.

As I lay in bed drifting off to sleep, I could hear the wet coals hissing on the fire and smell the lingering smoke. Concern for my mother kept me awake.

I tried to reconcile her gentle demeanour with the image of a bad German. I was afraid her flawless face hid a monster-mother. I didn't want to have to consider this possibility. I couldn't believe it. In conflict, I felt tight in my skin as if it would suffocate me. My scar burned. Even the love of Bobby Brand at school did little to calm my agitated heart. I had an awful premonition that my mother would just disappear, and I would be left with Leonard whom I barely knew and be sent to the children's home again. I was comforted by the sight of the black trunk on top of the wardrobe, the brass lock gleaming in the shadowy firelight.

Sometimes, apart from reading my books, I read squares of torn newspaper held together by coarse string tied to a nail on the back of the outside lavatory door. I found out about the diminished rabbit population in Britain as a cold draught blasted from underneath the door, and I discovered a man called John Christie had murdered three women and hid their bodies behind the walls of a house in Rillington Place; chilling piecemeal news to contemplate that sent me straight into the parlour where Sid was icing his cakes for company and comfort.

Sid didn't mind if I lingered in the parlour on my way from the lavatory. The instruments of his trade, the metal syringes and polished nozzles and gleaming palette knives were lined with considerable precision on the table. He applied the glossy icing with the deft movements of his palette knife, and then squeezed white roses from a fat icing bag, and then precious silver balls were delicately applied with tweezers. My mouth watered. I was always hungry.

I marvelled at the execution of Sid's craft. Bent over the table, stripped to his vest, cigarette between his lips, his large malformed hands with dirty nails would place the tiny plastic bride and groom under an arbour on the top tier, and then with precision place the pillars just so, and construct the masterpiece of glassy blue-whiteness, tier upon tier, glowing with an extraordinary light. It was love itself that commissioned such commemorative pieces for precious people who must be his favourites. I wondered how it would feel to be presented with such a cake, but I never asked Sid for whom he made them. You knew you couldn't. He liked to work in total silence. His concentration was grim-faced, threatening.

Gertie, however, was less reverential. Bursting in from the scullery, hairgrips studding her bright pink scalp in a crisscross fashion, accentuating her wolfish teeth and heavy jaw, she would bellow, 'Haven't you done yet, Sid?'

'Bugger me woman. Do you have to shout?' he protested, his teeth still managing to grip his cigarette between the corner of his lips, his hand trembling as he squeezed a fluted edge from the bulging icing bag.

'Language, Sid! Not in front of the kid. You're not in Billingsgate now.'

He glanced over at me critically; clearly, I was an impediment to his more colourful language, 'Ain't she meant to be in her room?'

'Oh, I know Sid love, but she's a fan of yours. You should treat your one and only with a bit of respect, you daft Apeth! And watch that ash!' With that she burst out laughing. Sid lifted the fag end from his lips and threw it in the fire.

Gertie turned to the mirror attached to a chain at an angle like a half-closed drawbridge. She spent a long time looking at herself in mirrors. She was always dyeing her hair different shades of black, bordering on dark plum, but never satisfied.

'I get sick of the same old face in the mirror,' she would tell it wistfully.

'Well, now you know how I feel,' Sid would say.

Without a doubt, her audacity gave her the authority to opine about life to my mother, whom she saw as a downtrodden Hausfrau. I remembered one of her tirades, the spirit of which went like this: 'Men! Don't listen to them, Sophie. They try to be the lord and masters but they're all useless. Look at my Sid. He thinks he knows everything. But what does he know about women and what women want? Look, I know he has this side-line in cakes, but I never see the fruits of his labour. Did you know that? They stick together, men. They walk all over us. I know.' Gertie tapped my mother's arm, 'Eh, it's true what they say. Behind every successful man, is a woman. Look at my Sid. I'd make him successful if he'd let me. What *you* need to do, Sophie, is please yourself a bit. Be more independent. We weren't born just for men you know.'

I heard all this in the yard, with the window wide open.

'Yer don't have to be dragged down by yer functions. No need to be a typical German housewife now. This is

England for crying out loud. We wouldn't have won the war if we relied on men!'

I heard china crash, 'I'm so sorry. I have made a mess,' said my mother.

'Don't fret, it's only me best china from Sid's mum. Right old cow she was! Sit down. I'll get ya another cup. You haven't spilt any on yerself have ya?'

My mother let Gertie talk and talk. I imagined it calmed both of them and my mother, distracted, forgot for a while Leonard's broken promises, the lack of money, and her homesickness.

'Look, why don't you get yourself a job. Have some money all for yourself. Pin money.'

'Pin money. What is pin money?'

'Money for yourself. Extra. For you, not for him. God, we deserve it. I clean Council Offices down the road. I just sweep round like and empty the bins. You don't have to talk to anyone if you don't want to. You could do that, couldn't ya? Oh lawd. Look, it's raining cats and dogs. We better get the washing in!'

After a year, we left Gertie and Sid and Mike in the marshes of Wandsworth and rented a ground floor flat in a ramshackle Victorian house in leafy Cambalt Road, off Putney Hill.

It seemed to me our lives were not only peripatetic, but cyclic. Here we were back on Putney Hill again. The rent was something we could ill-afford, but Leonard hoped once more that a flat of our own would help my mother's depression and that she would settle permanently this time. There would be less income to save for a house despite Leonard's two evenings of overtime at the office, so my mother, against Leonard's wishes, took a cleaning job for a wealthy Jewish couple in an enormous house on Putney Hill called The Clock House.

I sat at the table like a spy, listening, chewing on a dry, overdone ball of a lamb chop.

'You're working for *Jews*? What are you thinking of girl?' Leonard's face became severe and flushed.

'I feel sorry for them. Herr and Frau Stern can't have children. It doesn't matter if they are Jews. They are Germans.' My mother put down her knife and fork and wrung her hands.

Leonard continued. 'I don't like it. Look, I've got nothing against Jews. Believe me I don't. Stone the crows, I saw Belsen after it was liberated! But it's not going to work out. How can it? You say they lost family in the camps. The whole thing will blow up in your face. Don't ask for trouble, girl.'

'Ach Len. My family did nothing against the Jews. My Dad had many Jewish customers. My best friend Maria was Jewish. If I work for the English, they hate me as a German. I don't always understand English. The Sterns can tell me what to do in German.' My mother's voice was breaking up. She needed his approval, his support.

'Yes, but you're not making sense. It's not true the English always hate you. You should tell them the truth about your background. But what about the Sterns after what has happened to their people? Do you think they are going to respect you? Look, don't cry. Tell them the truth. The point is girl, I don't want you working. Not that kind of job. You'll be a charlady. It's not right.' With that he stubbed his cigarette looking depressed, his jaw clenched.

My mother had the last word. 'Len, please. The Sterns are good people. Actually, we are the same, the Sterns and me. Herr Stern just before I left said, "Mrs. Saunders, there are two most hated peoples in the world. Jews and the Germans."'

'There you are. He's putting you in your place already. Tell him the truth.' But my mother didn't answer him. She continued to quietly cry. All this went on without any recognition that I was their witness.

Despite her tears and Leonard's disapproval, my mother was set on working for the Sterns. Nothing Leonard could do would stop her. Leonard sulked for some time; mealtimes eaten in indigestible silence. But my mother looked serene as she cleaned her plate and a tiny smile played on her mouth. In any case, our spacious ground floor flat was only a ten-minute walk from The Clock House, which meant she could be home in no time. She was excited about going to work there. Unlike the manicured grounds of The Clock House, we lived in a large, neglected garden. The Clock House, my mother said, had a swimming pool and tennis courts. There were two gardeners, a cook, and a maid. I was less impressed with their setting as I was with our own after the baked clay of Gertie's backyard, the only feature being the outside lavatory. After all, we had a large jungle of a shrubbery and a ramshackle lean-to conservatory alongside a wall where I practised for Wimbledon with a tennis ball and wooden plank. On the first floor above lived the elderly Paxton couple who kept to themselves. On the top floor lived an

165

Irish widow with her daughter. Our new home may not have had the sophistication of The Clock House, but it was magic.

When we moved in the ground floor flat, my mother showed me the peach and pear trees spreading against the old garden wall in flower beds gone to seed. At the end of a long, overgrown lawn on the verge of becoming a meadow with tall grasses, wild oats and buttercups, a dense rhododendron shrubbery flourished beneath a huge horse chestnut tree, iridescent and fragrant. Sunlight poured through each leaf, surging through me like a knife, making my heart hurt. I would burst wide open like a sticky bud. I skipped about in euphoria. This was my very own secret garden where I could escape from the cold, cheerless indoors.

Earlier, before we left the bed-sit, Gertie said we had truly fallen on our feet. 'And you often get perks working for posh people like that. Clothes and shoes and stuff they no longer want.' She was proud to have helped my mother out of conjugal slavery. My mother was grateful and sorry to leave Gertie, but not sorry to leave the squalor of the Birdhurst Road scullery, and sour old beery Wandsworth.

On the morning of our departure, Mick had looked on with a sardonic smirk, lurking on the lower stairs. I hadn't seen the recluse for some time. His long sideburns were reminiscent of cowboys leaning on saloon bars with a look of insouciance, but Mick somehow managed to bypass the masculine look and appeared as soft and breakable as a breadstick. My heart went out to him.

Although he had deserted me, I had a soft spot for him. I wanted to put down the cardboard box of cutlery, go over and put my arms around him. He looked so unloved and yet guardedly defiant. He watched as we loaded the van with our meagre belongings. He kept his eyes on me. It was both uncomfortable and pleasurable.

'Keep up the two balls,' were his last words to me. I nodded and smiled weakly, hesitating, and then as if he sensed my childish yearnings, and the impulse to hug him, he turned his back and climbed the stairs.

After five miserable years, it was here, in No.8 Cambalt Road, that my mother was given a second chance to make a home and settle. With my eyes shut and hands together in prayer at school, I pictured her coming to life, rearranging the red three-piece suite this way and that, brushing the patterned Wilton carpet and measuring the tall windows for curtains. She had no time to be still; no time to read Romance magazines, sigh, or look up into the distant sky. Her hands were always busy sewing, scrubbing, darning and washing, and with a kitchen of her own, she whisked sponge cakes, stirred hot porridge for my breakfast and sprinkled sugar on top, melting to a caramel glue. On Sundays, she made Yorkshire pudding with roast beef and heated thick stews made on Mondays with old potatoes and left-over meat. We had our own larder, our own New World gas cooker in sky-blue flecked enamel like a blackbird's egg, and there was even a hot water geyser over the shining butler sink.

For my bedroom, Leonard found a secondhand wardrobe with shelves down one side in a junk shop in Lower Richmond Road, and my mother made me a dressing table out of an old pine cupboard by pleating pink curtain material around it and adding a swivel mirror. Leonard was busy measuring the floors for linoleum and carpets. He would involve me. My job was to hold one end of his leather cased Lufkin tape, keeping the loop tight against the door or skirting boards. He would mutter calculations, and I could feel the tug of the tape, a connection between us, and when he'd say, 'Let go, Fanny Adams,' I wondered how I could love a stranger. Then the moment, the hint of intimacy vanished as he wound up the tape and pressed the brass bolt like a locked door. I secretly coveted the tape. I loved the dark leather case, shiny and fresh as new conkers. One day I decided I would steal it.

We had a new paraffin heater for the kitchen and coal for the coal bunker. If it got too cold at night Leonard said I could wear his leather gloves to bed and read with my hands outside the covers. He blocked the chimney to stop the icy wind from whooshing down into the room and taped the cracks in the floorboards to stop draughts blasting up from the uninhabited basement. It was comforting to see him so considerate.

At first, it was strange sleeping alone after years in bedsits, where I'd found comfort in my mother's presence, but I didn't want to admit, least of all to myself, how lonely I felt. I read and talked aloud, refusing to be frightened by creaking doors, footsteps crossing the ceiling, and the wind blowing horizontal rain at the windows. In the past, living in one room for years, we found privacy behind a book or newspaper. But now if the air became tainted by hostility, I could escape to my room. My mother, after a time of banishing him from her affections, allowed love for Leonard to flourish again. This new strain of passion annihilated any enquiry other than their own, and I wondered what it was that bound them together. I believed love was a fixed state, not like theirs, mutable, blowing hot and cold by degrees, invariably smouldering with resentment and silence. Sometimes it was as if all three of us lived in our little capsules, meeting only at dinner. Then the rarefied atmosphere brought on headaches. Their relationship seemed so exclusive, dark and yet so full of light at times, I couldn't fathom it.

Like me, my mother liked it best outdoors. We were happy among the trees again. She planted ox-eye daisies, gladioli bulbs, and lupins, and sprinkled forget-me-not seeds all over the borders. We were together again, at last. 'Look, Susie,' she would say, 'look at the green shoots. Isn't it good? Everything grows for us.'

Yellow lichen and honeysuckle saddled the walls where behind the rhododendron bushes, I made a den and make-believed I was like Mowgli in the jungle, and could easily forget the past years and the dreadful last weeks at Gertie's place. It is difficult to banish the memory from my mind, that late afternoon, when my mother broke down, possessed by a shrieking demon and banged her head against the wall. I ran in from the backyard. Mike stood at the top of the stairs, mouth gaping. German words rushed from my mother's mouth. All the forbidden words. Words to curse and endanger us. I don't like to think about it. I felt terrified and helpless. Gertie came in from the yard stricken. She pulled my mother from the wall, and roughly manhandled her into a chair. I thought they would have to take my mother away and lock her up in hospital. I saw such things in films. But Gertie stroked her hair. 'Cry,

Sophie, cry. Cry it all out, girl. There, there.'

At the time, I made a pot of tea with shaking hands like Gertie said, and Gertie sweetened it with too much sugar, urging and coaxing my mother to drink up. And when Leonard came home, he took my mother from the armchair, guiding her to the bed, and laid her down, covering her with a blanket my mother used for ironing because you could see the singe marks on the place covering her stocking feet. And he soothed her with words.

'Now, don't you worry, girl. Stone the crows, I swear we'll soon get you better again, just see if we don't.'

# *Die Volksliste*—The Race Census, Germany 1938

They lay without a glimmer of light, in the slightest variation of shade that nightfall could offer. Each listened to the other breathing. Her rhythm was just a split second faster than his. He could hear her thinking, the mechanics of thought revealed when she held her breath and resumed after a sigh. In turn, she could tell his eyes were wide. It was if she was able to detect his blinking that made the slightest of movement of air. In the distance in the region of Bankenhorn's farm, a fox barked. The house contracted and began its nightly shifting and creaking as it settled further into the earth.

'Gustchen, are you still awake?' Robert eased himself closer as he whispered although there was no one else in the room. 'Listen, I spoke to Josef at market today. You know Josef Nowak who's got that smallholding up near Zwingli's farm. Josef was saying there are rumours the Nazis will make immigrant Poles register on the new Race Census.'

'What the children as well? Surely if they were born here, and German educated they won't have to.'

'Josef isn't sure. I've heard the Polish schools are being closed by Nazi officials. Immigrants must register and in return will get benefits. Some are being forced into the German army. Even that won't guarantee German citizenship.'

'Ach Gott. Poor Joseph. He has four sons he needs on

171

the land. All these changes are not good.'

They remained silent for a while.

'I suppose,' whispered Gustchen, 'they could pack up and go back to Poland.'

'And lose their land and livelihood?'

Gustchen drew herself up on the pillow. 'This Race Census. Is it just for the Poles?'

'For everyone living in Germany, I think. You know what I'm thinking, don't you?'

Gustchen touched his shoulder in the dark which made him flinch. 'What shall we do? Maybe we should just keep quiet about Sophie. Maybe no one will investigate. Her birth is registered in Ubstorf. They don't know where she is now do they?'

'True. Remember she is registered at school as Sophie Beck. We could officially change her birth surname from Chmielowiec to Beck, but that could alert the bigwigs to her Polish birth mother. If we change her name formally the officials might want evidence of Aryan ancestors and all that rubbish. I've heard Chmielowiec is a Jewish name.'

Gustchen let out a muffled gasp like a sob. 'I always had a feeling this would mean trouble. We were promised she was from a good family. If the Nazis find her, will they take her away?'

'No. No. We have brought her up as our own, as a good German girl. We'll have to tell her the truth soon that she is adopted. Sooner than we intended, and Erich will have to know she isn't his real sister. It will be a shock to them both. I'm not looking forward to telling them.'

'We must keep her safe. If we register her as a Jewish Pole she could be sent back to Poland. Why don't we just ignore the census.'

'We can't. Everyone has to register and put down their race.'

'We could just register her as our child, a German. She believes that in any case and so does Erich.'

'Tempting. Very tempting, but just think Gustchen. What if she has to show official papers? If there is a police-check for some reason, or she wants a passport. She will have to show her birth certificate. We can't fake that.'

'Who can help us? It's hopeless. I always knew she would bring us trouble. I sensed it.'

'She isn't the trouble. Who can help their race or birth? I know you don't mean things you sometimes say.'

Gustchen remained quiet feeling a little ashamed and guilty. Her own son Erich was very much her favourite. It is the blood that binds. She always did her best with her adopted daughter Sophie whom she found wilful, often deceptive and vain. She was a beautiful child, and growing into a beautiful, charming young woman, but that spelled danger. Robert spoiled her, and Erich always defended her. Sophie had that effect on men. She bewitched them effortlessly. But all Gustchen ever wanted was a loyal daughter, a compliant companion for the rest of her life, one who helped on the land, completed her chores without sulking, took interest in domestic skills such as crochet, weaving, cooking and housecraft. Instead, Sophie was reluctant to learn housewifery and had her sights set on city life, dancing and boys. It worried Gustchen. And now there was this wretched officialdom the Nazis kept bringing in. It was as if the state were taking over the children, and parents' authority stood for nothing. Under her breath Gustchen cursed the Führer, his cronies and the whole silly pantomime of boots, parades and saluting.

Finally, with his heart pounding Robert said, 'It will be for the best if we keep calm. I'll phone Cousin Oskar for advice. I can trust him. I think he will tell us to keep our heads down and say nothing to the authorities other than Sophie is German.'

Gustchen lay awake. She looked back over the years to when the doctor told her she would never be able to have another child after Erich's difficult birth. It became well known among the farming communities that the Becks were in search of another child, preferably a little girl, a sister for Erich. In the summer of 1921 Oskar visited with the news that there was a child available in Stadorf, a small farming community south of Lüneburg Heath. A Polish girl, called Marga Chmieloviec, a young student, had given birth to a baby girl in January of 1919 and left the baby with the Taut family hoping she would return at the end of her studies to claim the child when her circumstances had improved. The father of the baby apparently was a Swedish student who had returned home to Stockholm, and the girl's parents had no idea about the baby. That would have brought shame on Marga and her family. Sadly, the unfortunate circumstances of the young mother meant she decided not to reclaim her child. Instead, she thought it best in the interests of the child to have her adopted preferably by the Taut family, but this was not possible. Having survived the war, Herr Taut had returned to his farm in 1919, was struck by the Spanish flu and sadly died. His two brothers were killed in the war and so Frau Taut had to manage by hiring outsiders. In any case there were enough mouths to feed. She believed the orphaned baby would have a better chance in life if she could find it a secure family home. Word of mouth that Frau Taut was giving up the child excited the Becks. At last, their family would be complete and a little sister for Erich was possible.

Robert and Gustchen drove south to Stadorf through the woodlands until they came to vast plain of wheat and rye edged by pine forests, and finally to the narrow road which led to the tiny community of three or four farmhouses and workers cottages in flint-stone in the shadow of vast silo sheds. It was an anxious time. During the drive from home, Gustchen had negative thoughts. Would they take to the child or not? Would the child take to them? Maybe she would scream, and they would have to drag her from the foster family with whom she was familiar. Oh no, Gustchen couldn't bear that.

The table was set with white lace linen. Gustchen remembered the fine bone china with tiny rosebuds and the dusty spaces left on the dresser where they belonged. Frau Taut brought in the child, a two-year-old dressed in a blue smock over a white cotton dress. They were introduced to Sophie. Both prospective parents were taken back by the child's beauty. Golden hair, eyes the colour of forget-me-nots. Skin unblemished. Robert loved her immediately. He held her hand, kissed her cheek, stroked her fine head. Gustchen was more cautious, almost afraid the slightest move would frighten the child. Sophie is good natured, Frau Taut told them, so little trouble, and she had not yet suffered from any childhood illnesses, but no doubt they were yet to come. Six other children, all different heights and sizes sat on the long bench watching the strangers in silence. They brooded in their scant clothing, their colt legs twitching. They knew Sophie was going to be taken. It was unsettling for the younger ones, and alarming for the thirteen-year-old called Hilde that a child could be removed and given away with such ease. But she was a practical girl holding back her tears and consoled herself with the reality that with one less to look after once Sophie had gone, life might be easier. She told herself this to compensate for her pain.

On the chair was a small bundle of the child's possessions. It looked pitiful, barely adequate provisions for any living mite. In her mind as the pleasantries were exchanged, Gustchen wanted to suggest a trial period, in case the child became impossible and didn't settle, but Robert was confident and bold in bearing and the child went to him to sit on his knee, and she could tell he was smitten. After some coffee and homemade rye bread and butter, it was time to leave. The children were ordered to bob and curtsey and then to be off and see to their chores.

'They've already said goodbye to Sophie,' explained Frau Taut looking rather fraught.

The children rose and turned away without a sound. Little Sophie was held in Robert's arms and they made their way to the car. With the child's birth certificate in his jacket pocket, and shaking of hands, the child's fate was sealed. Frau Taut gave a brief wave and turned into the house. Robert passed the child to Gustchen while he got into the car. She saw a girl, about ten years old, spit in her direction and then bob behind the discarded wheel of a tractor. Gustchen climbed into the car with little Sophie on her lap and shut the door in time to miss a cloud of grit the girl kicked her way. The handover was disturbing and unsettling for Gustchen and yet her yearning for another child was strong. She felt sad for the Taut children. It must have been hard for them to lose the youngest of the tribe. Frau Taut had told them Sophie was returning home. They always knew she was being looked after temporarily. But that didn't make it easy for anyone.

What was going to happen to Sophie now concerning the Race Census? The Becks hid from her the truth about her origins. As far as Sophie was concerned, she was Erich's sister and German. The problem pressed down on Gustchen, brought on severe headaches, changed her moods. Is it possible as a Polish girl, she could be taken by the authorities and sent back to Poland, destitute and unloved? These were terrible times. She could feel it in her bones. Something was heavy in her heart, in the air, the wind, even the soil thickening with leaden clay. She had faith in Robert to sort everything out.

That weekend Robert went to see Oskar again after the market hours ended.

'Why don't you just phone him? It will save you a journey,' Gustchen said.

Robert said he didn't like to use the phone. 'You never know who might hear. It's safer if I go to Oskar and speak to him in private.'

Gustchen didn't argue, although she thought the idea that anyone would hear preposterous. She was afraid and wanted it sorted out. That day she found herself on edge. She hoped Oskar would come up with a solution to save them. She feared reprisals if they were found to be harbouring an alien child. Robert said that kind of official response didn't make sense and she was not to worry.

Gustchen changed the bed linen, plumped the feather mattresses, beat the rugs before preparing the vegetables for dinner. She fed the chickens and cleaned out the rabbits. Frau Kurtis came with more eggs. Gustchen was abrupt, saying she felt unwell and was going to lie down. Frau Kurtis watched her go into the bedroom and then, noting the fire of the kitchen range was low, went outside for kindle, banking up a good supply for the fire. In no time the new coffee pot was huffing and puffing, its lid hopping. She helped herself to coffee, then poured a cup for Gustchen.

In the bedroom Gustchen lay like a mannequin, on her back, eyes to the ceiling as if she had suffered a stroke. It was a relief to see her rise and thank Frau Kurtis with a whisper for the coffee. Frau Kurtis sat in the creaky wicker chair in the semi-darkness till Sophie came home with Erich, both hushed as their mother felt under the weather.

At dusk Robert returned. Frau Kurtis relieved of her duties, took her empty egg basket home and trundled down the lane with Sophie beside her as was the custom. It was only polite to make sure Frau Kurtis didn't stumble on the rough track. Her black cat came to greet them, tail up, mewling.

Robert sat on the edge of the bed.

'Close the door. Well?'

'It's settled,' said Robert. 'We talked the whole thing over. We thought about all the options and consequences.'

'Yes, so what did you decide? But keep your voice down.'

'The birth certificate says her name is Sophie

Chmieloviec and she was born in Stadorf. We will put her race down simply as German, adopted.'

Gustchen took a deep breath. 'But if they find out she is Polish and Jewish we'll get into trouble.'

'Listen. How are they going to find out? Her mother was probably a Polish immigrant. We know she was a student. She has now disappeared. We know nothing of the father apart from hearsay that he was Swedish. But who knows? There's no mention on the birth certificate of a father. He could have been German. So, we will leave it at that. We can claim she was handed over to us with little information, other than she was born in Germany, and that her mother was a German national. As for the Jewish thing, we keep quiet. Oskar says the thing to do is not draw attention to us. That's asking for trouble. We play dumb. If we get questioned, we stick to our story. We'll say Sophie's German birth mother emigrated to the States. We'll say we're not sure, it is only rumoured so we can't be accused of lying. Now don't fret so. Be strong. We will have to tell her one day when she needs to show her birth certificate, or if she needs a passport.'

'A passport? What for? She's not leaving us.'

'Keep your voice down. She will marry, have children. Boys flock around her. I don't want her to know about this race nonsense. We will tell her she is German. We'll tell her exactly what we might have to tell the authorities. Oskar says we must stick to the same story. All of us.'

'And Erich?'

'And Erich. We'll tell him later. Not now. It's not necessary.'

Unknown to them, Robert and his wife need not have whispered so conspiratorially in their bedroom in the evening dusk. Something happened when Sophie was ten years old. Her best school friend Lotte whispered in her ear as they lay in the warm grass after a long swim in the river.

'Sophie, I have a secret. Do you want to hear it? It is about you.'

'What? What is this secret you have about me?'

'You are adopted. I heard my mother talking to her friend. I heard her say, Sophie Beck is adopted. The Becks are not her real Mama and Papa.'

At first the words didn't make sense. They swirled around her head like demons, small but lethal and then they settled, burning and burrowing in her mind. Her heart began to race. Sophie moved her arm over her face. In the fierce dark, sunspots danced before her closed eyes. Her first reaction after the shock was the rise of a strong emotion, hatred mixed with anger and pain. She hated her parents for not belonging to her, for what she saw as a betrayal for not belonging, for not telling her the truth. She didn't respond to Lotte's revelation. She was tempted to save face by saying: I know. But she was dumb and let the moment pass so they could resume normality. Soon it would be time to skip along the path pretending to be happy on the long way home.

And yet home was not the same. She watched Erich, Papa and Mama with accusing eyes. The news made her worthless, an outsider, not a true Beck child. She searched for injustices and incriminations but saw none. Papa still adored her, Mama was her old strict, fault-finding self and

Erich her best friend. In time she tried to forget Lotte's words. But the truth was like a sharp stone in her shoe, sharp enough to draw blood. She learned to live with it and kept silent. Only years later, when a mysterious lady watching Sophie come out of the school gates, was Sophie reminded of her real situation. After that, whenever Gustchen was displeased with her, and punished her for not working hard enough after school in the house or in the fields, hope consoled her. One day her real mother would fetch her, take her away to a beautiful house in Hamburg or Berlin and she would be saved a life of miserable toil on the land. She imagined herself visiting the Becks and treating them to all kinds of wonderful things, beautiful clothes and food and making sure her adopted parents no longer had to work hard on the land. But a blessed abduction was a dream that faded with the disappearance of the beautiful lady outside the school. Sophie learned to bury the truth deep inside. She loved the strict and infuriating Mutti Gustchen and bore her nagging. She knew now she wasn't destined for this kind of life on the land. She wanted to be liberated from farm work and was determined to find a way. In any case, she loved her brother Erich and her dear Papa best of all, both of whom spoiled her and loved her in return.

2

# Putney 1953

Our first summer in Cambalt Road taught me how to live in a paradise of freedom without the rules and restrictions of being lodgers. I learned to walk the garden walls in bare feet, running along the backs of houses, leaping into corner piles of steaming cut grass, and trespassing in next door's overgrown garden. I swam in the wild grass, kicking my heels, rolling over and spreading my arms. Swallowing mouthfuls of green air, the past miseries powdered like dead moths on windowsills. I explored the neighbouring gardens under cover of shadow and overhanging trees, spying on gardeners mowing vast lawns, enchanted by hammocks swinging between stakes, tables with white cloths laid for afternoon tea served by maids in black dresses and white frilly hats to dowagers in bath chairs, and watched unsuspecting boys, home from prep-school, lounging in deck chairs hot from cricket and croquet.

Then over the wall again I trespassed in kitchen gardens to feast on stolen peas, rhubarb, blackcurrants, blackberries, peaches and unripe apples sour enough to make your gums bleed. Listening to foreign voices, laughter and the ping-ponk of tennis balls, I escaped home, critical looks, boredom, the oppressive silences, my clothes and knees green-flecked and my senses drunk with grass-liquor so that if in my new kingdom I met a leopard so exclusively dark in the dappled shade, I wouldn't flinch, but crouch low to watch and then continue on my journey. Because I was not there yet. I still didn't know myself. The mirror showed a girl on the outside, but nothing else, no clues of her becoming, of anything I might be made of, anything solid or real. Her eyes revealed only a blue glassiness. I was not yet Englished, but my disguise was good enough for that to matter less with urgency, even though I knew this to be unfinished business and I was yet to perfect my change. Grandmother in The Horseshoe would know what to do but we never saw her in those days. I tried to believe my Germanness was being diluted as my flesh and bones grew. At night my legs hurt. My scar prickled less often. I was on a rack, tortured by the slow wheel of time's growth. I needed to starve my German self so Heike would become weak, faint and dumb, capitulating and dying inside me.

Then something strange happened. Beauty might interrupt a steady flow of life, but so might an unforeseen intrusion when you are offguard, or fall down the rabbit hole, or suffer vertigo in the dark. My mother lay in the sunshine in a deckchair beside the bright green blades of the gladioli leaves just under the sitting room window with the net curtain billowing and threatening to snag on the outside wall. I was content; I knew this was the English life she dreamed about when she left home in Lüneburg and married Leonard.

I sat beside her on the grass, my legs pulled close to my chest held by my circling arms. We found no reason to speak. The silence we shared was different to the ominous, heavily laden, recriminating silences between my mother and Leonard. It was a togetherness silence; we were consonant, and our momentary closeness a tacit conspiracy against Leonard. I was against everyone but us.

It was enough to be at her side as the warmth soaks through our skin, listening to glitching gnats, the soft burr of bees and flies humming. Unexpectedly, I felt her hand resting on my head, and she stroked my hair. I looked up at her, screwing my eyes against the strong sun. It was so unusual for my mother to touch me.

'Susie,' she said, looking down, and after a pause, 'would you like to know about your father?'

My heart beat faster. I felt something in me close like a steel door. Everything was spoiled. She does this on purpose to unsettle me, to poison me with his Nazi poison, just when everything is good, and we are happy at last. Without a moment's hesitation, I blurted, 'No!' Fear made me protest too loudly. How could I be English when she dragged me back into the evil black hole of the past?

I didn't have time to think. I had to save myself. I wanted to hurt her back for hurting me. And I wanted to be ready with the answer as if I'd been prepared for this assault all along. But I knew the truth was a snare. Only moments ago, we were together and peaceful. How can this happen, this awful cut that severs us? Now we sat together but separate in a breached quietude. She had withdrawn her hand. I had denied my father whom I had never known. I had relegated his memory to a small word, a denial

My mother rises  from the deckchair and disappears inside. I run the length of the garden, through the shrubbery and leap  up, onto the wall leading to the overgrown garden next door. I jump down onto the long grass and lay curled with my knees drawn. A small animal wants to gnaw my insides. I try not to cry. It is silly to cry.

Full of anger, I hate myself for being cowardly and dirty and unworthy of a father who no longer exists but gave me life. I resent my mother. For her foolishness, her Germanness. For the brutal question without warning so I couldn't fortify myself or give myself the chance to consider her proposition. And yet I love her. It is impossible to be in command of conflicting emotions. They overwhelm and confuse with duplicity, smoke and fire. My scar burns. Then full of regret, I am too scared to go home and tell her I'd changed my mind; that I want her to tell me everything, but not now because I'm not ready. I wouldn't know when, but another time. Then I hear a voice, shrill and commanding.

'I can see you. You there, hiding in the grass. Be off with you, I say. I'll fetch the police! Do you hear me?'

I looked up with bleary eyes towards the distant house. All the windows were shut as usual, the blinds down, but on the second floor, an old woman in her nightdress, her white hair in disarray, waved her hairbrush like a handgun at the open sash-window. I stood, and called that I am sorry, slinking off into the undergrowth, jumping over the wall home.

Once indoors nothing is mentioned about my father, but that is little comfort. I am unsettled and have it in my head that my dead father has been a monstrous man. Weren't all Germans? I might be able forgive my mother. She is a good German. It was the German Nazis who were the unspeakable devils. I saw this in the cinema. I heard it on the lips and tongues of most English people. The memory of my dead father is placed in the shadow of war, in the concentration camps, among Nazi brutes and savages. I have his blood coursing through my veins. His absence is a presence I tried to fathom in the mirror: which aspect have I inherited: the voice, fingernails, hair, the shape of my forehead? Since I do not resemble my mother, it is a wonder she can bear to look at me. I know I must keep alert. His name might appear in the latest war criminal reports and set my heart galloping. I relegate him to the land of all the other dead Nazis, but Heike refuses to deny him. Heike wants to know. She pokes me with a conscience, and it hurts. At school, I behave as if nothing inside has happened. I smile to please the girls who do not like me. Perhaps the wrong smell emanates from me and with an animal instinct, they know I am not one of them. All the same I am careful not to upset them, not to show my feelings too unduly when they taunt me, or put me in Coventry, or nudge elbows if I say something, or cup a hand over another's ear and whisper about me, and then laugh. Whatever they do, nothing hurts as much as Heike's poking, taunting my cowardice and creepy sycophantic ways.

It isn't long before I discovered another intruder in our newly found paradise. It's the girl who lives in the attic flat. You can't help but trust perfection. She was a rare species of girl made from an exceptional template with the finest skin, a dewy bloom, the whitest teeth set in pink gums, with sparkling eyes and features arranged so that from every angle she was none other than exquisite.

Such was the beautiful convent girl in her moss-green blazer with yellow piping and school hat held down with chin elastic, and shiny, dark auburn curls, blushing calves and the whitest socks. Her sandals were cherry blossom polished with little tulip shaped holes on the uppers. Unlike my raggy cloth one with its rubber lining cracked and peeling, her leather satchel had the glossy patina of freshly fallen conkers and gleamed just below her hip. Standing behind her at the bus stop, I smelled the pungency of her perfection, her flawless Englishness, her fragrant Cussons soaped skin. She created a sensuous tension heightened by her disdain for me. But I expected nothing else.

Her beauty was potent. I imagined she possessed a heroic potential and intelligence I lacked, and although I yearned for someone to play with after school, I never had the courage to climb the stairs and call for her. I was convinced in any case, asking if she might like to come out to play would demean her. Although I had grown long-limbed and athletic, and stopped wetting the bed, it was my envy and inferiority that rankled and probably fed her superiority. After all, she must have known I was the girl who lived in the flat below her and she might watch me sometimes in the garden.

In the bus queue every morning, my green eyes wandered over her knife-pleated skirt, upright back, the slight turn of her head so that I imagined I could sometimes detect a faint smile of accomplishment. I wondered whether I should try and make friends, tell her my secrets, how I walk the walls, steal from gardens and burrow in my den to read *Heidi* in the dusk, but I knew I was unworthy of her, made of something different, something coarser and plain. I had poisoned blood. I knew my place, that I should stay away, remain cautious.

My mother was curious and cautious too, but had already been snubbed. From behind the net curtains, she stepped back to watch the convent girl's mother as she left the house and walked across the drive to the gates.

'She dyes her hair,' my mother commented, 'it is too blue to be a real black. Und ach, how she wiggles her bottom when she walks, and look at her long red nails!'

By my mother's standard, those were clear signs of having lapsed from what is natural and anything natural in her view, was moral. 'She's not a lady. A real lady says Good Morning, and Good Evening when you meet in the hall. She says nothing. It is rude, Susie.'

But the convent girl wasn't rude like that I told myself, following her down Putney Hill to catch the number 37 bus to St. Catherine's School, a bus that had taken on an enchanting significance for it carried my idol to her daily lessons while her minion lapsed into daydreams of being her friend. All through the spring term, the painful crush on the convent girl tormented me, but I kept my distance knowing I could never hope to befriend her.

Then one day, I was late and almost missed the bus. I bounded upstairs and as the bus lurched forward, fell blushing with embarrassment into a seat right next door to the convent girl. I didn't want her to think I am forward. I glanced at her with an apology on my lips, and noticed her smile, or was it a smirk, of pleasure.

We exchanged names. Theresa Behan made a point of telling me she was a Roman Catholic and taught by nuns. This made her special, she said. When she asked me what I was, I felt unsure, trying to summon an answer that might not encompass wider implications about my unfortunate heritage. I managed to tell her I went to St. Catherine's, a Church of England School, and I am was taught by Miss Lovejoy, who tells us brilliant stories. She doesn't look in the least impressed, crinkling up her snub nose and casting a lingering look at my fading cotton school dress and old cloth satchel. I blush. She says I am very fortunate to have such a nice Daddy because, she said, she didn't have one. I say nothing in reply. I don't want to reveal that Leonard is not my real Daddy and that my father is dead.

'My mummy is a secretary. She takes the Tube every morning, up town to a solicitor's office. What does your mother do?'

'Nothing,' I lie, uncomfortably, and shift in my seat. 'She doesn't do anything.' There was an uneasy silence. 'I never see you in the garden,' I ventured.

'Jeysus no! Nature is so boring.' She looked across at me with a faint sneer. I hid my disappointment. Then she said, 'We have a television. Do you have a television?'

'No, we don't.' After a long pause I provided a reason. 'My mother doesn't like it. She likes going to see films at the Regal or Odeon. Singing and dancing films with Doris Day are her favourites. She's mad about Doris Day and lots of other singing and dancing stars, like Debbie Reynolds.'

'Oh,' she said in a small puff of breath, and then as if to herself, 'I thought everyone had a television for the Coronation.'

I had nothing to say about this. But she was persistent.

'Did you see it? Did you go to someone's house to see the Queen crowned. I mean if you didn't have a television?'

'No. I could have gone to Gertie's friend's house in Alma Road where we used to live, but I had a boil on my knee, and it hurt.'

Theresa burst out laughing, but I didn't know why and was instantly offended.

'But' I added to impress her, 'I did see the Queen in her horse and carriage at the top of East Hill once and waved a flag. She wasn't wearing a crown, just a yellow hat and dress and I was disappointed.'

And then there was a ting-ting of the bell as the bus slowed for the Request Stop outside the Convent. Theresa stood imperiously, a sign I had to get up and let her step into the gangway.

'Cheerio. See you tomorrow!' she called, tripping down the stairs.

I bumped over to her warm seat by the window and watched her walk through the convent gates on East Hill as I normally did. Not much could be seen of the convent, hidden by high walls. There were rows of barred windows with dark glass peeping out from the eaves at the same level as the windows of the double decker bus. A nun marched across the courtyard, her face exposed, the rest encased in a frosted sheath. I was curious to find out what kind of teachers nuns were, their habitat and nature and what it must be like to go to a convent school. No wonder all the windows were shut. The convent was right next door to a brewery. I imagined the nuns would not approve of the men, bottles of beer and the bitter-sweet smell. I sighed as the bus droned on to Wandsworth High Street. I would willingly become Theresa's slave. Later she always kept me at a distance though, just as my mother always did, so I was lost, longing and beyond saving.

I was in my final year at St. Catherine's Junior School and had just taken the Eleven-plus exam to determine what kind of child I had become. We were ignorant of the official categories: Golden children were academic, gifted and capable of abstract thought; the Silver children were the future office workers and professionals, and the Iron children of limited ability, destined to become semi-and unskilled labourers or apprentices.

Miss Lovejoy, however, left our intellectual development to nature and concentrated on our imaginative, spiritual and moral enhancement. Or as I suspect, unaware of her own prejudices, lumped us all together as the hopelessly poor offspring of the proletariat, unworthy and possibly incapable of academic rigor. But she seemed to love us the way we were, even though she ought to have had more faith in our intellectual potential. I sat the exam and read the questions. I knew there was a code to crack but didn't have the key or time to discover answers. It was gobbledygook. I couldn't fathom the odd one out between startlingly disparate objects such as: *kite, cake,* and *code*. Innumerable other conundrums in which words were compressed into neat rows, their relation to each other impossible to decode. I remembered reading in *Alice in Wonderland* the Mad Hatter's riddle: 'Why is a raven like a writing desk?' and Alice's indignation when the Mad Hatter said he didn't know. I felt indignant, too, that these riddles had in my view no answers, so I didn't see the point. Disappointedly, the exam papers failed to offer the opportunity to write stories or poems or psalms as springboards to other worlds. Only infinite numerical conundrums, and linguistic obfuscations fogging the brain, frustrating and confusing. Clearly, I was not clever enough to seek the right answers. I had to learn to live with a limited brain, and it was hard to accept.

Theresa said the examinations were easy. I expected nothing else from her, aware that my dream of attending the warm red-bricked, ivy-clad grammar school, set in a neat lawn lined with broad plane trees on West Hill Road, faded from my sights even before the results came through. I would have to face the future of Theresa's success, my longing threatening to make me sour, discontented and jealous.

I took solace in the garden and escaped into other worlds in books. Enid Blyton's *Malory Towers* series offered me distraction. I read during the chilly springtime evenings in the den I made in the shrubbery, and sometimes if I were walking the walls at the bottom of the neighbouring gardens, I would ignore my mother's call at dusk and sneak in later through my bedroom window because indoors was not to become the safe haven I hoped. Despite my disappointment and unhappiness, something surprising happened.

That summer term of 1956, my eleven plus failure miraculously rewarded me. I was allocated a place at the grammar school of my dreams. As a London County Council experiment, the school had been recently turned into a comprehensive, one of the first of its kind for girls in London. As a member of the new intake enjoying the spanking new airy buildings, I knew my inferior place. The older girls had an aura of intellectual authenticity. I watched them as if they were of a different species, confident, well groomed, and beautifully spoken. Here at last there was hope of achieving my ambition, to be clever and acceptable. This was my chance to learn, and become one of them although the seniors kept themselves apart from us, a herd of ruffian failures to be tamed and educated. But before attending the new girls' comprehensive, my education continued in a different vein on the top of the 37 bus during bleary mornings when I rubbed little crusty balls of sleep from my eyes.

Theresa's special curriculum began with the darkness of Sister Mary, who brandished her cane, causing the girls to be alert during religious instruction. The inattentive daydreamers were striped with the mark of the cane on the knuckles where the pain could be felt more intensely. Pity for oneself was not tolerated since the punishment was always deserved. I pointed out to Theresa that in our school no one received lashings or were beaten. It was enough to be sent to Mr. Newman at St. Catherine's. His name alone made the backs of my legs weaken. No one was quite sure what happened in his study but there were rumours. One that he kept a slipper in his stationery cupboard with which he beat the boys' backsides, but girls were never sent to him for punishment. Miscreants were few and far between and it was often left for Miss Lovejoy to punish the disobedient with a severe talking to. Mr. Newman's imagined secret power was more terrifying than the slipper. The thought of being sent to him was always enough to keep us in check. Anyway, Theresa was unimpressed with Mr. Newman. Hadn't I heard about eternal hell fires for the wicked and how all the children had to attend weekly confessions in a curtained box in the Convent chapel to allay the possibility?

'But what if you've done nothing wrong?' I argued, trying to recall what sin I had committed that week. 'What if you have nothing to confess? What then?'

'Oh, Father Leary says we are all sinful girls, and we must look into our black hearts, because there's *always something* we have done wrong. It could be an evil thought, or a lack of prayer, or back chatting our mothers. God is all-seeing and all-knowing so you can't hide anything from Him.'

'Why do you have to go in a box, then?'

'Eejit! It's not a box exactly, but a curtained off space with a grill you speak into where Father is listening. You have to tell him all your sins, and then he tells you how many Hail Marys we have to say to atone for the bad things you have done. It's called going to confession, don't you know? If you don't confess, you are impure, and you can be cast out from the church.'

I sighed. It sounded all rather hocus-pocus to me, not unlike a story about wizards and witches and spells, and I turned away as the bus droned along Upper Richmond Road, the conductor pounding the stairs singing his refrain, 'Any-more-fares-please!'

I didn't like the idea of an all-spying-God. I wanted my privacy. I wanted my secrets if I should happen to accumulate some. It seemed to me everyone in my small family had secrets. Certainly, my mother had hers, and I sensed Leonard had his because as I grew older I found my mother and Leonard furtive, constantly hiding truths, covering up with non-sequiturs, or talking what I considered to be nonsense in front of me. If I entered the room unexpectedly, Leonard would hide papers, or turn away and their conversation would tail off to an uneasy quiet.

'Toodle-doo,' Theresa would abruptly say as the bus slowed to stop outside the convent, leaving me to wonder how anyone could avoid the fate of excommunication, even for the smallest of misdemeanours. It came to me then, the terrifying possibility that my mother and I had already been cast out for the sins of the German people. Is this why we have come to England hoping to escape censure but only to find ourselves cast out? They were no good the Germans, other than my mother. I knew that much. Everyone knew it and told me so. I felt scorched with guilt and felt my body tighten as if to squeeze the breath out of me. I stood and rang the bell to get off the bus at the next stop, and then I ran to school to burn off my fear and apprehension.

A few days later, I decided to test God's omniscience and hid a girl's pencil case behind a tall cupboard after morning PE. I chose Daphne's pencil case left on her desk because I was jealous of her beauty and brains and she looked well fed and cared for so I imagined she wouldn't suffer too much. But she did. She wailed like a poor rabbit caught in a trap.

'Everyone must look for Daphne's pencil case,' said Miss Lovejoy who was tight-lipped, very annoyed and clearly determined to expose the culprit. I flounced about the room pretending to search, my face burning. What was

God going to do now?

'No one is going home until the pencil case is found,' announced Miss Lovejoy. But God did not strike me dead or expose me as the thief.

All day, pupils searched between lessons afraid we might have to stay in the classroom forever like prisoners. Miss Lovejoy could be severe, and it showed in her face. A sinful act such as stealing had consequences for everyone else. When home-time came we were told to search again and not allowed out of the classroom. By this time, I felt dreadfully broken and ashamed. How would God reveal to me that he *saw* me steal with his very own eyes? I waited anxiously for a sign, my heart beating fast. Finally, we were told to go back to our seats. 'Silence! Sit up straight, hands on desks!' Miss Lovejoy meant business. In stalked Mr. Newman. Stiff, erect and imposing, he addressed us cowering in rows.

'I'm very sorry and disappointed to hear that a thief is among us,' he boomed.

Daphne resumed her sobbing from her seat in front of me. I could see her shoulders trembling.

'Hands together and eyes closed. We must pray to God to reveal the nasty culprit, an enemy in our midst. We ask Him to forgive the child and we must pray it will never happen again. And remember God works in mysterious ways and in the end the thief will be punished. Now I want all of you to make one last effort to find the pencil case otherwise you cannot go home.'

The time had come. There was a loud scraping of chairs and frantic searching presided over by the formidable, frightening Mr. Newman and Miss Lovejoy who rummaged in her desk and searched behind the blackboard.

I bounded over to the tall cupboard to the narrow gap by the wall and cried out, 'I've found it!' as I pressed my face against the wall and slipped my hand down to retrieve the pencil case. Daphne snatched it from my hands and hugged it to her chest without a word of thanks.

'Stand still everyone. We hope this kind of thing will never happen again children. Chairs on desks, and then line up by the door, but make way for Mr. Newman to go out first,' called the relieved Miss Lovejoy above the excited din.

Before he swooped majestically through the classroom door Mr. Newman and Miss Lovejoy exchanged a look. Neither praised me or thanked me for the discovery of Daphne's pencil case and Miss Lovejoy avoided my eyes. In retrospect, they probably knew I was the culprit. I ignored this knowledge at the time; I hope I had pulled it off blamelessly, but in my heart, I knew Miss Lovejoy and Mr. Newman knew the truth. I waited to find out if God had known too. There was no message from Him in the way I was expecting. I thought he might strike me dead, or prevent my legs moving, or slit my tongue. I confessed to no one. But I felt a deep, unshakable shame.

Needless to say, there were no more thefts, and Daphne, the Golden child, went on to a prestigious grammar school; I imagined her blonde ringlets bouncing all the way.

But before I left St. Catherine's School, I came to more serious harm. Posing as a friend, Theresa dragged me into a murky pond of imponderables, a grey swamp between God and the Devil, both advocates of punishment and cruelty. Daily, she left me floundering and wretched on the top of the number 37 bus, and since I was made of fire, I could feel my spirit die under the weight of ash with its acrid stench rising from the fires of people who burned their detritus in backyards.

I had no choice but to listen to her daily lessons as my scar sent needles of pain down to my ankle, and the bus blindly rattled towards Peckham, lurching to deliver my personal oracle to her beloved convent school. Over the weeks, the subjects became increasingly wide-ranging as if she was on a demonic mission to cram me with as much ghastly information as possible before I escaped her clutches.

Or maybe, disturbed by her own discoveries, she had to exorcise them, relieve herself by unloading onto me as an act of indisputable obligation. Did I know women sold their bodies for sex? I wasn't sure how this worked, whether they could have their bodies back again. That men liked to look at 'dirty' magazines full of naked ladies was what men were about. Boys had a floppy *thing* that could grow thick and hard to shove up girls' front bottoms and actually enter their bodies, which was a sin. And I must know all about the Nazi concentration camps she had heard about and seen on television with her very own eyes, you know the SS forcing inmates to thrust women and children *alive* into hot ovens, or gas them in the showers, naked and screaming, their hair already shorn off? All this told to me glibly as if she was recalling a recipe for a chocolate cake. My scar deepened.

Appalled by her revelations, I wanted to stop her mouth with my hand, but I sat rigid while she whispered so close to my ear; I could feel her moist breath gather inside the shell. Her words had a duel effect. Not only were they carriers of horrendous truths—for I never for a moment doubted her source: the venerable BBC—but they stung me with the paralysis of further unspeakable shame. She locked me in a nightmare where it is impossible to move or scream. She took my innocence, my hope, my faith in human nature. But maybe not. Maybe she told me what the real world was about and the nature of the human race. Her means were brutal. She told me to hurt me. I knew as much.

'Do you never go to Ireland?' I asked her one morning, in a pathetic attempt to allay further terror, details of which repeated in visual form at night on the black screen of my closed eyes.

'Jayzus, yes! But mummy gets tired of all the relatives coming to gawp at us and ask about our London life as if the city was Sodom and Gomorrah, you know, wanting the gossip and gruesome details. Of course, there's little to report in boring Putney. Won't your Daddy get you a television?'

'No,' I said sadly, but it was an act. The last thing I wanted were programmes about the horrors of the world. Theresa commiserated. 'There are fantastic programmes on TV. Last night I saw *Dixon of Dock Green*. And Mummy loves *I Love Lucy* and *Hancock's Half Hour*. You should ask your Daddy for a television then you won't have to run wild in the garden...'

But I had already stopped listening, remembering her

information about how the Germans threw babies against the wall, made lampshades out of human skin, and stuffed mattresses with human hair. I was horrified by these heinous acts, and plotted ways to avoid meeting her and sharing a bus seat. Everything she told me was unforgettable, and the pain continued between innocuous accounts of popular television shows.

'I would invite you up to watch... but Mummy wouldn't allow it.'

'Oh,' I said thoroughly miserable and yet relieved. The punches to my stomach, dealt by the loathsome Wright boy after school, was nothing compared to this. As the bus trembled past Wandsworth library, I stared at her exquisite profile and watched those supple lips shape her words.

'You know, the truth is, Mummy would have a fit if she knew I was talking to you. She says people like you and your mother shouldn't be considered part of the human race, and you should go back to where you come from. That's what my mother says.'

I froze, unable to respond. I had no truths with which to defend my mother, only my love for her, threatened by the idea she was evil. I refused to believe my mother was evil. Theresa leaned her face close to mine and whispered in my ear: 'We know all about your mother!' Then she threw her head back so violently her school hat fell back, her auburn curls let loose over her forehead.

I couldn't look at her again. Her beauty was God's gift, and he had sent her to torment me. I decided to skip school. I sat in Bishops Park across Putney Bridge on the Fulham side, watching the river traffic and wishing I had never been born; but as the lonely day wore on, my escape was futile. It simply gave me more time to dwell on the horror and wonder if Theresa knew evil things about my good mother I dare not ask about.

I contemplated calling on Mrs. Bailey. I could see her house clearly over the brown oily water as I leant against railings, my eyes settling on the boathouse across the river. I fantasized she would guide my spirit to a safe haven of guiltless joy, and we would sit and eat sugar mice till we were sick and our teeth fell out. Then I would beg her to adopt me till I remembered the little paraffin lamp and the rats tumbling over my back. Then I thought of Ida. I wondered where she was now when I needed her, but how she betrayed us. Gertie would defend me. And if I agreed to kiss Mike now that I was relieved of my brace, surely he would befriend me? But in any case, I told myself, how could I leave my mother? We were joined by blood and bones, secrets and love.

I walked through the leafy park, sat on the edge of the sandpit and then went for a swing. I couldn't wait till St. Mary's clock struck four thirty, and I could make my way home.

That evening, while Leonard listened to a *Paul Temple* episode on the wireless, his head leaning over to the speaker, and cigarette glowing in the fading light, my mother put her feet on the sofa and darned the worn elbow of my school cardigan under the standard lamp. I watched as she wove the needle in and out, over and under the lines of stitches she had already patterned to make a miniature trellis. Her darning, composure and contentment calmed my agitation.

She looked very lovely, and I had an urge to go over to

her, put aside her darning, and rest my head in her lap. I wanted to feel her arms close around me. I felt she loved me despite herself, that her love for me was a secret she kept from everyone for a reason I couldn't fathom. Maybe I *imagined* she loved me when she didn't, being mostly distant and undemonstrative. I never understood her. I even entertained the idea that she might want me to grow separate from her, to be unblemished as if drawing me to her might in some way contaminate me. Maybe this idea was just as fanciful as the possibility she didn't like children, or didn't like the way I looked, or that I reminded her of something or someone she would rather forget. I didn't think all those things at once. Over time I would try to fathom her feelings for me.

I watched her mend the sleeve of my cardigan with such precision and care, I shifted closer and had to believe she felt something for me; she pulled the wool firmly through the webbing and I tried to lean my head against her thigh, but the needlework basket got in the way.

'What is it Susie?' She looked down at me with a frown and then looked over to Leonard in the armchair.

I could feel tears well. I hurt for her, the way she was being slandered, although I had no way of knowing what made her sad apart from homesickness. And yet thinking about everything Theresa told me about what the Germans did, how *could* my mother sit there in the glow of the firelight and calmly sew? I wanted to beg my mother to tell me what Theresa had told me wasn't true. I wanted to know what part my mother played in the war and its crimes. But I was timid and afraid. I was afraid I would hate her, and my late father, and myself. The seeds had already been sewn.

'Susie, you don't look well. Ah! Your head is burning. Feel it yourself. Do your legs hurt? Can you breathe all right?' She was worried about polio. There were pictures of children in the newspapers encased in iron lungs in hospital.

'I've got a headache, and I hurt here,' I said pointing to the centre of my chest. Then my body contracted, and I bent over and sobbed.

'No school for you tomorrow, Susie. Here take this handkerchief and wipe your tears and blow your nose. Go and have a quick wash and get into bed. Len will bring you in a cup of warm tea, won't you Len?'

It was all arranged behind my back. I was to be sent away on an unwelcome visit. When I found out, it left my dry mouth and protest stuck like a lump in my throat.

'It won't be so bad, Susie. You can take your books and sleep in the spare bedroom. It will not be new for you. You are not going to be with a stranger. You are grown up now.'

Almost twelve years old and all the fears and dread of my four-year-old self resurfaced.

'She's an old lady. There's nothing to worry about. Dolly and Harold are going on holiday, and they don't want to leave Grandmother by herself. You can keep her company. It will only be for a week. She's seen so little of you.' That was Leonard's coaxing.

Lying in bed at night before my departure, memories of The Horseshoe came like a blood rush to my head. I remembered how the walls trembled in the snowstorm, and the smell of old dinners congregated in the corner of the bedrooms. The house loosened and rotted like an old tooth in its socket through the winter. In a panic, I tried to recall the rules: straight back at the dinner table, elbows in, peas on the arch of the fork. Speak English! Speak English! The out of bounds larder. The persistent hunger and someone pounding the door. Marching boots. Nightmares. Black holes filling with blood drilled in the snow.

My very person had caused offence. How could I go back there now? The sound of Grandma's clip-up handbag like the vicious wire springs on the mousetraps, the disapproval in her rheumy eyes, and her unkissable mouth, that hard, unforgiving rictus made me sick with fear.

I reasoned I was older and spoke English fluently. I understood how hard it must have been to have Germans in her home, and such an unforgiveable German who came with nothing but the black suitcase, the brass lock and a fur coat, and a child dressed like some showy Nazi offspring in her buttoned-up boots and unearthly white plaits.

My mother said I could pack Leonard's small leather suitcase. I threw in various toiletries, clean knickers, a couple of vests, three pairs of white ankle socks and a fresh summer dress. I didn't forget to pack pencils, writing paper, back copies of *Girl* comic and *Wuthering Heights*.

To my mortification it was Harold who met me at Croydon Station, looking exactly as I remembered, only a fraction more human. He was as bald and pink as ever, his pinkness accentuated by the glossy black leathers, his piggy eyes gleaming like a butcher's hatchet, hustling me into the side car, pressing the suitcase down on my lap. After some rocking and paddling of the pedal and revving up the engine, we were off in a blast of cold air pouring through the ill-fitting PVC windows. I rather enjoyed gazing at the misty world through the plastic lens, private in my own container, my green-stick bones absorbing the jarring all the way to Coulsdon, the Brighton Road gobbling up by his hungry chrome rattle-machine.

Grandma, pale and etiolated, stood in the doorway squinting like someone who had emerged from years in darkness. Face to face; this time my eyes levelled with hers and a smile was triggered briefly on our lips. I couldn't but obey my four-year-old self and look down at her tiny feet encased in black velvet slippers with pink bows. Was this a sign of less austerity, Grandma being openly lavish and frivolous?

'Here she is. Delivered safely,' puffed Harold with my suitcase under his arm.

'Thank you,' I said turning to him and taking the case from him.

'Can't stop, Mother. Best be off. Dolly's waiting. You know how anxious she gets when there's any change in the arrangements.' He tossed his head in my direction. 'Ring Leonard at work if there is any problem and don't forget to put the chain across at night. Cheerio now.'

'I'm listening. And there's no need to go on and on the way you do, Harold. I'm not stupid.' Grandma waved him off and without waiting for him to drive away, beckoned me in and shut the door, putting the chain across and slamming the bolts top and bottom. For a moment, the violence of her actions were alarming, but I took in a deep breath. I was incarcerated with the person who gave me the first experience of being unacceptable for reasons then unknown to me. As a child you don't wrack your brains to find the source of hatred. You accept it as your fault for simply being who you are.

'You can take your suitcase upstairs and unpack in my bedroom. You'll be sleeping with me. I've not been sleeping well on my own ever since Bertie died. I'll put the kettle on for a nice cup of tea.' She shuffled off into the kitchen.

I stood beside the coat stand. Grandma's hat hung on the usual peg as I remembered, and Grandfather's hat and scarf in a state of rigor mortis, hung on the other. His furled black umbrella and galoshes occupied a space close to Grandma's pointy going-out shoes. In the oval mirror, I saw a girl. With the light behind her from the little front door window, she looked haunted in a faded black and white photo, straight, blonde hair and shining eyes. It was impossible to approve of her. She had no substance. Thin and ethereal. Plain but passable.

The top of the stairs was now visible. Beneath the window of Tudor roses was my small kingdom waiting for me, a landing space that had shrunk to the size of a pillowcase, where once I had tried to make sense of the salty islanders, their comings and goings. It wouldn't be any use to me now, but I still had a soft spot for the space as if it recognized me.

Grandma's once forbidden sanctum, her bedroom, relieved of its 1940s clutter, looked fairly hospitable. I noticed the dressing table with its silver-backed brush and mirror. The photographs of ladies in absurd icing cake hats had disappeared, and so too the forbidding array of creams and jars. I don't know what made me do it, but I opened the top drawer. It seemed to open in my hand without being touched as if a spirit compelled me. It was stuffed with small envelopes. Curious I opened one and read a letter to dearest Granny about passing the Matriculation and wouldn't Daddy be proud. *I'll be meeting him soon, and I'm so excited.* It was signed *Your Chrissie.* I thought no more about these letters and assigned them to the past, to part of Grandma's life, a place that naturally excluded me. But I was stirred and made anxious by this discovery so soon into my visit.

The truth is often like a drug. It takes time to get into the bloodstream, take effect. Two words, *Daddy* and *Chrissie,* preyed on my mind although I dismissed them. I scratched at the itchy scar on my leg before I closed the drawer gently so as not to disturb anything and began to examine the room. The bed, once towering above my chest, appeared a little sunken with a cream eiderdown perched on top of blankets like a pastry crust. But the little footstool was there offering familiarity, and the windowsill ledge that had once only just reached my nose if I stood on tiptoe, now cut across my waist. The garden no longer stretched a long way off and bounded close to the house. Grandfather's rose bushes long gone, had been replaced by wide beds of lavender and catmint tangled over the path.

I put my suitcase under the bed, beside the china wee-wee pot. I brushed my hair. How pleasant it was to think that being allowed in Grandma's room was none other than a mark of her acceptance at last. But the thought of sleeping beside her in her bed made me uneasy. An electric sensation travelled down my spine and spread to the backs of my legs. I thought they would buckle any moment the way they did when I was afraid of heights.

I decided to be careful and keep myself to myself as

much as possible. I would close myself up, keep my limbs close to the main body. Lower my eyes. That was something she had taught me, to will myself invisible. I was going to be her best pupil. My thoughts were interrupted by someone calling, 'Are you up there?'

I crept down the stairs. 'Come and have some bread and butter, and a cup of tea.'

'Now,' she said, pouring tea. 'You like it weak and sweet with plenty of milk. There. Help yourself to bread and butter. Your Grandfather liked his tea strong and if I didn't watch him he would help himself to six lumps of sugar. No need to comment, dear. Your mouth is full.'

I kept my back straight; elbows tucked in and smoothed the napkin over my lap.

'I want to know everything,' Grandma announced imperiously, 'all your news. How is your beautiful mother? I haven't seen her in an age. Is she well?'

'Yes, thank you, very well,' I replied in my best English. I fancied I could play the role of Alice in Wonderland while Grandma took on the green tint of the Caterpillar who insisted that I explain myself.

'Now, tell me all about school and what grades you are getting. Your father was always so good at Mathematics and English, but he wasted himself when he was young chasing the girls and going for the easy option.' By *father* I assumed she was referring to Leonard. I had no idea what 'easy option' was, but Grandmother soon enlightened me.

'Your grandfather wanted him to enter the insurance firm in the city and work his way up but just to be difficult he chose to become a cabinet apprentice. He wasn't suited to it. We told him, but he remained reckless. Harold was always such a good boy, but Leonard was my favourite and difficult. Adorable child, but I only confess this to you. Your father often led Harold astray when they were boys spending their pennies for the church plate at the sweet shop, that sort of thing. Then your father got pleurisy which weakened him, and Harold had a weak heart so neither were called up to fight in the war. But your father joined to help with the liberation and occupation of Germany. Oh, they suffered for that, my boys. People called them cowards and shirkers. I felt for them but what could I do? I told them not to stand for it. I told them to explain they were doing important work at home for the country. Someone had to!'

Grandma paused and gave me a long look. 'You're like your father, dear. You have the same blue eyes. They're mine you know. Your Grandfather had grey eyes. You're nothing at all like your mother!'

Although this was true, I was disconcerted. I sensed that Grandma was confused and had forgotten who I was. She seemed to think I was someone else related to her. I couldn't think straight. I was so intent on being a good child and pleasing her, something I had always wanted to do because her manner and person commanded it, so I couldn't fathom where she was coming from. To make sure she knew who I was, I found myself saying: 'Grandma, I'm Susanna.'

Her face crumpled and I thought she might cry. I almost panicked, sensing a catastrophe neither of us could control. But she saved the moment. 'Oh, it doesn't matter. What difference does it make what they call you? You're here now,' she said rather graciously.

I wanted to reassure her and felt sorry for her. I touched her unresponsive hand. She thought I was another girl perhaps, the girl who had written her many letters I'd found in her dressing table drawer, so valuable to her she kept them all. Before I had time to fathom who Chrissie was, the author of so many letters, the hall clock struck its mellow four. Grandma rose from her chair.

'Is that the time already? Time for a walk. Quickly button up your cardigan. We'll go to the park and then visit the cemetery. Fetch the flowers wrapped in newspaper on the draining board. Come along.'

Wearing a round felt hat like a sunken chocolate sponge, Grandma held my arm to steady her legs all along Woodcote Grove until we came to St. Andrew's Church. She seemed to have forgotten we were to visit the park first. At the gravestone I read out loud:

*Herbert Saunders*
*Loving Husband of Rosina Saunders.*
*Died 1953 aged 70*
*Asleep*

Grandma sent me to change fetid water in the jug. There was a single tap sticking up at the end of the path. Then she arranged the roses with rusted petal tips in the jug and placed it on his chest. There was nobody else about.

'We were childhood sweethearts,' she confided. 'I met him when I was ten years old. He was a handsome boy and the cleverest in the class in our school in Sydenham. I had eyes for no other boy.' She mumbled to the grass. I tried to stop her rambling. 'Grandma,' I said so she would pay attention, but she was deep into her story which I couldn't hear properly or understand so I skipped away between the graves and sat on the bench. I sometimes caught her murmurings on the breeze. I swung my legs and had the urge to do a few handstands in the clover, but I had a notion the dead didn't like playfulness or fun. In the graveyard the birdsong of sparrows and a robin rose above the faint traffic noise and the trees rustled their seared leaves. From time to time, I left my post and read a few more graves wondering what the dead once looked like with their old-fashioned names like Ethel, Florence, and Matilda before Grandma and I slow-motioned our way home. Tried as I might, I couldn't conjure an image of Grandfather. But I saw a pale frightened child. She cowered in the kitchen corner growing smaller and smaller so small she was easily flicked away by a fingernail.

That evening Grandma wouldn't allow me to help in the kitchen. She made shepherd's pie with cabbage boiled to a green pulp.

'You sit at the dining room table and do your schoolwork,' she insisted. But I played at schoolwork. I created story titles like: *The Last Leaf, A Crooked Key*. I wrote notes on each title in an unfamiliar hand, sloping the wrong way with hooks and tails. In this fugue, I sat on the stool by the electric fire while she read the newspaper on the sofa. 'My eyes are beginning to strain. Read the Obituaries would you?' The word Obituaries sounded like a book of devils in answer to the Bible. I saw it heavy and black with flame-coloured pages about to combust. A brief list of names: Baker, Bates, Burroughs ending with memorial quotations: *Never to be forgotten. We will remember Thee* comforted her.

Grandma seemed to like the freshly dead. They nourished her. Her ears sucked them up like musical phrases. He eyes watered, her lips were scaled like a disease. She leaned her head back as if my disembodied voice was elixir. I stopped reading when I thought she had dozed off, but the silence woke her. 'You might as well read me that book you have on your lap.'

'It's *Wuthering Heights* by Emily Brontë.' I pronounced it *Bronty*. 'I haven't started it properly yet.'

'Well, now's the time. Open the book and begin.' Her eyes were cold, predatory as if I had denied her something. Wasn't that always the case? But I already knew what I denied her was something I couldn't give. Certainly not trust or admiration. She left me drained, impotent. To muster up solidity I would have to hide but I was trapped by her wishes, by her commands. I read boldly at first, but as her eyes half closed, I dropped my voice. I swear she heard little of the second chapter. I received no help with the pronunciation of difficult words that I stumbled over. Without her corrections, I assumed she had fallen asleep again beneath half-drooping lids, which was a pity because I had hoped she might tell me what some of the strange words meant. I grasped enough of the novel to be disturbed by the savage aspect of the wolfish dogs and Heathcliff's brutal treatment of his guest and tenant, a Mr. Lockwood with whom I sympathised entirely. Wasn't I just like Lockwood arriving at a strange and unwelcoming house?

Then the clock struck nine and late summer's dusk filled the room. Grandma woke. 'You read well. You're good at English. Just like your father. You both write beautiful letters. I keep them all. I reread them when I miss you both. Time for Ovaltine, then off to bed.'

Sinking beside me in the feather bed, she didn't bother to say goodnight, so I presumed it was because she had left her teeth on the bathroom windowsill preventing her from articulating words. Her mouth looked large, sucked into the middle of her face grown soft and supple. I thought of a sandstone wall scooped away by waves in a storm. She switched off the bedside lamp. I felt the warmth of her body, although we didn't touch.

Then a terror of contact with her skin came over me. I thought over her words during the day and renewed the connection I made between Grandma mistaking my identity, believing I was someone else. It came to me as a shock. I lay there in the dark beside her.

It was not difficult to examine the clues, make the connections hooking each person together in the family puzzle: I was Chrissie in her eyes, and Chrissie's father was Leonard, and Leonard was her son, the brother of Harold, the favourite son, the wayward one. And Chrissie, Leonard's daughter was her granddaughter who wrote hundreds of letters to her grandmother on blue writing paper in a plain, tiny hand with the news of her success at school, her dark hair no doubt like her father's and her grandmother's blue eyes. Now I knew Leonard's secrets. He had another wife, he had a daughter whom he loved.

I was betrayed all over again, an imposter in Grandmother's bed. I trembled. Thinking of Leonard, I tried to understand my feelings for him. The distance between us now made sense. His heart was elsewhere. I felt abandoned by him, although we were always quietly hostile, and I was jealous now of Chrissie whom he undoubtedly cherished. I looked towards the window. I hoped I would not have to look at the moon through glass. Grandma said she never slept with the curtains shut. I searched for an anchor of light to ensure my eyes were not closed but wide awake, and in time I found a single pinpoint of a star upon which to fix my gaze. I didn't know how I was going to survive the daily bruising of my mistaken identity. A sadness fell on me. I could never forget Grandma's unassailable authority, the ambivalence of loneliness and security it provided. And without the tiny star, Grandmother and I might have been buried alive, the empty universe pouring through the little diamond shaped pane of glass silently silting up the house.

After a week in her company, I was virtually silent again; once more my existence was denied for the second time, the first when mother and I arrived here at The Horseshoe hungry for love, shelter and sustenance. And now her second denial, that only her granddaughter had the right to be respected for herself, which left me empty and bereft. Maybe Grandma was determined not to like me, the way I'd been determined not to accept Leonard. Despite his early cajoling, his secret life made me feel I was right all along not to have taken him into my heart. But because I was hurt by his other life, it seems I already loved him despite myself. I wouldn't admit it, partly perhaps out of fear. I don't know.

After quiet days of boiled fish, visits to the graveyard

and evenings of reading the local obituaries, I waved goodbye to Grandma, my face turned towards the motor-bike sidecar. I had a notebook of short stories and lists of the dead in my head. *Wuthering Heights* had yet to be finished. I left with a sense that I was of no use. My efforts to gain Grandma's approval and affection had been futile. It was the last time I ever saw her. So much was happening, my new school, the tensions at home, I barely thought about her. Leonard visited her every Saturday as if she could only endure a private audience. Dolly and Harold eventually took her into their home where she occupied the converted dining room, and The Horseshoe was sold. Some years later, Harold reported his mother had become impossible; it was common knowledge in Purley that Grandmother took money out of her savings account and handed out pound notes to strangers. Leonard often asked her for money, which I believe she gave freely; he prematurely bled her of his inheritance to supplement extra expenses that didn't involve my mother and me, but rather his other life, which he kept secret from us. So the mystery of how impoverished we were, became clear. Grandmother died in hospital in 1965 just after one of Leonard's visits. I loved her and was sorry she died alone, especially as Leonard had promised he would always stay at her side. I wouldn't have minded being Chrissie for her if it meant she had some company. I regret I wasn't brave enough to thank her for what she did for us. And yet, I wonder sometimes if loving someone can be a waste; especially when it can't be expressed or demonstrated. After the funeral, which my mother and I were not invited to attend, Leonard said I could go to Auntie Dolly's house, and pick out anything of grandmother's I'd like to have for myself from The Horseshoe before everything was auctioned off. In the politest way possible I said I didn't think so. Even the beauty of the loyal grandfather clock in the hallway or the little bedroom stool or the silver hairbrush couldn't tempt me to take possession of anything that belonged to her.

It took almost twelve years of life in London to find Bonnie. She says I am her mirror image, except her hair is white and unruly, gathered in a clutch of tight curls bound by an elastic band, whereas mine is white and straight and I'm growing it so I can have a ponytail like hers. I first set eyes on her in my Set 3 English lesson. I gazed at her back directly in front of me, the thin strap of her school purse diagonally cutting across the bones of her spine tucked under one of her shoulder blades. I can see it now like some intersection of torment, a mark of vulnerability and submission and I wanted to protect her. But it was her voice that had at the time the most memorable effect. It was husky and warm, and with the help of Tennyson's alliteration, a tingle beginning at my neck, spread through my body. *'Willows whiten, aspens quiver, Little breezes, dusk and shiver...'*

Coincidentally, it's the incarcerated Lady of Shallot in her state of loneliness and isolation, who binds me to Bonnie. I'm certain our English teacher, Mrs. Kirk, also liked Bonnie's sensitive and beautiful rendition because she didn't ask her to stop reading to allow the girl in the next row to take over after a few stanzas, which was the usual practice. At the end of the lesson, I gently poked Bonnie's back. She swept round with a wide grin without a hint of indignation. We recognized each other immediately; we were friends.

Now, we're inseparable and I'm so sure of her friendship, her loyalty and attachment, I never mind girls hanging on her arm during milk break, or those gathering round her on the lawn begging to be in her netball team. I'm never jealous of girls who try to entice her from me. Naturally, my crush on manipulative Theresa faded some time ago, and although I continue to admire her, I've abandoned the desire to be her friend. When Theresa and I met in the communal hallway now and again, we walked out of habit down Putney Hill together, but her interest in me had waned too. Clearly she still finds me a bore, finding nothing more with which to shock or hurt me for the time being. But there might be more to come, although I can't imagine what.

Bonnie and I are different. We don't dwell on the dark side of the moon, or on the Cold War, or riots in Notting Hill Gate, or the fact a satellite, the size of a grapefruit, is orbiting the earth to no purpose as far as we can ascertain. Neither do we burden each other with our unhappiness at home. She knows my mother was brought up in Germany, but we don't talk about its associated afflictions and recriminations. For example, I never talk about spiteful comments made about my mother by girls at school, and I never refer to my mother's depression and how the doctor gives her a bottle of tonic from time to time with no effect, and how, just recently, he has supplied her with new wonder pills to ease her angst.

'You be careful, girl, with all that crying,' says Leonard

under his breath, 'you could turn into salt.' The reference is lost on my mother and at the time, on me. His little jokes to himself could be very cruel.

And I never complain about how things unsaid, poison the atmosphere at home so that even the sun stops at the windows, and how secrets in the cellar threaten to infest the house like maggots worming through rotten meat.

Bonnie knows nothing about the appalling Saturday morning when my mother opened the front door to find a large black swastika daubed on the front door. I remember the shock on her face, and the stricken stiffness of her body as she scraped the swastika with a kitchen knife while Leonard attempted to calm her with practical advice.

'Stone the crows! It's useless doing it that way, girl. You'll never scour it away without digging into the wood. We'll paint it over. I'll go straight down to the hardware shop and buy some green paint and do the whole door. Then I'll call the police.'

'No, no,' my mother insisted. 'Not the police. The police will make it worse. And no Len, if we paint over it, I will always know it is there, underneath the new layer of paint. Then it may slowly show through again in time. No, I must scrape it away.' She had a point.

'The paint hasn't even dried properly yet,' said Leonard playing the sleuth. 'It must have happened only a short while ago while we were all in bed. And look here, along the hall wall. There are more of them as if they're breeding.' He turned to me, still in my pink flannel pyjamas. 'Look at you. Standing there like a lemon! Get a knife and help your mother!' I stepped back, my mouth gaping. In the end my mother did all the scraping away of the main swastika because there wasn't room for both of us to work at it without slicing off fingers, but at least I was at her side absorbing her distress to add to my own misery and horror. When she is hurt, so am I.

Finally, after a weekend of shame, they called a painter in to redecorate the hallway and blow torch the smaller swastikas away.

'What lunatic has done this?' the painter and decorator asked my mother, who shrugged and continued scraping at our defaced front door. 'You needn't do that. I'll burn it off with my blow-torch.'

'That's very kind, thank you,' said my mother.

Then, because the door remained green but with a burn mark in the shape of a jagged swastika, my mother asked the painter if he would blow-torch the paint off the whole door to even it all out. She gave him slices of freshly baked sponge cake and cups of hot tea.

Now the defiled front door is a fresh green, a *Gesamtkunstwerk*—a total work of art-—I'm still wary of it. I have the notion a ghost swastika will spring up again through the new paint, because the swastika is a branding mark that sears into my retina. I remember the first time I saw it on the flag in our suitcase under my bed at Ida's house, and had an idea, even then in my innocence, that it was something interminably linked to Germanness, but not goodness as I had thought because now I was better informed. My scar on my leg seemed to correspond with the branding mark, and it began to prickle.

The incident disturbed my mother's efforts at settling down, and she suffered an intense bout of her old *Heimwheh* causing that insatiable restlessness that always put me on edge. My mother said she was one of the unlucky ones whose past catches up with them. I had no idea what she meant. I couldn't think why the swastika was linked to her past in any definitive way. I thought it was all to do with being German generally, a nationality synonymous with bad. So many more in the past might be doubly guilty, yet they escape. This worried me. And I wondered what else might come to light concerning my mother's past. Meanwhile, Leonard reassured my mother nothing would come of the swastikas daubed on the door and walls. It was the mark of a coward. He promised her the hatred for the Germans would die down after Remembrance Day. 'It always does,' he said, 'people get all fired up beforehand. It's only natural.'

But my mother, even allowing for the outrage and grief felt by others, continued to be nervous and depressed. This was because she hadn't yet experienced *Vergangenheits-bewältigung*, which means conquering the past, coming to terms with it. I taught myself the word, fascinated by the lengthy compound explaining why she had mood swings between joy and clinical coldness, and when she was icy I always felt guilty, as if it was all my fault because of something terrible I had done. My mother's state of mind was locked in that word.

Then I do something shameful. One afternoon, still in my first year of secondary school, as I'm leaving the school building, making my way towards the path along the tennis courts, a cloudburst made the girls ahead shriek as raindrops made black spots on the felt fabric of my blue blazer, causing it to smell of damp mould. I could hear groups of girls laughing and protesting behind me as we surged towards the narrow side-gate. I didn't mind the rain. It refreshed my face after the chalky atmosphere of the classroom, and then the wind brewed up brushing the tops of the horse-chestnut trees.

Waiting outside the narrow side gate, I was surprised to see my mother in her beige trench coat brightened with a peacock blue scarf, standing under a white umbrella, searching for me among the groups of girls. She looked rather lovely. She was smiling at the passers-by. I swallowed hard. I wanted to cry. I wanted to run towards her and kiss her. But I couldn't. I would look such a baby in front of the other girls. If she spoke, they would hear her accent; there would be questions and I would be an outsider all over again and have to face a barrage of abuse about concentration camps, Nazis and the war. I emptied myself of love; it was quickly replaced by anger. I blamed her for my shame. I blamed her for coming. It was her fault I was made to pretend she didn't belong to me.

And I did a terrible thing, I averted my eyes and walked straight past her. I could feel her eyes on my back as the rain poured down, dripping from my beret down the back of my neck as I walked along the road. My shoes squeaked. I became angry with myself. I tried to think of the worst self–punishment imaginable, but I had already unknowingly harmed myself. I was too terrified to look behind me. I didn't want to see her. I wished we had a different life. She followed me home wordlessly. I wept in the rain. Her silence told me something poignant I didn't understand. She was a mystery to me. There was a darkness in her; a darkness Len possessed too. But my mother's darkness was the deepest, the more terrifying. I didn't want her to be like that. It made me afraid. It made my love for her more unbearable. Why hadn't she pulled me back in the street, shouted at me, expressed her anger? Called me an ungrateful spoilt brat? Slapped my face? I let the rain soak into me. I wanted it to pound harder, to break my skin, to wash my blood away. When I got home, I took off my sodden clothes, and hanged them in my bedroom to dry. The air tasted musty and stale as they dried. I ate supper quickly, asking Len if I could leave the table. I couldn't look at my mother's sad face. He was not pleased. He said, 'Stone the crows! Eating food so fast will make you ill. Mark my words. You'll have an ulcer if you're not careful!'

In my room, I suffered. I pulled at my hair, cried and bit the pillow.

Months later, I came home to find my mother ironing and shaking with sobs in the kitchen. I let my satchel fall to the floor, already defeated, but I kept hold of the strap like a lifeline. Her look of contempt intensified my guilt. I watched her tears fall onto the cotton sheet and the hot iron was smoothed over to make them disappear. When a tear fell on the hot iron it sizzled into a mercury ball and vanished. She was struggling underwater. I didn't know how to save her. Unable to run, I stood there, useless. I felt I was to blame, I was a bad child to cause her all this pain, and as if she could read my thoughts, she told me to leave her alone. I knew I was making her unhappy, and I was sorry, but she never allowed me to comfort her. Dragging my satchel to my room, I fell into bed fully dressed and waited to hear Leonard's key in the lock. Then it would be safe to come out.

When I'm ill though, she won't leave me alone in the flat. Instead, she wraps me in wool like an orphaned lamb and I have to follow her to the Stern's palace on the hill; well, it seems like a palace. My mother has a key to the side door where the rubbish bins are and the rows of wine bottles. We enter the hot kitchen. It is snowy white with an enormous refrigerator and a silver bar handle; all the cupboards are fitted together. There is no larder, or kitchen cabinet with its little fold down shelf, and I can't find a cooker.

I stand shivering.

My mother calls, 'Guten Morgen, Madam!'

A tall lady, statuesque, enters the kitchen. She has enormous feet in brogues, which are very unbecoming. Her brown hair is arranged in a loose bun piled on top, and her face is long, with a prominent mouth. She wears a tweed skirt and grey twin set.

'Forgive me, Madam,' my mother says, 'Susie is not feeling well. Can she sit in the kitchen this morning?' My mother is putting on a pea-green nylon overall. I think she looks beautiful even in that horrible thing. The lady smiles down at me with kind eyes. They are warm and brown. 'Hello, Susie. Of course, Ingrid.'

Ingrid? I wonder why my mother is being called Ingrid. Is it a name bestowed on her, the way slaves were given names by their owners? The lady offers to help me take off my many layers of cardigans and old sweaters. She hangs the gabardine school coat on a hook beside the utility door over my mother's coat and takes my school cardigan and scarf. The kitchen is tropical. The lady bends down and

226

unlaces my shoes. She puts them by the back door. My mother is in a cupboard. She emerges with a large bag stuffed with cleaning cloths and dusters, and tins rattling. I can't find words. My throat is painful. I feel hot and dizzy. Mrs. Stern guides me out of the kitchen towards a vast room in the bright sunshine. Everything gleams. The wood of the occasional tables are like dark mirrors reflecting silky, yellow sofas. There are large golden lamps, a glass bookcase crammed with beautifully leather-bound books, and footstools, and chandeliers sparkling. My blood shot eyes burn with the needles of light. Mrs. Stern gestures that I must sit. I hardly dare.

'Now, Susie, what can I get you? Lemonade I think and some coffee cake?'

I nod and smile appreciatively, wondering how I might manage to swallow, but it is rude to refuse. When she leaves, I hear her talking to my mother in German. It does something to me. It sedates me, pins me to the edge of the sofa. I don't think I will be able to move again locked inside this unimaginable sumptuous luxury I never dreamed existed beyond the studios of technicolour films and listening to a language I could once speak buried deep inside me.

Mrs. Stern enters with a tray and sets it down on a little side table she brings forward. I have never seen wall to wall carpet, a deep mossy green, without a mark, bar our footsteps from the door to sofa. On the tray is a tall glass of lemonade with a straw, a plate of cake with several layers bulging with coffee cream. She places a white handkerchief on my lap.

'So, there you are. I vill put some music on for you.

Something light and cheerful. A little Chopin, Fantasie Impromptu in C sharp minor is exquisite.'

While she takes the record out of its sleeve, my mother passes by carrying a large contraption to connect to a power point in the hallway. It fires up. I am embarrassed and uncomfortable to be treated like a guest while my mother is doing the cleaning for Mrs. Stern. I understand Leonard's protests now. I nibble at the cake; I sip the lemonade. It is sweet and sour like the music. I'm left alone for some time and venture towards the bookcase to read the extraordinary titles I have never known. And then I fall asleep half swallowed by the feather cushions on the sofa.

When I wake, the light has dulled. It is raining outside. My mother fetches me to put on my coat and go home. She smells sickly and sour. Mrs. Stern follows her footsteps to the sitting room to fetch the tray and plump up the pillows where I nestled in a fever. I want to go to the lavatory, but I'm too afraid to ask. My mother washes up my glass and plate in the kitchen sink before leaving. She dries them on a cloth and puts them in a cupboard. Mrs. Stern remembers to give my mother some of her blouses to handwash and iron in a paper bag and offers me a book. *Christmas Books* by Charles Dickens. It is bound in red faux leather with golden tipped pages.

'You may keep it. A present from me for being such a good girl. Your mother is very proud of you.'

My mother looks away. I thank Mrs. Stern in a croaky voice, which she finds amusing. I am genuinely pleased for an instant and feel myself flush hot. Despite the luxury, I'm pleased to be out of the house. My mother and I walk down Putney Hill to our cold flat. 'Don't tell anyone, Susie.

Don't tell anyone what I do.' My mother puts a match to the paraffin heater in the kitchen. It smells toxic at first, blue smoke rising and then it gives off a good heat once the meshed half-globe is glowing.

'No mum,' I say, so I know she is ashamed. And I am ashamed but for different reasons. 'Why does she call you Ingrid?'

'Ah. Mr. Stern said I look like Ingrid Bergman. So, he calls me Ingrid. He was the one who gave me the job. Mrs. Stern didn't like me at first. But she's kinder to me now. Every time I wanted to leave, he gave me money, slipped a five-pound note into my pocket.'

'Do you like her?' I rasp.

'She is moody. Some days I can do nothing right. She follows me and watches me work. She looks for faults and I have to do things all over again. Once she made me cry. But I feel sorry for her. She has no children, and she escaped to England before the war. She lost all her family in a war-camp.'

In my bedroom, tucked under the blankets with my clothes on, and the school scarf round my neck, I open the book. Inside it is inscribed: *To Susanna, Best wishes from Mrs. Stern.* Despite my hostile feelings towards her for being unkind to my mother, I can't bring myself to feel anything but pleasure. I open the first page to *A Christmas Carol,* Stave One, Marley's Ghost. 'Marley was dead, to begin with.' And I hide myself behind and inside the book while my body gets on with its business of healing. But I can't help remembering what Leonard said, about working for Jews and how it would be unadvisable to work for the

Sterns. It troubles me.

Later, when I recover, I visit Wandsworth library and search among the history shelves till I get to a section labelled the Second World War. I find a book called *Hitler: A Study in Tyranny* by Alan Bullock. I begin to read. The print is too small, but after a few chapters all about the rise of fascism, I make a note of the page and return to the library as often as I can to continue reading, hoping no one has taken the book out. I don't want the book issued in case my mother finds it. I sense she wouldn't be pleased. I find a pleasant corner near the reading room window, and no one disturbs me. But the history disturbs me. I work out all the dates and realise my mother and her brother were caught up in the maelstrom and I wonder what my Opa and Oma thought. They must have been Nazis I tell myself. Everyone was a Nazi, weren't they? I remember the sword and the flag in the black suitcase with the brass lock. When I go home, I'm aware of the suitcase's sleeping presence on top of my mother's wardrobe. It appears blacker, more foreboding, less of a comfort. Yet it seems to have grown smaller, and my mother eventually finds a blanket to cover it. I find myself watching my mother and listening to her closely. I watch her for signs of her turbulent past as if her past beliefs might leak out of her as evidence. It is important to me to have a good mother. I must find out the truth.

In a daring moment one afternoon home from school, I ask her if she ever saw Adolf Hitler. To my surprise and relief, she seems willing to answer. Yes, she did see Hitler. She and her best friend, Lotte, took a train from Hamburg all the way to Berlin to see him speak at a rally. It was exciting she said, and they managed to find a place right in the front so you could almost touch his boots. I don't think this is funny, but my mother laughs but because of the lectern, she says, we couldn't see his face, just his arms sticking out and waving about as he bellowed it seemed without a script. She said his speech was very rousing, impressive, and masterful. Afterwards two young men followed them and bought them drinks in a bar, and they danced all evening to American jazz. Oma was so angry when she came home late and grounded my mother for a week. On another occasion I asked what kind of man Hitler was if she and her friend Lotte took the train all the way to Berlin to hear him speak. She said Hitler gave generous grants to farmers. Opa's business boomed, and new roads and houses were built. Everyone was impressed with Hitler's social policies. Later on, he did awful things. I don't ask her about the awful things. Theresa has already given me examples. I'm beginning to learn more in Wandsworth and Putney libraries than I can from my mother who closes the conversation with a look of admonishment.

I never talk about my mother to anyone. At school, none of the girls talk about home.

Bonnie would understand if I confided in her, but I can't bring myself to speak about the tensions at home and burden a friend with my troubles. I'm never able to find the proper words. I don't tell her I have started attending ballet classes either.

In ballet class, I don't have to speak or pretend to be anyone. I lose myself in dancing, in the rituals of exercises at the barre, feeling my feet and limbs contort in an effort to conform to a choreography of beauty I might never achieve. My mother is pleased I'm taking up a hobby. I asked her if I could have piano lessons as well and she said, no. I had to choose one, not both. Learning the piano would have been the better choice as I could play for the rest of my life but not so when it came to dancing. Without that forethought or advice, I choose dancing at a ballet school in Barnes on a Saturday morning. Later I found out Mrs. Stern paid for the expensive lessons mother could never have afforded.

I allow myself to be bullied by the teacher, as do all the other aspiring dancers because we are partly in awe and partly afraid of him. Alexander abuses our efforts, makes us watch his lithe leaps into the air, his supple grace and immaculate footwork are in our view impossible to copy, despite the fact he demonstrates in his scruffy desert boots. He has the body of a gifted man, and I wish he would dance for us rather than just show how we should perform. The ballet lessons have become my escape; I can express my moods in mime and dance, and all the tension from home flows out of me.

I have made a dancing friend, Debbie. She is American and has attached herself to me. We change into our leotards together and slip into our ballet shoes. There is something strange about her, other than that she is from Washington, and her father is some kind of diplomat. She is always on edge, with a tense expression, and petite, delicate so I feel like a giant beside her, graceless, whereas she has the lightness of a nymph. Her face is angular, sharp under thick black hair cut into a severe bob. After a while, she likes me to give her a cuddle and sometimes we walk across Putney Heath instead of taking the bus, and she then makes her own way towards Manor Fields where she lives, while I continue down Putney Hill. One day, on such a walk she told me her father has sex with her. She says she likes it. I am so astounded I can't say a word. I'm unable to imagine what sex entails and think back to Biology lessons and the science teacher Mrs. Godly describing the reproduction of rabbits. Not long after her confession, Debbie disappeared. Alexander said she had gone back to the States. I remain disturbed by her confession and her absence. I wonder if that is the sort of thing American fathers do. I am beginning to find men frightening. They seem to break the rules, at least what I would call rules about being human beings. Revelations about my mother's country folk, the Nazis, the persecution of Jews and gypsies fill me with horror and guilt. I feel the guilt in my bones. I am of her and so I must inherit the guilt as a punishment for the bad blood in my veins, and like her, walk alone. All these ugly things accumulate in me like pockets of poison. I think I will be poisoned to death soon enough.

The remaining girls in the ballet class do not speak to me. Most of them are in attendance with their mothers who braid their hair and help them into their ballet outfits throwing me a hostile or pitying look. No one smiles. I walk home alone now across the heath and save the fare money for some new clothes. I often think of Debbie and wonder if she is happy, ballet dancing in Washington. And what her mother must think, whether she knows or not about the affair her husband has with his daughter. It

233

seems friendships are dangerous. You never know what they reveal, which is disturbing and sad because I instinctively knew Debbie was troubled despite her devil-may-care attitude and bold show of pride and we were beginning to love each other as friends.

The dance studio is a beautiful room of mirrors looking out to an apple orchard, which is often sunlit. Even on a winter's Saturday morning, it glows. The mirrors repeat the light so that the room is always richly golden and silky. To the right sits Miss Koval at the up-right piano. She remains in profile, a slight grey figure in a tight suit, a woman with infinite patience, stopping and starting according to Alexander's interruptions. We always have to say 'Good morning Miss Koval' when we arrive at the barre, and at the end of the lesson 'Thank you Miss Koval' with a slight curtsey before we flitter in single file towards the door to the changing room, a door which is also mirrored and very heavy to open so no one really likes to be first out.

I watch myself repeated in the room of mirrors, each time growing smaller and deeper until I'm nothing but an intense spot in a tiny silver speck of glass about to disappear into my own black hole, so I don't care if my arabesques are clumsy; if Alexander shouts at me to keep my head up, if my plié displeases him, I almost relish his displeasure. He rarely praises so his critical attention is perversely satisfying. I am a bad dancer and I know this. The only nice thing he says about me is that I have lovely arches as my feet make a point. But he is not the only reason I like to attend to watch him dance, or the beautiful room of mirrors. Afterwards, I feel a deep relief and although it is clearly an illusion that I'll ever be a dancer, I enjoy a sense of achievement washing over me and the release of all my bad feelings about myself as I struggle to achieve grace

Bonnie suffers at home too. She never actually talks about home, but I soon learn about her Dad's facial disfigurement. She gave me no warning. I wonder if she was so used to his misshapen face, she no longer saw it as visitors or strangers might. I found him difficult to look at the first time because I imagined the pain he must have suffered. His skin is stretched like white linen patchwork over his cheeks and around his eyes, one more deeply embedded than the other; the skin on his forehead is lurid and shiny. He wears black, think rimmed glasses that magnify his rheumy eyes. It's Davy, Bonnie's younger brother, who told me his father's merchant ship blew up in the Atlantic in 1942 and his Dad was severely burned. When I stay the night on Fridays now, Bonnie and I babysit her brother Davy, and by the time her parents arrive home, we have already put ourselves to bed, I listen to Bonnie's parents preparing for the night. Later, I'm woken by Bonnie's Dad screaming out from a nightmare, and then Davy makes his way to Bonnie's room, slapping his bare feet on the lino. He always comes to my side of the bed because Bonnie, sleeping deeply, invariably pushes him out of the bed onto the floor. I shift to make a space for him. He puts his freezing cold feet on my calves to warm up and his arm hooks around my waist so it takes me ages to get back to sleep because I can hardly breathe, and we lie wrapped together waiting for sleep to take us.

In the morning, Bonnie's Mum, Carol, is already in the

kitchen. I sit at the table waiting for Davy and Bonnie to wake. I marvel at the ease with which she carries on as if I were not there. There are no awkward moments, false smiles, or shows of antagonism or dislike. She simply doesn't register me, or she has the skill of a trained actress able to deny the world around her if it impinges on her performance. Strangely, this makes me feel at ease. I watch her backcomb her hair in the mirror on the windowsill just above the sink, and dab orange pan-stick makeup to smooth over her face and over one or two bruises on her neck. Then she puts kohl around her eyes and applies mascara she wets with spit and applies with a little brush to make her lashes long and curly. You can tell she takes pride in her long lashes because she blinks furiously at herself in the mirror. Then she coats her lips in pale pink lipstick and presses them together. If I think she might throw me a glance, I look away in a flash. It's like shadow boxing. It's a strange business. I don't want to lock eyes with her, afraid of how she might look at me. But before long, I'm watching her again.

She wears a white shirt tucked into her tight pencil skirt with a large slit at the back. She checks her stockings have straight seams and puts on white high heels, which she has whitened the night before with a small sponge dipped in whitener and left to dry overnight on newspaper on the draining board. Then she lays the table for three places, but not one for me. Just as she is putting on her coat, I stand and go to the little hallway. 'Thank you for having me, Mrs. Aiken.' I have an inkling she hates me but is controlled enough to simply pretend I don't exist. I feel guilty about Bonnie's father's burns. I know by now I am not welcome.

However, if I stay over, she feels Bonnie won't mind babysitting her brother.

When I politely thank Carol, she never properly acknowledges me, and lifts her head like a reversed nod, slaming the front door on my words. I can hear her stilettoes sparking the path and the gate closing. She works in the local grocery shop just around the corner on the council estate, serving behind the counter and pressing down the cash register keys with her long pink fingernails that look as if they could tear cloth. At the moment of her departure the house brightens. Even *The Green Lady* (by Vladimir Tretchikoff, I learn later) above the fireplace looks uplifted, a little brighter and less oppressed.

'Do you think my mum's a tart?' Bonnie asks at breakfast, pouring sugar puffs into a bowl for me.

'No! Don't say things like that.'

'Well, she is according to *Woman's Own*. The problem page is full of women writing about being married and falling in love with other men, and she always says, you know the Agony Aunt, Mary Grant, you have to resist temptation and stay loyal to your husband at all times.'

'Falling in love with someone doesn't make you a tart.'

'Well, a slag then?'

'What's the difference? No. Don't be daft. Is your Mum in love then?'

'I don't know,' she says, but looks as if she knows something. 'She's not nice to Dad and creeps round the manager of the shop. You know, touching his arm. I've seen her.'

Whatever Bonnie says I feel for her Mum, having to relive her husband's nightmares at night. It must be hard for her to marry a handsome man and see him broken when he returns from the war.

I can hear someone padding on the landing. I don't want it to be Mr. Aiken coming down the stairs. He is always truly kind and polite to me, but I remember the disturbing noises he makes in the night, like an animal in pain, and remain dead still with my mouth full of cereal. The door bursts open, and I jump out of the kitchen chair.

'Ah, ha,' says Davy, springing into the middle of the kitchen floor, arm raised to announce his presence. 'It's me!'

I gulp a mouthful of sugar puffs. 'Davy, you gave me such a fright!' I place my hand over my heart.

'Hey? Are you pleased it's me? Betcha are!'

'Shush. Don't wake dad,' says Bonnie.

'Of course, I'm glad it's you. I'm sorry though, I've pinched your place.' I fetch him another bowl and spoon. I'm glad I can spend more time with Davy, just the three of us. I have a secret dream Carol might adopt me, which I know is absurd, but that's the nature of dreams, elusive and often ridiculous . I know my mother, Leonard and I do not make a proper family. I don't know why. Something is wrong.

'Don't worry about Dad. He's stone deaf without his hearing aid and can't see anyfing without his glasses. He has a lie-in till lunchtime on Saturdays. C'mon, give us some cornflakes and then we can watch Roy Rogers, or play Draughts.'

'Susie hasn't just come to see a brat like you. We're gonna practise our hand-jiving. We could put "Smoke Gets in your Eyes" on really low and have a smooch dance, and then afterwards we'll put on Cliff Richard's "Living Doll".'

Bonnie and I would like to be someone's living doll, but that's long before we understand what it means. Then we play the Everly Brother's 'Bye Bye Love' without registering the meaning behind the words.

'Yeah. Can I jive too?' asks Davy. 'I'm good at jiving.'

Bonnie and I laugh at him. He has such a sunshine face, broad with creamy skin and flushed cheeks. I already love him. I want him to be my brother. We manage to dance, and watch Roy Rogers, and play Draughts. Then I have to go home before Bonnie's mother comes back from her shop assistant shift. I sense I must. If I am there when she returns, the atmosphere would change. The air becomes heavy with her silent presence. I say goodbye to Bonnie and Davy, and I walk home down Putney Hill unhappy at the prospect of finding my mother in a sad mood.

# Gütersloh, March 1942

The letter below is from Sophie Chmielowiec-Beck to her best friend Lotte. Both young women are completing their compulsory Philchtjar—the duty year or training year, which every young girl must complete to ensure she becomes a good German mother in the future. This usually entails being sent to serve as a nanny to a family and thereby learning the skills of housecraft and motherhood. The aristocratic and upper-class German girls manage to evade this duty with excuses that they are already contributing to war work either typing or driving officers around, providing so-called proof from influential friends.

At first Sophie likes the idea of the Philchtjar because it means she can live away from home, and experience independence, escaping her mother's harsh surveillance and demands. Although she misses her friends, father and brother Erich, she knows she won't miss the gruelling work on the land made worse by the constant shortage of workers.

It is also pleasant to live in a charming house in beautifully kept grounds and observe the wealthy; she relishes the sophistication and luxury of her own room next door to her two charges, to sleep in lovely soft linen sheets, and eat well with the cook and housekeeper despite the shortages. The war seems far away as if a gracious life is sufficient to keep it away by magic or witchcraft.

While Sophie is working as a nanny for Dr. Franenarzt's family in Bismarkstrasse, Gütersloh, she meets a friend of the doctor's wife's nephew, completing his

Luftwaffe training nearby. His name is Klaus Groth, a Berliner. Some details are blanked because of security and censorship and Sophie is mindful about what she can write. She knows traitors can be arrested and imprisoned. Secretly, Sophie is appalled and afraid that she has been called up to serve in the Luftwaffe; surely it goes against the Nazi ideal of women as good housewives and mothers. Rumour has it Nazis are running out of manpower and need to recruit women to keep the massive war machine in operation. The safest and wisest way is not to question anything or make a fuss. Her father has taught her this.

Bismarckstrasse,
Gütersloh.

March 22nd 1942

My dearest Lotte,

How are you? I think of you so often and all the fun we had going to dances. This will be my last letter from here. My training year as a nanny is being cut short. I have been called up. I can't say what I feel. Can you imagine? My father wrote to tell me that I have to end my service with the Franenarzt family and begin my auxiliary Luftwaffe training near home in May, but I mustn't mention where. I never thought this could happen and I am dreading it. But this is just as well as Klaus my boyfriend will be returning back to the city after his pilot training here, and now that we are unofficially engaged, I feel particularly sad. We don't know when we will see each other again. I will try and get a photo of him in his uniform to send to you. He is so handsome and charming and from Berlin.

We are expecting bombing raids any moment, so Frau Franenarzt is taking the boys to her sister's summer house just outside Vienna. Her husband, the doctor will remain here with the housekeeper Luisa as he must work in the hospital. I feel so cut off from the world. Little outside the normal domestic routine happens. In town you wouldn't know there was a war on apart from the boys' noisy skirmishes—they are always playing war and fighting with wooden swords. I had one horrible visit to the hospital with a message for Dr Franenarzt to come home immediately as little Heine almost died with a high fever. It was so different inside the hospital. The floor was slippery with blood and the medical staff faint with exhaustion. There were wounded men left in the corridors, some on the floor, trying to catch my ankles as I passed, begging for help. It was terrible. Then outside again, to people in the cafes sipping coffee and eating cake just like normal, it was crazy. The wounded can no longer hope for the kind of victory you read about in the papers. Heine survived his fever thank goodness. It's so scary knowing the Tommies will be coming. The Franenarzt boys Otto and Heine seem fearless. They play war at every given opportunity, which can't be healthy, but I can't seem to distract them from it. Luisa says they probably hear all kinds of talk about an invasion.

I long to go out in the evenings, but I don't like to ask permission. Anyway, there is nowhere to go. The old town is picturesque, with beautiful parks, but many shops are boarded, and I'm sent out to queue for hours with Otto and Heine, for bread and whatever cook demands. I thought the point of my service with the Franenarzt family was to learn the basics of motherhood and housewifery, but I'm not given instructions on how to look after the children, to cook, or run a household. With the help of the housekeeper Luisa, I just muddle through. The boys are quick to tell me if I'm not doing things right and no one checks or supervises me. I'm growing very fond of Otto, who is seven and little Heine is only four, so I try to stop myself loving them too much knowing I'm only here for a short time in their lives.

Frau Franenarzt is friendly and pleasant, but she's always sickening for something and likes me to wait on her. She's about sixteen years younger than her husband. She told me having the last baby, little Heine, took it out of her mentally and physically. She is always sad. I think she has given up on motherhood. When the boys are in kindergarten she plays the piano at lunch time in the music room. Her favourite piece of music is Chopin's Nocturne in C and F minor. When I hear this in the future, I know it will bring back memories of this family and my time here. I found out Frau Franenarzt has recently lost her younger brother. He was in the 6th Army driving the Russians back into the city of Stalin. I feel so sad for her, I do everything she asks because she never interferes with me or makes me feel beneath her as a servant, despite her demands. When her nephew, who is in the Luftwaffe stationed near here, came to dinner with his friend Klaus, she allowed me to join them for dinner. It was her nephew Rudie who invited me, which was rather naughty of him, but I think he did this on behalf of his friend Klaus. I was so nervous hoping I would do the right thing at the table. In the end it was easy as I just copied Frau Franenarzt. Klaus gave me such a sly smile and a wink as if to back me up!

He kept making eyes at me. I felt under his gaze the whole time. I felt excited but uncomfortable when Louisa the cook came in to serve us. She didn't express resentment when she served me, but it made me blush. I couldn't look up from my plate. I was glad to be excused as the boys were crying for me.

Dr. Franenarzt is very much in demand at the hospital, so he doesn't have time for family life, although he insists on total obedience without exception when the boys are in his presence. I don't have much to do with him and keep out of his way, but he is always polite when we meet, clicking his heels and bowing his head, you know all that formal, old fashioned kind of thing.

Lotte, please write and tell me your news. How is your cousin? You are so lucky to be doing your training year in the town where your aunt lives so you can go visiting. How is your handsome boyfriend Wolfgang? I've not heard anything from our friend Tia. The last I heard she was going out with a U-boat captain from Dresden! That girl always falls on her feet! I haven't heard from my brother Erich. His bullet wound just above his lip healed well and he has returned to active duty. I worry about him often. My Dad writes occasionally. My parents have Poles working for them now in the fields and one or two Dutch women. I miss you. I miss home despite the hard work I had to do in the fields. We used to have such fun going to parties and dancing on Saturday nights.

After the first meeting at dinner, I met Klaus in town. Now sometimes we meet in the park. The boys are usually with us, but he doesn't seem to mind. He is charming and funny, but I feel so shy with him, I can barely say anything at all. It is difficult as he often has to get back to camp and soon he will be sent away. I don't want him to go. Things are too unsettled to consider anything serious going on with him. I have only known him for a short while, so I don't know if it is love. How can you tell? I'm worried about my training. Have you been conscripted too? I wish you could be with me. Please write as soon as you can. I send my absolute best love to all your family.

Love Sophie xxxxx

Sophie leaned back on the pillow and reread her letter to Liselotte. She always did this to make sure she hadn't missed out words or said anything compromising in her haste to get the letter sent. She felt unsettled to the point of not being able to keep still, read, or sleep. Inside her head and heart there was constant turmoil. It was difficult to adjust to the constant changes the war brought and the struggle to remain optimistic and cheerful. She glanced over to the boys in their beds tucked under the sloping ceiling. Their bodies always seemed smaller in their stillness. They slept well but by morning, both were frequently nestled beside her in the double bed. Otto was adorable, so affectionate and articulate. He wanted nothing more than to fly a plane in the war to shoot down Tommies. He took after his father in looks and temperament, a steely, self-disciplined lad. Little Heine was more diffident, shy and delicate like his mother, but in the incessant war games the two brothers played daily, little Heine held his own as if he had a cruel streak that might one day save him. As violence was less expected of Heine, when it did surface it was shocking. Sophie recalled the time Heine lost his patience with his older brother, tricked him to go down to the cellar and locked the door knowing Otto was particularly afraid of the cellar since he heard Luisa talk about the rats. Heine ignored Otto's cries for help, ignored the hammering on the locked door, and calmly went into the garden to play on the swing. It was only when Sophie panicked about the missing boy, and insisted Heine her tell her where Otto was, that she rescued him. She saw the glint of pleasure in the younger boy's eyes. Sophie decided not to tell anyone about this incident. Afterwards, however, she felt differently about Heine, and he knew all right. Her cooling affection made him withdrawn and sulky. But now it was all coming to an end.

What was to become everyone? Frau Franenarzt was about to escape the Allied bombardment with her boys whom she can barely look after having such a delicate constitution. And now Sophie was called up to work in the armed service. Everyone sensed the nation was heading for disaster. And to complicate everything Sophie found herself in love. But she had her doubts. How is it possible to be certain? Maybe the feelings churning inside her for Klaus were a romantic delusion, maybe she was simply infatuated, wanting love and attention far from home. Sophie certainly lost her appetite, day-dreamed of Klaus, playing over and over in her mind when she first set eyes on him walking with Frau Franenarzt's nephew Rudie in the park, and Otto recognizing him, bounding over the grass into his arms. Klaus was beside him, laughing and opening his arms to catch little Heine on his way too, but his eyes caught hers and locked and she felt a rush of blood to her head, and blushed deeply. Otto introduced her. Klaus said he hoped he would see her again at dinner. They had been invited by Dr. Franenarzt weeks before as Rudie and his division had almost finished their training and would be flying off to a secret assignation.

It wasn't usual for Sophie to join the Franenarzts for dinner. She normally ate in the kitchen by the warm tile-stove with Luisa; they were like two lonely spinsters abandoned by men at war. Luisa took to secretly listening to BBC accounts, which made Sophie nervous. She didn't understand much English and was afraid if they were caught, she would be arrested as an accomplice. Luisa reassured her that no one in the sleepy little town out in the sticks could be bothered to monitor her misdemeanours. All the same it thrilled Sophie to hear what Luisa managed to translate. Luisa was certain the Allies were on the way any moment and had warned Frau Franenarzt, not telling her from where she obtained this intelligence. It was best not to ask. Without thinking about it, Sophie knew Luisa was Jewish. It was also highly probable Frau Franenarzt knew this. She suspected Luisa was up to no good listening to the wireless but welcomed the benefits of being better informed.

Luisa also wanted to know all about Klaus. Sophie liked to confide in her. She sowed the seeds of doubt in the young girl to prepare her for heartache. 'War romances never last. Be careful. I had my heart broken in 1918, the year before you were born.'

When the guests Rudie and Klaus arrived, Sophie had

already put the boys to bed, and helped Luisa in the kitchen. She asked Luisa's permission to go upstairs and get ready for dinner. Her wardrobe was virtually empty. There was a straight skirt, and plain black jumper. It would have to do. She brushed her fair hair and put on lipstick. She had so little left, she used a matchstick to dig some out and paint her lips. After the introductions in the sitting room, they all moved into the dining room. Sophie knew her place and did not join in the conversation that began lightheartedly about the boys, how they had grown, and Otto would soon be ready to have a private tutor.

At the table it was difficult for Sophie. She was unsure how one should eat in middle class company. In the old Hollywood films, film stars barely ate at all. At home everyone tucked in as soon as the plate was put before them. She watched and copied Frau Franenarzt, who ate reluctantly, and from time to time put her knife and fork down, leaned back, and chewed. Then she took sips of red wine while the men talked war. Dr. Franenarzt was taciturn, broody while the young men amused Frau Franenarzt with tales of their flying exploits, and fear of being sent to the Eastern Front. Sophie felt the doctor should have made more effort to keep up his spirits for his wife's sake. At the table at one point Frau Franenarzt rested her hand on her husband's as if to say she understood. He looked exhausted and didn't respond to her touch.

In the presence of the ladies, the conversation was desultory, full of bantering and teasing. Frau Franenarzt kept embarrassing her nephew with memories of his childhood, his fear of lightning, and toads. Didn't the devil have a toad for a heart? Klaus tolerated the lady's treatment of his friend, but his eyes pinned Sophie inside his gaze, making her hot and nervous. Only occasionally did she dare meet his blue eyes. He was breathtakingly handsome, with a broad forehead, his hair swept back with auburn tints but closely shaven at the sides and back. He had an upright bearing and the sophisticated manner of a city man, which made Rudie seem boyish and gauche.

Luisa entered to collect the plates and serve pudding. Afterwards, Sophie rose from the table, asking to be excused so she could help. She didn't like Luisa waiting on her, but Luisa tapped Sophie on the back and indicated that Sophie should sit down again. Frau Franenarzt nodded and smiled in approval.

Later, as the evening took on a more serious mood with the doctor bemoaning the lack of medical supplies and how the numbers of those injured were insufficiently reported, Frau Franenarzt took this to be a cue for the ladies to retire and leave the men to smoke and discuss the war. Later when they all reconvened in the sitting room Frau Franenarzt offered to play the piano for her guests. Sophie thought this was the best time to rise and explain she must check on the boys. Afterwards, climbing the stairs Sophie realised she had been rude to excuse herself when she did, and ought to have waited until Frau Franenarzt had finished her performance, but it was too late. Before she slipped away, Klaus and Rudi rose to bow their heads, and Klaus moved to the door to open it for her and whispered, 'Tonight. Near the gate. Under the lilac.' Sophie laughed quietly. It was like a silly romantic novel.

She wasn't sure whether to take Klaus seriously, but that night asked Luisa to leave the back door open and met

Klaus under the lilac, a little way from the gate by the wall and there he kissed the beautiful girl, a girl of innocence, a country simplicity the girls in Berlin could never aspire to. For Sophie he was the Berliner, the urbane man of the city who would promise her a life she dreamed about. And when he took her in his arms, she received his kiss, first tentatively, a little on the defensive, and then as she relaxed, she couldn't stop kissing him. It was not just lustful petting she had half expected, but transcendental, when she became aware of him breathing into her his magnetism, his very life. This was her first true kiss. A kiss that confirmed the universe was aligned to love. The poet Rilke wrote of love consisting of two solitudes that meet, protect and greet each other. Love was unutterable, the whirling world did at that moment indeed stand still; the turmoil, the killing, the war, consigned to the darkest place of fear and dread.

# Putney 1959

Bonnie says she is waiting for Mr. Right. She wants to flounce down the aisle in a cloud of silk taffeta, or organza froth, and if she's rich enough, tiers of ruffled Chantilly—the names of fabric making her eyes cloud with dreams. She desires a nipped waist and a peter-pan collar, virginal and chaste. And babies and G-plan furniture, a television, car, caravan and holidays in Dorset or Hastings with the occasional visit to a Butlins holiday camp.

I don't want a white wedding. I don't want a wedding at all, but I don't say that. I haven't thought about the future. I accept I will probably marry someone, but I want him to be a god. To be exceptional like Heathcliff is for Cathy. Thoughts of being possessed utterly fill our daydreams and send us into euphoria, blind to our mothers' day to day unrelenting drudgery, the handwashing, cleaning, dusting, scrubbing floors, carpet-sweeping. We escape from our home lives into dreams, but find ourselves trapped in each other's domestic turmoil.

What I love most at Bonnie's house is the record player and dancing to Cliff Richard and the Drifters, Elvis Presley's 'Heartbreak Hotel' and 'Jailhouse Rock', The Everly Brothers, and Adam Faith's 'What do you want if you don't want money' at full blast until Davy drags me down onto the sofa for a play fight, and we all lie exhausted on the floor unable to stop giggling. When Bonnie comes to my house we have to be more sedate, quieter, and spend the time in my room fantasizing about boys who hang around the school gates. These boys, tired from a day at school, come to look at us as a leisure pursuit. We like it. Some send us into a whole flurry of pleasurable sensations, as if fingers run down our spines, fluttering deep inside us to make us giggle and blush.

Sometimes, distracted from longing for boys, Bonnie corrects the lines I have to learn for drama class at school, a job she relishes. In English I'm playing Portia in *The Merchant of Venice*. Bonnie doesn't let me get away with my own variations of the script, hesitations or what she called a lack of emphasis.

'Look old Shakes won't mind if I get tiny words wrong. The gist of the thing's the same!' I protest.

But Bonnie doesn't care. 'Look, he wrote it this way with these words, so you have to say it the way he says you've gotta say it.'

It's thanks to Bonnie I'm not thrown out of drama club for being slap-dash or lackadaisical. When the day of the performance arrives, I'm nervous and feel sick. A group of girls in my year, but another class, sneer and whisper about me in the toilets. I hold my head high and push through their coven of spite. With luck I manage my lines, thanks to Bonnie, and perform in front of the school. I think it was painful for the pupils to watch *The Merchant of Venice*, despite the fact our English teacher had drastically cut the play. It's the nervous tension that's exhausting, trying to give the role impact, but I think many of the dramatic parts are lost on most of the audience. The pound of flesh is nothing more than a pound of meat as far as the girls are concerned. I'm aware of fidgeting, chair scraping, and whispering in the audience, but try to whiten them out in the bright lights. There was only one curtain call and a small bow during less than a minute of half-hearted clapping. And there's another performance due in the evening for parents. Somehow, I don't expect my mother or Leonard to come. I didn't dare ask Leonard because I couldn't bear to watch him search for an excuse or make some joke or comment about my futile attempts to tread the boards. I take it for granted my mother won't attend. How would she cope with the intricacies of Shakespeare? My mother says she will fetch me from the gate at the back of the school if it gets too dark to walk me home and I don't protest this time.

I'm pleased to see her after a mediocre performance at the side entrance of the school hall. Everyone else is milling around searching for their parents and siblings, calling and shouting, and then there she is in her flowery summer dress, a white cardigan over her shoulders, smiling and looking round, quite at home. My heart lurches in love for her.

We walk in silence along Chartfield Avenue in the dusk. Once home, she asks if I would like a ham sandwich. I answer yes, as I haven't the heart to tell her I don't feel like eating. Leonard is listening to the news on the radio in the living room. Together like old times when we lived in cramped bed-sits, we ate our sandwiches in silence, a habit from those days when in crowded houses everyone had to be quiet. She doesn't ask me anything about the performance. I don't expect her to.

Lying in bed that night I'm relieved the play is over. The speeches no longer need to stay in my head. I can open the little port holes of my memory and watch words float away in the dark and soar like small birds on a migratory route somewhere exotic and magical where they can be free. But something inside me is wrong. I'm troubled and can't sleep. Bonnie comes into my mind, mouthing the lines in the audience, and her brilliant rendition of Portia's quality of mercy speech in her cold, bare bedroom keeps replaying. She infused the lines with passion and conviction. The words came from her, not Shakespeare. She took total possession of the speech:

> *The quality of mercy is not strain'd*
> *It droppeth as the gentle rain from heaven*
> *Upon the place beneath; it is twice blessed;*
> *It blesseth him that gives and him that takes…*

I know she is more precious than I am, she is very beautiful with her mass of white curls, pear shaped face, and perfect complexion. The role of Portia will always be hers, not mine. Many years later my mother confessed she watched the performance, hiding in the back row of the hall, but didn't dare tell me in case I protested, her presence being unwelcome.

I was secretly ashamed I hadn't asked her. To make it worse, I felt fraudulent, like I had stolen the role meant for Bonnie. I was a spoilt brat and Bonnie should have had the part. In reality, this was nonsense because Bonnie refused to join the after-school drama club. Nevertheless, it was my belief I was miscast, second-rate in most things, and Bonnie's gift undiscovered. This didn't stop me continuing with drama club. I could forget myself in a role, just as I could in dance, and if I performed badly, I didn't care. I tried to do my best to lose my misgivings in movement and acting.

It's summer again, and my mother treats Bonnie and me to musicals like *South Pacific*, at the local Regal, but Shakespeare has given us a taste of hardcore realism perfected by *Room at the Top*, and *A Kind of Loving* and the suffering of adorable James Dean in *East of Eden*, which sends us into paroxysms of sympathy and grief for the boy cruelly misunderstood. Knowing so little about men, we hope to gain some understanding about how different relationships work. My mother puts up a defence against the *schrecklich* kitchen sink films. 'They are too hard to bear. I want to see the happy films.' She likes *Calamity Jane* and *Gigi*. But Bonnie and I are for the full bloodied and brooding males, like Marlon Brando and Montgomery Clift; emotionally mixed up, intense, physically strong, alluring and above all, dangerous.

In my bedroom we experiment with makeup, and backcomb our hair. We mince about and pose in the mirror and practise kissing with each other, so boys won't think we are hopeless virgins when our lips latch. Sometimes we can't stop laughing about boys on the low wall outside the gym who wait for girls to leave school to follow them home. They make their way from the boys' school in Earlsfield. They are without doubt a strange species with their broken voices, pimples, soft down just under their noses, loping along as best they can. Growing so fast, their etiolated bodies defy gravity and the restrictions of their uniform, ties loose and shirts unbuttoned. They looked wanton, louche, knowing and strong. Their otherness is the catch, the lure.

But we are proud of our feminine selves, too. We like to dress up and learn the flirtation game, the use of eyes, the grinning and blushing, the come-hither body language, thrust of hips, the coy downward movement of the head and eyes, and the connections of the occasional mistaken-deliberate touch. The power we have over the boys makes us heady, silly. Except Bonnie and I hate the hidden paraphernalia of girlhood, suspender belts or *roll ons*—elasticated tubes to keep our bums and tummies flat and *being on* with tummy cramps, and sanitary pads that chafe the inside of our thighs. With school exams looming, we're often moody and morose. And we're not ready to change the world because it all appears irredeemably and universally fixed. We are living dolls until we get the hang of things, and then maybe we might try some variations of the feminine theme, learned from books and films. We might even try becoming tarts for a day, but not just yet.

'Miss, Miss, can you tell us about contraception please Miss?'

Bonnie was brave. She had put up her hand but didn't wait until Miss Godly nodded her head giving permission to speak. We were in the Biology room with its usual smell of gas or bad eggs. The room fell unnaturally silent. Miss Godly turned puce, twirling her chalk in her fingers. She had just described the basic mechanics of 'sexual intercourse', first in rabbits and then humans. We looked at the diagrams in the little blue book. The penis was arched and hung down, and the vagina looked straight. The logistics struck me as odd. It seemed all to do with strange plumbing. I couldn't understand how the penis, so obviously downward arched, could be placed into the vagina so the sperm could swim off into the fecund, blood-padded womb when the vagina appeared so plainly straight.

Then I thought of the serpent in the garden of Eden. I guessed the penis was snake-like and could bend itself to slip into the vagina. Miss Godly missed out the erection bit, as she did ejaculation. We all waited for Miss Godly to liberate us.

'The best contraception,' said Miss Godly in answer to Bonnie's bold question, 'is *not* to do it.' We groaned in disappointment, or was it in protest? Protest that it was up to us to be in control, and not a boy's concern. After class the girls swapped stories as we huddled around the radiator. There was talk of a rubber cap thing that you had to shove up your vagina, and there were rubbers for men called French letters for an unfathomable reason. As far as I could tell, I had no vagina. It seemed I couldn't shove anything up it. In fact, there was no obvious *hole*. Biology diagrams insisted there was another hole near the hole we peed out of, but I was yet to discover it, the monthly blood flooded my pads. Tampax sounded like medicine for constipation. Some girls reminded us there were lots of other things you could do to boys and keep safe from getting caught in pregnancy. It was overwhelming; too graphic even though the term blow-job wasn't in circulation then, and sucking off a boy, less of a euphemism, too shocking to imagine. And imagine the taste of the thing! Bonnie and I decided no decent boy would expect any 'nice' girl to perform such an absurd and outrageous act. That couldn't be natural, could it? We thought of our parents, many of whom never exposed their flesh to the air, and the thought of them engaging in sexual intercourse was both vulgar and unpleasant. They were just too old. Listening to some girls talking 'dirty', Bonnie and I would flounce off arm in arm, heads in the air, repelled by all these speculative sex acts with boys.

And yet much later in my next year, I found myself equally repelled by Jane in *Jane Eyre*—on the GCE English Literature syllabus—and her sanctimonious air of righteousness. For me that was the other end of the spectrum and equally unappealing. She never put a foot wrong in her philosophy of adhering to the truth. A prig, she seemed an impossible act to follow. Bonnie and I needed different role models, independent women who lapsed from time to time in touch with their bodies and sexual desires, and we didn't want our heroes blinded or dilapidated before we had permission to love them. We wanted whole men who would love us with all our vanities and faults, our frailties, who would satisfy our minds and bodies completely. In turn, we would love them and forgive their faults and devote ourselves to them.

After exhausting weeks of revision and examinations in every subject, Bonnie and I look forward to the holidays. I performed well in my exams. My mother reads my school report of which I am proud. She folds it slowly and puts it back in the brown envelope addressed to her and Leonard. 'This is good, Susie.' I respect her quiet response, but I wonder if she really cares or whether I am genuinely good enough for praise. She seems pensive, distracted and puts the report in the walnut bureau in a little drawer. I certainly don't earn a hug. It was only years later when I collected my own children's school reports as precious objects did it occur that all my school reports vanished. I never thought to ask where they might be or what became of them. They simply disappeared and I assumed my mother threw them away.

I'm sorry that Bonnie failed in all her subjects, but she brushes off her failures. Because I have done well which is a surprise, I will be going into a higher class in the autumn term to study GCEs and she will go down into the lower sets. We don't talk about this separation. I know she could have passed her exams if she wanted to, but Bonnie says her Mum thinks she would make a good hairdresser and so there wouldn't be any point in staying on at school. I panic, afraid she will end the friendship, so I make things worse by being sycophantic, clinging, and especially attentive. Her reaction is to become quiet and distant, but once the term ends, we look forward to a holiday together in Cornwall. No doubt it was Bonnie's idea to ask her parents if they would take me. They hire a small cottage in the corner of a fallow field just outside Taunton. It belongs to a dairy farmer a good mile away. Carol agrees I can join them provided I pay my way, or rather my mother pays my way; this includes a contribution to the accommodation and food, and petrol for the journey. Bonnie is the spokesperson because Carol never talks to me. When I hand over the money to Carol one morning in an envelope from my mother, with a short letter of thanks from Leonard, she says humph, and puts the envelope in her apron pocket without opening it.

The night before our departure, I stay the night at Bonnie's. We are woken by Bonnie's Dad, Graham, at about one in the morning and there's no time for breakfast. The boot holds our small luggage, and the three of us squash into the tiny Austen in the back seat. It smells of old cracked leather and petrol. The journey is slow and seems to go on forever, the night rolling by as the little car nudges through the darkness. Sometimes we fall asleep but when we wake, we don't utter a sound. Davy slumps over and his head falls into my lap. Bonnie's head leans against my neck as I watch the suburbs give way to the shadowy countryside of looming black trees, the grey road like a calm river lit by the ghostly tunnels of the car's headlamps. This is the first family holiday I have experienced and I'm overly excited. At last, after taking the wrong road and cursing the lack of signposts, Bonnie's dad finds the farm. By now it is dawn, and we are greeted by the most magnificent sunrise, the sky livid, and the sun pushing up over the inky sea like a giant blood bag. I'm astounded. I have never seen the sun like this. It is awe inspiring and thrilling. The farmer, a morose, stout man, climbs on a tractor and we have to follow him in the car. The cottage turns out to be a dilapidated caravan poked in the corner of a field obscured by high grasses and overhanging elms. But there is a little gate and an attempt at a cottage garden with seeding lupins each side of wooden steps in the long feathery grass up to the doorway. Inside there is only one bedroom at the back with a double bed and a chest of drawers alongside a bathroom, with rusty taps and a brown stained bath. And then a living room with two narrow divan beds hugging a central table and chairs. On a sideboard there are two electric hotplates.

'What kind of cottage is this? What a bloody dump.' Carol pushes at a chair. 'How am I supposed to cook on that thing? Oh, for God's sake. I could kill that farmer! You wait till I see him. I'll give him cottage. This is no cottage. I hope you haven't paid a penny, Graham.'

'It said a cottage in the paper.' Graham is equally disappointed and mortified.

'It said a cottage in the paper,' she mimics. 'This is a rip off. I'm not staying here. I'm not. What a place to choose, Graham. Can't you show me some respect. At least think of the children. You should have left it to me. It's horrible. It's depressing. It stinks.'

With that she sat on one of the divan beds and burst into tears, her head bent over her lap. She sobs loudly. Graham strokes her back. 'There now, there now.'

'Oh, get off me!' She moves her shoulder away from him. 'Don't touch me!' she says, her voice thickens.

Bonnie takes my hand, and calls Davy from the back bedroom, 'C'mon Davy, let's explore!' We escape through the little front door to the outside.

It's lovely in the field. At the back of the caravan there is a running stream where we paddle our feet under the elms. Crows announce our arrival. As if in a tin drum, we can still hear Carole firing off her abuse at Graham. We find a gap in the hedge and run across a field of cows, then keep to the edge and down a hill, and find the sea. We gasp at the sight of it: a blue expanse glittering in the sun. I catch my breath. I'm filled with exuberance. Bonnie and Davy roll down the hill and end in a hedge. We cross the road and take a sandy path to the dunes and lie there in a huddle looking up at the blue sky.

'I bet pirates come this way,' Davy leans on his elbows. 'C'mon lets, explore.'

In the distance, further along the coast is Par harbour,

and what looks like a factory, the China clay works carved out of the rocks. Davy takes off his socks and sandals and goes to explore the rocks and pools. He shouts for us to come and see all the sea creatures and when we follow to please him, he insists we put our finger on the sea anemone for it to suck at us and draw us in. It makes us laugh and we wonder at its strength.

Then we hear Carol's distant voice calling and make our way back to the caravan. In our absence, Carol has tried to make an effort. She has reorganized the main room by putting the two single divans together over by the main window, and the table and chairs are now in the centre. She has unpacked a bag of cereals, milk and bread.

'Kids, your bedroom's in there. Go and unpack your stuff. Then come and have some cornflakes.'

Bonnie and I go into the back bedroom. It smells stuffy, like bad breath. It only has a tiny window high up covered in a square of red material pinned across. Bonnie switches on the light. Davy jumps on the double bed. It has little resistance, thin and unsprang. I unpack my shorts, a couple of white blouses, and my school plimsolls. Bonnie has two summer dresses, one with a large blue flower print, and the other her school dress. She is already wearing her white shorts and pink blouse. That there is only one double bed doesn't trouble us in the least. We always end up sleeping together at Bonnie's house. Carol is cross with Davy because he has left his socks and sandals on the beach. After a small bowl of milk and cornflakes, we run off to find them, and then forget to return because the sea commands us to stay and Carol is so sour the atmosphere in the small caravan is grim.

The beach is stony in places and there is a fetid smell of drying seaweed, but the sea smells sweetly of fresh fruit. Bonnie and I want to lie in the warm sun in the hollow of the dunes out of the breeze, while Davy explores the rocks. We are careless with him, insensible to the fact he could easily fall. But he is agile and intense in his explorations of this strange, exciting alien world. I would like to stay like this forever beside Bonnie with whom I have never had a cross word; I want to take possession of her in this place; take possession of sands, the rocks, the sea and sun. I momentarily remember the time when I was very young playing in Auntie Dolly's garden with the *Hund* and believed you could possess things by the simple statement: you are mine, without knowledge that the world was for sharing. We are only tenants on the planet, after all. The beauty of the moment passes, its contentment and wholeness fused into all living things. My expectations are threatened by failure, by a feeling of being as light as a wisp, a fugitive. And home is now here with Bonnie. When I strain to recall my mother's homeland, all that comes to mind is a train journey, the cold winter sea, white cliffs and snow. The faces of my grandparents, Oma and Opa, are like stone statues that have had their faces destroyed by time. I am falling in love with England, resembling the ancient Sphinx with wings of an eagle, and the body of a lion, a bi-species on a beautiful island. The powdery blue sky arches over us like a secluded dome and we lie falling into a half sleep, woken by Davy's desperate cries. He has cut his foot on the rocks. He limps towards us, and we examine the side of his foot. The blood is already congealing. He is fascinated by the blood smeared over his skin and wants to go back to show Carol.

'Go into the sea and wash the wound. Mum will have a fit if she sees it.'

We help him towards the water's edge. The water is cold, and he cries out and laughs at the same time as the saltwater bathes his superficial gash. It is only a surface wound.

'You're such a big baby, Davy. It's only a graze.'

Then Bonnie and I take off our stockings and roll them up inside our shoes. We paddle in the waves to keep Davy company. I like the way the waves suck the sand from under our feet to make us almost topple. We watch the waves for a long time. Then slowly make our way back to the caravan through the hedge and field and over the little rushing stream.

For supper Carol has opened a couple of tins of beef stew she serves with tinned potatoes, and Marrowfat peas. We wolf down the food and the greasy taste is lost on us, then prepare for bed. Lying very still for a moment with Davy in the middle, he begins to tell us funny school jokes. In no time though, Bonnie is fast asleep, so Davy and I read some of his *Hotspur* comics, but he doesn't let me read. He keeps saying, 'Hey Sue, look at this! What a whopper space ship!' I have to look and admire. We are both lonely, grateful for each other's company. Soon, a hand opens the door and stretches for the light switch to turn it off. The door quietly closes again. In the darkness the sound of the bubbling stream outside grows louder. We can hear Bonnie breathing hoarsely. The total darkness gives us a new lease of wakefulness, and Davy whispers about school, the teachers he likes, and the naughty boys who gang up on weaker ones, until his half-voice croaks and grows distant and immediately it is morning and it's as if he is still talking, 'C'mon, let's go down the beach!'

Bonnie has already disappeared. We get dressed. We pass Carol and Graham tucked in their separate divans, and find Bonnie outside, sitting on the little wood steps. 'Shush!' she says indicating a flock of sheep nibbling their way closer.

'You scared or something?' scorns Davy, speaking low. Bonnie shudders.

'No, it's just they're weird. Look at their little pokey eyes. Davy, stop. Don't go in the field. Keep the gate shut.'

'They're not man-eaters. I can tell,' says Davy. We don't manage to titter at his joke.

We can hear stirrings, hollow footsteps on the boards inside. Carol appears in a man's stripped flannelette pyjamas. I know at home she wears black and pink lacy nightdresses. She looks younger without her makeup, even though she has her hair in pink plastic rollers.

'You lot! Inside and get dressed. Oh no. How are we supposed to get out this field with that lot? Graham! Graham! Come and look at this!' Davy and Bonnie snigger at her distress. I keep a neutral face. I know she doesn't like me. Graham peers from gloom in his shorts. He laughs. 'Don't worry, I'll soon see to them.' He claps his hands. Instead of the flock of sheep dispersing, they raise their heads and stare, still as if rooted.

'Oh quite the shepherd aren't we!' Carol flicks her hand over Davy and Bonnie's head, and we have to go inside. We have bread and margarine and dark red jam for breakfast which is so intensely sweet the fruit could be anything.

Then Graham leads the way through the field, flaying his arms about so the sheep do not attack.

'It's quite unnecessary to do all that waving, Graham. You look ridiculous,' says Carol. We make our way to the car parked in a little side turning from the narrow main road. In the back between Davy and Bonnie I know to remain silent. The morning is already oppressive. Graham starts the car which chokes and wheezes, but before Carol complains, we move forward, and Graham drives us to Mevagissy. We wander through the little streets. I notice people stare at Graham, but quickly look away. I'm used to his disfigurement now and feel sorry for him because Carol is bitter and cold. I would like to visit the cake shop, but when Davy suggests this, Carol says no, we are all fat enough. Instead of leaving it there, she begins a tirade about kids always wanting things without being grateful for what they have. Davy mumbles under his breath that that's the whole point because we haven't got 'no-fink.' Bonnie nudges his arm to make him stop as she senses another outburst from Carol. In a trinket shop full of shells, and plaster figures of dolphins and toy white cottages, I buy a postcard to write home. Then we drive to Polperro, a tiny fishing village, full of stalwart stone houses, day trippers and finally, weary from sightseeing, we return to our field. Bonnie says she has come on and has a stomach pain. She lies on the bed with her legs drawn up to her chest. I stroke her shoulder, but she brushes my hand away.

Davy and I go down to the beach. We take with us a piece of bread each, folded over to keep the jam inside. There are dark clouds over the horizon. The sea pounds in among the rocks. Next time I tell Davy we'll have to find a bucket or pudding basin to catch shrimps and small crabs. Davy chats all the time. He wishes he had a net. We squat together and look beyond our reflections into the pool, but I find it hard to get truly excited by the creatures. I have a strange feeling I have eaten something poisonous. It sits on my chest like a stone. When the sun goes down, we make our way up the hillside to the caravan. The sheep are clustered underneath an oak tree alongside the hedge. They look up and stare at us with inscrutable expressions.

We have fish and chips for tea. Graham has driven to Polperro for them. Carol puts rollers in her hair and lies on the divan under a blanket reading a romance magazine. Bonnie is still on the bed and refuses to eat. She turns her back to me. 'Leave me alone. I'll be all right in the morning.' Graham says we can have her share of fish and chips and he cuts the cod into three and divides up the chips which are limp and cold. I write my card home to Mum and Dad. I want to write Dear Mum and Leonard, but that might give rise to questions from Carol and Graham so I write Mum and Dad. I look at the Dad for some time. It looks strange like a foreign word. I write that we are all having a lovely time in Cornwall; that we visited Mevagissy and Polperro, which are both quaint and pretty, and that we have sheep in the field.

Because there is no TV, Graham gets out a pack of cards and teaches me and Davy games. I don't like it at first, but learn to get involved with Gin Rummy and Fish out of sheer desperation. Later, Graham teaches me Solitaire. Davy and Graham liven things up because they are keenly competitive so there are mock fights, and name calling and mockery between them. I don't care if I win, but I go along. This diminishes the long evening wavering under the dull, yellow light and soon we are told to wash and go to bed. The light disturbs Bonnie, so we slip in the bed like shadows and Davy whispers that he wants a story. I tell him the story of the *Snow Queen* and before I finish, he is asleep his head slumped on my arm. I carefully take my arm away before it goes dead and remain lying on my back. I can hear the brook outside burbling. It is an exquisite sound like a blackbird's song that rarely repeats a refrain. I miss the sounds of home; the soft rush of traffic, and distant clicking of the tube trains, and the line of lamp light under the curtains from the street. The darkness is so thick I can barely breathe. I remember this suffocating darkness in Grandmother's house at night. I wish I could read something. Instead, I pretend I'm reading and rewrite the story of *Black Beauty*, but that becomes too disturbing. I can hear Carol and Graham moving in the next room. She is making small mumbles. The stone on my chest is still there. I sigh and sigh again, but it won't go away. I have a sense Bonnie doesn't want to be here with her family, or me. I am so grateful for Davy. But I wish I could go home but tell myself everything will be new and interesting tomorrow. It occurs to me that here in the caravan, Graham hasn't had a single nightmare. And then I fall asleep.

The following day is cloudy, and Carol insists we continue touring. We spend most of the morning in Looe, but Bonnie says it would be good to go down to the beach later and have a swim once we get back to the caravan. I play a silly game of trying to catch as many boys' eyes as I can and count the times I receive a quick welcoming glint. I like the mutual touch of looking. If we spot a good-looking boy, Bonnie nudges me as if to say, look at him. I know she feels better. We all spend the afternoon on the beach. Carole and Graham lie on a blanket they take from one of the divans in the caravan, while Bonnie and I occupy a sand dune and sunbathe. Later, Graham says, 'None of that, young ladies. I need you both as fielders.'

We reluctantly play cricket to please Graham. It is impossible for Davy to bowl Graham out. He throws down his ball in the opposite direction in despair and is then made to fetch it. 'I'm not a dog!' he shouts, but we all laugh. Then we climb the hill back to the caravan. We have fried eggs on toast for tea with some Heinz baked beans.

The following day it rains. The sheep cluster under the dripping trees staring out, a void behind their eyes. Carol doesn't bother to take her rollers out, so I understand that we are not going anywhere. The rain gets worse and thunder rumbles over the sea. Davy goes to the bedroom to read his new Eagle comic. I have come ill-prepared. I have no books, magazines or writing paper. Graham plays Solitaire at the table while Bonnie and I sit on the outside step beneath the broad lip of cover over the door, looking out at the sodden field. She looks up from time to time to check the sky, for some breach of cloud, change in the light. I love the sound of the rain pounding on the roof. I feel liberated from the strangely unsettling atmosphere inside, and yet Bonnie's aura is tainted by it. I wait for her to speak.

'Sorry about Mum, Sue.'

I pretend I don't understand. She continues keeping her voice low. 'This was all Dad's idea. He wants us all to be a happy family, you know. He tries.'

'Your Dad's nice.'

'You can tell Mum hates it here. I don't blame her. She probably wants to be with her fancy man at the grocers.'

I say nothing. But tears well up. I swallow hard and find myself shifting closer to her.

'Are you getting all wet? Hey, look the rain's easing off. What shall we do?'

'I dunno,' I say. 'The sheep don't know either.'

Bonnie laughs. 'Let's run away,' she says, 'I can just see the newspaper headlines. Two girls vanish in Cornwall, both suffering from a disease called boredom.'

'We can't just wander off, what about Davy?'

Bonnie scoffs. 'The rain's stopped. Let's go and look for boys. There must be some around here, some lusty farm boys to snog in the hayloft.'

We take Davy with us on the walk. The hedges and country road are steaming in the sun. We have our bathing suits wrapped in towels tucked under our arms and wind our way along gorse bushes towards the sands. The sea looks rough with sea horses far out, but loses its vigour as it reaches the shore. The waves are frequent, small and gentle. The dune grasses are full of sparrows. I undress and get into my swimming costume. Bonnie lies on her towel and sunbathes. She says she can't swim because she's still 'on' but hitches her skirt to brown her long legs. Another small boy about Davy's age approaches with a lilo and invites Davy to play with him in the water.

'Don't go out too far Davy,' says Bonnie looking over at a couple, presumably the boy's parents sitting some distance away.

Eventually, I join the boys in the water. The newcomer is called Christopher. They act as though they want to exclude me from the game, pushing me off their boat. But when I turn my back and attempt to swim, they call me back, 'Hey you, the pirate, come and get us!' After a long game of chase in the sea, I try to teach myself to swim but fear grips me. I prefer to have at least one foot on the sea bed. I pull the boys on the lilo nearer the shore. Davy goes off with the boy to make sandcastles near his parents.

Bonnie and I lie side by side in the sun and she falls asleep. Bonnie turns to lie on her stomach and Davy is digging trenches with the boy in the distance. I shield my eyes with my hand to scan the rest of the beach. Here and there are small groups of people. The boy's lilo lies at my feet. I decide to borrow it, and wade out up to my waist. The land looks different from the sea, expansive, green and beautiful, the low cliffs sculptured by nature, by the winds and sea. Swifts skim the grassland on top, and gulls cry in the distant harbour. The wind has dropped. The sun is hot. I jump onto the lilo with its strong smell of rubber, and stretch out as it slowly drifts; the waves carry the sound of people talking and laughing on the beach. I like it on my own for a while. I have missed moments to myself. I appreciate how intoxicating the countryside is, how calming. As I drift on the gentle undulating waves, I fall asleep.

When I wake, I realise I've drifted quite far out, but not too far to be dangerous. A bank of cloud hides the evening sun. I can see a boy on the rocks who looks like Davy, although the small family with the other boy has

271

disappeared. I feel guilty that I have taken the lilo and intend to leave it in one of the dunes. Bonnie, too, seems to have woken and gone. I decide to jump off the lilo and wade back to the shore. But I don't know that I am out of my depth and I fall into the icy cold, bottomless sea. The shock prevents me from taking my last breath. My eyes sting with salt. A strong current takes hold, and I seem to swirl, twist and turn as water invades my body. My first thought is that I have had a short life but I must be grateful for trees. I don't know why I thought that. Maybe I had some kind of root-lust in fear of drifting. Why I didn't worry about my mother, what the news might do to her, or what it might be like to be present as one's own church memorial, I can't imagine.

My life does not flash before my eyes. Trees. Only trees. The water rushes down through my nose and mouth and I begin to drown. The noise is like a thousand waterfalls exploding inside my head. My arms flay, fighting against the surge, and I kick at the water but descend deeper into the black depths. I have my eyes screwed tight, but then I stop fighting the current and let the sea take me. I don't feel upset to die. I feel grateful for the brief life I have had. An arm locks around my chest, and I am lifted up in one strong sweep, to air and light, my eyes burning, my throat stinging with salt. I cough. I can't stop coughing as I'm dragged to the sandbank. My eyes sting and weep, my throat is raw. I'm on all fours, the sand dragged away from my knees by the waves. My hair hangs like string, encrusted with salt. I vomit salt water. I manage to stand, my back bent, vision blurred. I can make out a boy about sixteen or seventeen beside me. He is tall and I know it is a boy because he has strong gangly limbs and pats me on the back and then lopes off over the dunes. He and I are wordless. I try to call him back to thank him. My mouth is open, but my voice gone. Davy has gone too. The lilo is bobbing on the waves, drifting far out from the bay, looping back towards the harbour. I find my towel and wrap it around my shivering shoulders, gather up my clothes, and make my way across the road and the fields to the caravan still in shock. I open the door, and I'm now shaking violently. They are all eating at the table. Carol gives me a frozen look and then quickly looks away.

'I'm sorry,' I mutter down my nose, 'I fell asleep.' I'm made to feel ashamed for being late, for causing Carol to interrupt her meal and open another tin of mince to heat up.

'There you are,' says Graham. 'We thought you had gone off to swim the Channel. Come and sit down and have your tea.'

After the week in Cornwall, Bonnie and I are not the same. We try to make ourselves the same, shifting from one falsely optimistic mood to another, but there is a difference between us. She is dismissive, as if I have let her down. I'm too afraid to admit to myself, I feel she and her family let me down. A nugget of pain in my head just above my eyes tells me I am hurt, that she abandoned me to the sea, that both Bonnie and Davy made their way back to the caravan without me. It is odd that   Bonnie makes me feel increasingly guilty. I hate myself for being needy and insecure. I love her and can't let her go. I know she won't be coming back to school and our paths will diverge, but I can't see why that should mean we won't still be together. I try to work out if she is rejecting me in anger, or resentment, or maybe I have done something to disappoint or hurt her. She is calm, amenable and gentle as always, but no longer has any interest in me. I'm beginning to see these traits as cruel, as a form of affected indifference, a dishonesty. But I won't let her go yet. She is my extended family. Would I dare admit these people are my only family? And there are my feelings for Davy whom we have to look after before September when school starts.

I don't tell anyone about the accident on holiday when I was left to drift out to sea. I want to put it behind me as a lucky escape, but somehow it rankles that Bonnie didn't wade out, or call me. Maybe she did. I will never know because I can't bring myself to tell her I almost drowned. Instead, I tell myself that the boy who saved me may have been a dream even though I know he was real because I am alive. I will always remember him but he haunts me because I want to tell him how grateful I am that he saved my life. I don't tell my mother what happened. I fear a thread of indifference in her but hope to imagine she would hold the whole family responsible, and hate them for not properly looking after me.

Despite growing apart, during the last days of the summer holidays, Bonnie and I loll in the long grass in my garden, suck lollipops and read Carol's *Woman* and my old William books. We remain together like a couple who can't bear a divorce. We play tennis with Davy, saunter to the river and share an ice-cream and watch the boats, or visit the park near Mrs. Bailey's house and spend an afternoon on the swings. You would think if you saw us we were close friends again. But we are changing and hunger for new experiences; it's no surprise then we find ourselves knocking on my neighbour's door and asking to take Baby Pickles out for a walk in his pram.

In this way we graduate from playing and dancing around like dolly birds, to being responsible grown-ups, or so we like to believe. As if to save our friendship, Baby Pickles is our shared project, a distraction from the rift between us. Baby Pickle's mother, Mona Pickles, is very pregnant and looks ready to burst. She's suffering from swollen ankles. Baby Pickles comes to Bonnie and me without resistance. He's about nine months old with dark blue, mournful eyes, a wide mouth and fat, red cheeks I can't stop kissing. Mona dresses him in little knitted suits with short pants and tucks him into the pram with a white sun canopy at half-mast. Under his pram blanket she tucks spare nappies, some rusks, and a bottle of baby milk. She arches her back and she looks in pain. She shows us how to put the brake on and take it off on the pram, which is often difficult to manoeuvre round corners.

'Thanks Mona. We'll bring him back at tea time.' She gives us a flick of her arm as if swatting gnats to wave us off.

We wheel Baby Pickles to my house. The pram is like jelly, springing up and down. I like the way Baby Pickles grips the padded sides with his little podgy, dimpled hands, as if he is in a boat. Bonnie, Davy and I take turns to push him. Baby Pickles looks around happy to be out and about. In my house we raid the kitchen for biscuits, make jam sandwiches, and collect lemonade bottles full of Dandelion and Burdock from our den among the rhododendron bushes, loading the provisions into the pram to set off to the river to show Baby Pickles the swans and have a Thames side picnic. On other days, we walk to Richmond Park and take Baby Pickles out of the pram to lie in the long grass and look up at the blue sky. On one occasion, we all fell asleep, Baby Pickles wedged between Bonnie and Davy, and we woke to find a deer with magnificent antlers watching over us.

Soon, I'm less anxious under the cloudless summer sky, but mostly it's Baby Pickles who distracts me from what I fear. We fetch him every day. I can't live without him.

'He's been waiting for you at the window since six o'clock this morning,' says Mona. 'I've packed him some mashed up dinner in a jar with his spoon. Rusks are in the paper bag next to his bottle and nappies. Bring him back if he frets.' Mona looks washed out, with dark circle under her eyes. If this is pregnancy, I want nothing of it.

'All right, Mrs. Pickles, don't worry.'

But Baby Pickles never frets. And off we go. My mother keeps her distance when we take him into our den. She watches Bonnie and me fuss and feed the baby and change his nappy on a blanket she provides on the lawn. How strange that she is not tempted to fuss him, take him in her arms. He never cries except when we take him home and hand him back to Mona. We learn his real name is Derek.

'*Derek?*' spouts Bonnie once we leave the entrance to the flats. We enjoy making up names for him, Chubby chops, Mister, Handsome, Pudding and Pie, but then suddenly he's Baby Pickles again. But he's never Derek.

After a while Davy lusts for boyish adventure. Fathering Baby Pickles has lost its allure so he spends the rest of the summer weeks with his cousins and granny in Streatham.

When we are denied Baby Pickles, if he has gone a few days with Mona to see her mother in the Isle of Wight, Bonnie and I decide to pick up boys, and abandon our Martha and Mary roles, tart ourselves up, white lipstick, pony tails high, summer skirts billowing with petticoats, ankle socks and plimsolls, and take the 168 bus to Clapham Junction where a short walk up Lavender Hill finds us in a café with a juke box and chain-smoking boys.

The air in the café is thick with smoke and steam. The glass coffee cups are shallow and smeared. Self-consciously we sit at a table and check out the talent. There are three boys at a table, slouched over their coffee smoking, commenting on people passing by and enjoying endless in-jokes. One is playing on the juke box and grinning across the cafe at us. 'Don't look now, but that boy by the juke box, I think I know him. He keeps staring. I'm sure I've seen him around the estate.' Bonnie is all breathlessness and pink.

'When can I look?'

'Don't, not yet! Oh my God, he's coming over.' Bonnie turns to the window while I glance over my shoulder. The boy looks familiar. Maybe he has hung around the back gates of our school. He is stocky, mature, with black hair oiled back and a white shirt open at the neck. I'm not sure yet whether he is a contender, but when he asks if he can sit because he thinks he knows us from somewhere, we can see how good-looking he is with his genuine smile and clear skin.

This is Paul. He lives on the edge of Bonnie's council estate in a high rise. His family moved from Battersea, and he lives with his sister and her baby and his parents. He went to the local Secondary Modern School and has a job as a motor mechanic's apprentice mending motorbikes. He delivers all this like a CV, pausing to ask where we live and what we do. He is open and doesn't try to show off. Bonnie flirts for his sole attention but he doles it out equally between us. I feel silly pitching my voice higher, fluttering my eyelashes and playing with my hair, so I abandon the act. Once I do, Bonnie plays her part even more as if to compensate. I prefer to watch him. He has lively eyes and expression, and his gestures are unsure, which suggests he is not as confident as he pretends. He leans over the table with his shoulders hunched and keeps his head down so he has to look up to meet our gaze.

'You two sisters then?'

Bonnie giggles and asks suggestively, 'How old d'you think we are?'

'I'd say,' he pauses, leaning back and looking us both over. I'm shy and embarrassed and look down into my coffee cup, but Bonnie holds her breath.

'Sixteen,' he lies.

'No, we're both fifteen,' says Bonnie, complimented that we look older. In truth we are fourteen and Paul probably realizes this. We exchange a brief knowing look and then he glances away. It makes me collusive, party to his thoughts. Then Paul wants to know if we go to this café often and what singers we like and what school we go to. Bonnie provides the answers. But I sense, now that the introduction is over, he is waiting to talk about himself, to impress us with his London worldliness although I know he's hiding something. Maybe he is hiding his loneliness; his lack of self-worth. He tells us his job mending bikes is only temporary. He's going to travel and see the world, apply to join the Navy. Bonnie makes the appropriate noises to show she's impressed. Then he rises and asks to take the bus with us and walk back with us to Putney Vale. I leave Paul and Bonnie under the plane tree doubtless arranging a date. I wave them goodbye, but they are too engrossed in each other to wave. I know this is how I'm going to lose Bonnie, because that's the rule of the game. Once you have a boyfriend then friends must take a back seat or disappear. But it's not just that. I know she is disengaging herself; she no longer needs me. She's growing up faster. I'm still the baby, needing her and immature.

Walking down Putney Hill, my thoughts are on the diverging paths Bonnie and I are taking and how it will all turn out and whether we will end up the same in any case, married with a husband and family like everyone else we know. The paths seem predictable and confining. I want other paths. Then I hear someone breathing heavily behind me, and Paul races by and slows down, and walks me home to Cambalt Road. He tells me Bonnie is nice. I say Bonnie is nice. This makes him laugh.

Outside my gate, I let Paul kiss me. It's a clumsy effort because I'm not expecting it, and he has to twist his face round to catch my lips. The kiss tastes metallic mixed with salt. My face grows hot, and I hope my mother isn't looking out of the window or Theresa in the attic flat preparing a lecture on promiscuity, and sluttish street behaviour. In my confusion, I guess Bonnie has rejected him. Why else would he come running after me, the second best?

'Bonnie and I are meeting up tomorrow. We thought we could go to the Windmill on the heath. Can you come as well?' He looks me up and down. I feel uncomfortable and hunch my shoulders trying to make myself small. I wish I didn't have breasts.

'Oh, I can't. I promised Mona to take Baby Pickles out for the day.' The words came straight out of my mouth. I know I sound foolish.

'Mona and Baby Pickles?' Paul laughs. 'Who are they for crying out loud?'

'Mona lives over there.' I point to the opposite side of the street. 'Her husband's in the police—no don't worry, he's a nice man. He often gives me a lift on his motorbike to school. But Mona needs rest. Her new baby is on its way so we look after her other baby to give her a break. His name is Derek, but Bonnie and I call him Baby Pickles.'

Paul stares as if I have hypnotized him. I'm talking too much because I'm uncomfortable and nervous. I want him to go away. Finally, he says, 'You're really weird—no I don't mean weird, but sort of funny. Different. Oh, I don't know!' Paul laughs again. 'Look come, and bring Baby Pickles, eh? Meet us on Tibbet's Corner about ten.'

'Yeah. See ya then. Bye.' His step is jaunty. I like watching him walk up the road, head down, hands in pockets. He surprises me, turns, winks and waves. He does this several times and it makes me tingle and laugh. Finally, he's gone. I think I'm supposed to like him, but I don't know if I do. He is on my mind and his words repeat in my head.

The following day, as arranged, I set off with Baby Pickles to meet Bonnie and Paul, and after introductions to Baby Pickles looking lively in his pram, we make our way across

Putney Heath to the Windmill where you can buy tea and cupcakes. We sit in the grass, awkwardly and sedately at first, and let Baby Pickles crawl all over us, and then we become silly, giggling and crawling all over each other. Calming down, Paul amuses us with stories about his schoolboy antics such as cheeking teachers, playing truant and getting caught stealing sweets in Woolworth's. Bonnie is more smitten, glowing with admiration. It suits her, that look on her face, angelic, beautiful, as if she were cast in heaven.

When we are alone, Bonnie confesses her love for Paul. I like him, but I know from the outset he will never be mine. All the same, I'm aware that rivalry between us simmers just beneath the surface of our conversations about him, speculating on whom he likes best: 'No, it's you. No, not me I know it's you...' we insist from time to time. But I'm plagued with glimmers of hope. At first I make myself believe I do like him and might be falling in love with him. This love play or love game is catching. I like his attentions, the way he includes me, but it disturbs me because it seems wrong I should encroach on Paul and Bonnie. I wish I could simply leave them alone, but I'm reluctant to lose Bonnie, and in any case how is anyone to know if the love they feel is real, or an infatuation, a crush? The truth is I've become competitive. I'd like to hurt Bonnie. Part of me wants Paul, not to possess him, or to be loved by him, but to make him prefer me to punish her.

In spite of doubts about whom Paul prefers, we find ourselves in his company most of the summer. He is reluctant to exclude one of us. When Paul doesn't have bikes to mend he joins us on our London excursions. We visit Bishop's Park for the swings and sandpit, Wimbledon Common and Richmond Park for enclaves of green to nestle in out of the wind, and take train journeys to Hampton Court. A few times, without Baby Pickles, we take a train to Brighton and lie in the hot sun starving hungry but happy on the white stones before plunging into the cold sea and drying ourselves off with a single towel. Paul goes off on a few ventures to steal chocolate. It's always the train journeys I remember the most, the windows wide, the warm air rushing into the separate carriage, the seats hot and dusty, the smell of smoke, and Paul leaning out and singing. In his company we live mostly on air. Happy with him, I often forgot to compete for his affection. I didn't mind if he loved Bonnie most.

Then as the summer fades, and the air has that autumnal whiff of decaying leaves, the world darkens, and I grow sad. Our time together is coming to an end. Paul has become the divine intermediary; Bonnie and I are together again in his presence. Soon I'll have to go back to school, and Paul may disappear from my life because my mother doesn't allow me out in the evenings.

I lie in bed and rewind the summer in my head, remembering when Bonnie held his left hand, and I his right hand as we walked along Upper Richmond Road, and a lorry driver at the lights leaned out of his open window, and called to Paul, 'You greedy bugger,' and laughed and tooted. We were happy then, the three of us, or five if we include Baby Pickles and occasionally Davy. I loved them all. I wanted the summer to go on forever. But how long could our little family stay glued and consonant? The world of flux and catastrophe pressed, and we did what we could to survive.

Months later, I'm worried about the stockpiling nuclear weapons and concerned about the publicity of the Adolf Eichmann trial. I don't want to read about the 'banality of evil', and the measly ferret of a bureaucrat, who signed the papers for the slaughter of innocent Jews. It has an effect on my mother. Her nerves are bad so she goes to Dr. Miller for another prescription of sedatives. These calm her; she is serene and distant, but I'm not aware that the pills will lead to addiction. She works hard as a cleaner to the Sterns and comes home with little gifts from Mrs. Stern, things we don't need like thin linen napkins, or better still bed-linen thought to be on the verge of tearing to shreds but never do, and food leftovers from the fridge when the Sterns fly to their second home in New York. My mother is trusted with the house keys and expected to water the plants and attend to the house, together with the retired housekeeper who no longer lives in. Her name is Florence. She often comes to the flat for a cup of tea in the afternoons. She has a large pimple on her tongue, visible when she speaks, giving her a lisp. She has lizard like eyes, the lids half open, and despite her plump, diminutive figure, she is always immaculately dressed in expensive clothes. She scrutinizes me and makes comments about my appearance as if I were absent, which makes me uncomfortable and self-conscious. But I'm happy my mother has a good friend, and they work well serving the Sterns so I don't tell anyone I don't like Florence. What is good about her is that when German war atrocities appear in newspapers and on the news, Florence never changes towards my mother. Her only fault as far as I'm concerned is that she rarely speaks to me directly: 'She's looking tall now. Have you told her about the birds and the bees?'

'O Florence. A long time now!' My mother manages to smile pouting.

'Has she… You know?'

By this time I make my excuses and squirm my way to my room.

Bonnie, my Lady of Shallot has left school and is now working in a shoe shop called *Mansfield*. It's depressing when I remember how we lay planning our future in whispers on cold wintry nights, delighting at first at the prospect of succumbing to domestic servitude and the taste of marital bliss to escape the confines of our dreary home life, and then changing our minds, plotting our escape by vowing never to marry but have serial love affairs. We fantasized about living in our own family with Paul and Davy and Baby Pickles.

At night, instead of pitying Bonnie, I try to redefine her, or reinvent her as someone I love without a guilty conscience for staying on at school to study. What luxury and indulgence, I tell myself, to work among shoes, that pungent smell of new leather and glue, the elegance of heel and pointed toe, bearing little resemblance, if you think about it, to the shape of a human foot. I love the contrasting textures of calf skin, grainy and matt, patina sheens, soft as satin and silks. I try to persuade myself that she loves her job.

But when I visit the shop on a Saturday morning, Bonnie looks doleful, unhappy to see me and I feel guilty for my insistence, my intrusion. She looks tired, her eyes small and lacklustre. My heart misses a beat and aches. More fitting to see her in a pre-Raphaelite woodland setting where *she weaves by night and day/ A magic web with colours gay*, her hair a bright halo of webbed gold. I pretend I want to buy plastic, pearly winklepickers with two-inch heels.

'How's Paul? I hear you're engaged?' I ask, trying not to move my lips under the watchful eye of the diminutive, bald Manager in his glass alcove.

'Oh, he's all right, and we're sort of engaged but he hasn't bought the ring yet.' She shrugs and her face flushes. I know she feels uncomfortable.

'How's your mum and dad and Davy?' It's difficult to make her talk. I haven't seen them in ages and miss them. I'm no longer invited to her house.

'We're all the same. And you, how are things with you?' Her voice is deadened by lack of interest. I know she is lying.

I stand in the shoes and parade in front of the mirror. The shoes make me look deformed. I don't want to tell her I'm miserable. I miss her and Paul, miss my visits to her home, and I can't bring myself to confess I have often called for her at weekends like a love-sick dog, but no one answers the door. I'm desperately lonely. I love her and want to be friends again, as we were. I miss her and Davy and I even miss Carol's dead, expressionless face, her animosity.

I return to my seat. I won't let her take the shoes off my feet as she sits on the stool, brandishing a tortoiseshell shoe horn. I don't want her to touch me.

'They cripple me,' I say pulling off the pearly heels, and

putting on my old shoes. 'I'm thinking of dying my hair red or pink.' I know I'm being ridiculous, but I want some kind of reaction. I want to shake her and ask: what has love done to you—this life? What about our plans to live better lives than our mothers? Why have you collapsed like a rag doll? As she puts the pearly shoes back in the shoebox, covering them with tissue paper, I stare at her familiar small hands and think there's something infantilized about her, sitting there obediently, waiting to serve, unable to admit she wants to be back inside the magic web we wove to protect us from harm. Divided against herself, she raises her head with a contemptuous look.

'You're daft,' she whispers, 'You always were a bit funny. You've got black stockings on. Why are you all in black? Has someone died?'

I stifle a sob and take in a deep breath. 'I'm in protest about nuclear weapons. And yes Baby Pickle's dad is dead, and they have gone away.'

Bonnie looks upset. 'How? Did he have a motor-bike accident? I can't bear it,' she says. 'Why do you come here with that kind of news? The manager's looking over. You better go.' I haven't the heart to tell her Mr. Pickles hanged himself in the garage at the back of the flats, and Mona has taken Baby Pickles and the new baby to live with her mother on the Isle of Wight.

I have a feeling Bonnie wants to say something else. She is smiling softly like her old self, and I'm expectant that she is about to reveal something significant and honest at last; I watch her mouth gape for a moment in hesitation. She takes in a mouthful of air, and changes her mind about a disclosure, and touches my arm.

'There's a customer waiting. Better go. See ya.'

It's a stocky man with a college scarf who looks over expectantly.

I leave the shop, and cry along Werter Road. I'm too upset to even argue myself out of my feelings of self-pity and wretchedness. The pavement is crooked and cracked. Mounds are formed beneath the plane trees as if the roots have come up for air. My lonely steps pound the paving stones and bring on a fresh wave of crying. You can do that in London. You can smile inanely at traffic or bawl your eyes out. Passers-by either don't notice, or pretend they haven't, because naked emotion belongs to the insane and frightens them. Instead of going home, I backtrack and make my way down Disraeli Road to sit in the library seeking the solace of musty books.

Here the silence is soothing and protective: shoes softly pad and make cushioned squeals on the parquet floor; traffic hums outside; there is sibilant hushing at the desk; drawers and tomes open and close like velvet lids to boxes; papers rustle and there is a discreet clicking of the Librarian stamping dates in books. A comforting orchestration, a lullaby, a haven from the troubled world outside as I try to hold myself in one piece in here.

I lean on my hand at the reading table and picture Paul laughing, his white teeth and clean mouth I want to close with a kiss. I miss his warm hand, soft inside like the belly of a small animal. I can see him lifting Baby Pickles from his pram with the sunshade decorated with silky tassels half folded down and pressing the baby close to release a chuckle. I stare into empty space between the bookshelves filled with a green light from the trees, and picture Bonnie, the comforting Madonna on the serving stool, full of humility, attending to the pilgrims' feet, with her tiny lily-white hands and wonder who will take her into theirs. I don't understand why, even though we have taken a different path, and Paul has chosen her, Bonnie finds it necessary to turn against me. Maybe she is frightened he might change his mind. But I wouldn't accept him if he hurt Bonnie. I always knew Paul would choose her; I rebuffed him enough, but if he had chosen me, if he had insisted, I would still love her and give him back to her. Then I remembered the terrible holiday when in retrospect I saw her disengage, turn from me before Paul entered the scene.

My trust in friendship is fragile. It would never be the same between us. Friendship is subject to severe testing and hardship, it seemed to me, which asks too much of any person. I'm glad I didn't know then I would never see her again, otherwise I think my heart would have burst. I grieved for her for a long time. I heard some years later Paul left her for someone else and joined the Navy just as he had always wanted. Although I searched for her on social media, I never found her. I continued to love her, but she disappeared from the face of the earth.

# Lübeck Luftwaffe training camp 1942

## Extracts from Sophie Chmielowiec's Diary

1st December—Arrived last month after a brief time at home. Papa brought me here to the Luftwaffe Women's Auxiliary training camp outside L—deep in the forest. My fingers still raw from farm work at home, harvesting potatoes so forgive this bad handwriting. I have heard nothing from Dr Franenarzt in Gütersloh and nothing about how Otto and little Heine are doing in Vienna with their sick Mama. It is their bedtime now as I write. Luisa the housekeeper promised she would keep in touch, but she has not written either. They all have my home address. Maybe the post is severely disrupted. I am worried something may have happened to them all. I wonder if Dr Franenarzt closed the house and moved to be with his family in Vienna. Maybe Luisa went with him. It was very difficult for the housekeeper and a spinster too. I know Dr. Franenarzt will help her. I miss them all more than I thought. They have taken pieces of my heart away! I wish I could be with Klaus. I keep picturing him in the rain waiting for me under the lilac tree in Bismackrstrasse, his collar turned up, opening up his coat to enclose me inside. I put my arms around myself to try and get the feeling of his loving touch. I hide this diary under my mattress which is too obvious. I must find a better hiding place.

4th December—The camp culture is shocking for me. The other recruits, who shrieked with laughter at dirty jokes when they got here, and seemed happy to escape misery at home, and personal problems such as unhappy love affairs, now look pretty crushed and miserable. But we have to make the best of it. We're woken by music blasted through loudspeakers. We just about have time for a quick wash and inspection of the billet by the NCO, who has a voice like a she-wolf. Her abuse is utterly demoralizing. She calls us sluts brought up in the gutter. She has no right to say these things. No makeup is allowed, and some are marched off to have their hair cut. Luckily mine only just touches my collar if I keep my head slightly down, so I haven't been shorn. Afterwards there is marching practice in the freezing cold. We have to keep shoulders back, upper bodies stiff and hips still. Chest raised, chins high. But our legs must scissor the ground. March. March. March. Right foot! Right foot! Right foot! Right! I can't see the point of marching. What is it meant to achieve? We are not going anywhere but kept as prisoners.

9th December—This morning, I went into the latrine to silently cry. Everybody does from time to time. Inspections make us feel like tins in a factory. We are footsore. I think they want to keep us exhausted so we don't rebel or run! My calves kill me. Later we had long lectures on ranks in the armed services. Then all about Rules & Regulations. I hate this communal living. Wanted to be on my own. Today we had, what I call, a forced letter-home writing session as if we're ignorant children. It is difficult to know what will get past the censor. And hard to be sincere knowing everything we write will be read by someone else first. My letters are flat and dull because of it. The food is getting worse—cabbage soup and potatoes. NCO She-Wolf reminds us to forget men. This only makes us yearn more for someone human and loving in a pair of trousers. Not allowed to write to brother Erich or Klaus. No news filters in from the war. Or from anywhere, so we are so hungry to know what is going on.

14th December—I made friends with a girl called Liska from Hanover who whispers bad comments to me under her breath. She keeps me from breaking down. I ask her why we have to do all these marching drills. They don't serve any purpose. If they run out of men, said Liska, we'll end up fighting this bloody war. We have to be careful. Some recruits believe the training is part of a patriotic greater good. We, the Apostates, must keep our mouths shut. We had tests all morning on how to recognize ranks in uniform. I couldn't keep my mind on the task. I think only of Klaus in his Luftwaffe uniform. This afternoon, we had lectures on the history of Germania, full of invasions and battles, killing and looting. I nearly fell asleep. Another NCO says we have a responsibility to assist men—fathers, brothers and husbands—in their struggles. I daydream about my Mum's apple-cake with cream and strong coffee. I wish I could go home and would happily let her nag me for hours about how useless I am, which would be kindness and affection to my ears compared to the verbal abuse from She-Wolf.

December 24th—No one is allowed leave. We all shared our food parcels from home for Christmas. Delicious stollen, and almond biscuits. In the morning we cleaned out the billet with mops and brooms. After inspection, there was marching drill, then we decorated the concert hall with holly and ivy from a wheelbarrow outside the main hall door. A letter from Klaus got through. How I don't know. It was given to me by a man who sees to the plumbing and everything else if things go wrong. He is thought to be a bit 'simple' because he doesn't have speech and grins at us all the time. Klaus is not allowed to write any details—just how much he misses me, and he wants to get married as soon as my training is complete. I panic a little. Everything is happening too fast—it makes my head spin. I'm frightened. I'm not sure I want to get married while this war goes on and on and on. It changes the way you see things. It distorts everything, disguises mistakes. I'm not sure the news is real. I'm anxious and unsure. But it was lovely to get Klaus's letter. I kept reading it as if by magic it would reveal more to me, that somehow words between the lines would magically appear. Yesterday a recruit ran away. The NCO said she has been caught and sent to work camp for rehabilitation. Liska and I were too afraid to exchange looks.

Beer flowed in the evening. We watched films about how brutal the Soviet men are, how cold the English are, and the Americans cruel, despite the fact we knew Tarzan was a gentle giant. If ever we have to face the enemy down a dark alley, we all agreed, Oh God let it be an Englishman. There was a lot of singing and dancing after the film. But no real joy without men. We made the best of things. I tried not to think of Christmas as it once was in the past, with Mutti and Papa, and Erich singing round the tree. My mother decorated the tree in secret, and then locked the living room door so we couldn't see the tree until Christmas Eve. I remember I looked through the keyhole and saw it. Denied to us I thought it looked as if sent from heaven by the angels. A card Klaus made for me in red crepe paper with a little gingerbread house made me cry. I've kept it since my time in Gütersloh. We all dropped to our beds drunk and disorderly, without undressing and we didn't care.

Jan 22nd, 1943—We all thought the war would be over by now. I haven't written much, too exhausted and demoralized. We all have to study for exams, punch drunk. Our mental reserves are low. Lectures on moral hygiene and singing from the Soldier's Song Book: 'Oh we'll go marching onwards, till nothing's left but shards. Today, we're lords of Germany, Tomorrow, all the world.'

I have such a bad ear for music, so I just open and shut my mouth. I'm sick of marching and uniforms. Liska and I, and some of the other recruits, don't want to shatter the world—ridiculous words. There are others who lap it all up and can't wait to help the war effort.

Soon we shall hear where we will be sent to serve. We are allowed post now. My dear brother Erich writes. He is marrying a girl from Belgium, Helga, but will be sent to fight again soon. I write to Klaus every week. He would like me to join him in the town where he is billeted. That would probably mean working for the Gestapo in some way or another. Don't relish policing. Snow falls.

March 8th—The exams over. Now we're to be assigned to specialized training courses. A few girls who have not made the grade, left for another camp to take up menial duties. They cried their eyes out all night and the more successful girls told them to shut up, so a miserable, disturbing night. I feel sorry for those who have failed. Who wants to clean the latrines in some training camp?

I was sent with Liska to Hut 16 with a small group of women. We are to be trained as telephone and wireless operators. Liska said thank God. She is relieved we don't have to do dangerous work. Klaus is the only sane voice: I think of you constantly, he writes, and wherever you are in the world, I will find you and take you in my arms.

No news from my dear friend Lotte. I don't know if she and Wolfgang are still together. I wonder if she has been called up. There is no news from her. At the end of training, our group will be sent to F-----. Others are being trained as typists and an elite group with members who can speak foreign languages will do intelligence work.

March 22nd—My Mum is ill with flu. 23rd March is her birthday. I sent her a letter and drew a sunflower for her. Papa writes to say Frau Kurtis is helping in the fields. Two Polish workers have absconded. I worry that Mum and Papa aren't coping. Papa said not to wear black at all costs because it doesn't suit me. I know what he means. He has warned me before and it just makes me nervous all the time that I have to keep up family standards.

We have no outside news. But there are rumours the city is getting heavily bombed and there are terrible firestorms lasting days. Klaus writes nothing about this. In all this madness his single voice saves me from distress: I think of you my darling. I think of you to distraction, he writes. He is such a romantic.

April 14th—Lectures on how we are to behave when we graduate. We have to salute officers and must appear smart at all times. We must do nothing *anywhere* to cause the German nation to fall into disrepute. We must never associate with the local population, and in public should not be seen with German servicemen. We girls must not hold arms in public. A shy girl called Siggie sobbed all night. Her finance got killed in Stalingrad. We are all feeling wretched for her.

April 28th—Papa came to the camp to bring clothes from home and say goodbye. It embarrassed me. No one else had family visitors. It was surprising he was even allowed to see me. I thought something had happened to Erich or my mother. It was such a shock. He had driven all the way from Lüneburg with a parcel containing my best summer dress, some white socks and a cardigan, which smelled of my wardrobe at home. He looked thinner and tired with dark rings under his eyes. But he brought good news. Erich is married to Helga, a girl he met in Belgium, and she is expecting a baby soon. I listened to all his advice about my duties, and he made me promise again never to wear black.*

The girls all thought he was my good-looking boyfriend and pretended to be suspicious when I said he was my Papa. They did nothing but constantly tease me. I have not told anyone about my family circumstances. In these difficult times, it's best to trust no one. I trust Liska with all my heart, but I keep my secrets. I expect we all do. We are meant to report anything suspicious immediately. Poor Papa. He looked nervous and edgy. He told me there are no more Jews in Lüneburg and no news from Maria. I cried when Papa left. His concern touches me deeply. I told him not to worry. I told him I am in the best and safest place, serving in the Luftwaffe. I sent my love to Mum, and Erich and Erich's Belgian wife, Helga. We embraced. It was sad to see Papa leave. Then the women crowded round wanting to know what news he had from outside, and I had to show them my best summer dress. Then they all wanted to try it on. I thought the buttons would split the button holes when some of the bigger girls wanted to try it on too. Tomorrow off to the big city!

* See Endnote

# Putney, 1961

Troubles, they say, come in battalions, often crushing love in their wake. It's my sixteenth year to heaven and I feel like a fish floating belly upward, slowly turning, brushing against the skin of stone. I want to be mothered, comforted while my blood burns. But my mother is occupied, always in the process of patching and plastering the defects in her marriage. I want her to confide in me. I want to befriend her. To be in a state of constant renewal. But she sees me as a child and guards my innocence as if I have no idea what is going on. The hostility between my mother and Leonard creates another forbidding presence in the house. It makes Leonard surly, cantankerous; he sometimes gives off a stale odour. Their strange wedlock, their brief alliances full of endearments fondling and canoodling, is no less disturbing. During their arguments, Leonard's voice is always like someone walking backwards. In retreat, he stumbles and mumbles. I can't make out the words through the wall dividing them from me. My mother is loud in her various protestations, but about what I can never fathom. I can hear her tears gathering in her throat. It breaks my heart to hear her pain.

It disturbs me so I can't settle to sleep. I want to rescue her, but I don't know how. They live in their own special white noise relegating me to the other side, the *out*-side where I like to escape and sit under the mossy wood-wormed beams of the lean-to conservatory and daydream of escape and read my books. But the escape is temporary. Even though I manage to read, their unhappiness is always present and occupies my mind.

I let myself be seduced by the writing of D. H. Lawrence, the poetry of John Betjeman, Dylan Thomas and Emily Brontë and find solace in existentialism as far as I can understand it. It advocates we have the freedom to become whatever we want to become.

I don't see this. Leonard and my mother are trapped in their painful relationship. I don't have the ability to become whatever I like. I don't even know what to become. But the writers give me hope that I might English myself further, and hope a comfortable English identity is still possible. The will to power is the secret; was that Nietzsche? I remember Simone De Beauvoir's *The Second Sex* about how women are defined by men and other women become dangerous competitors. I wonder if I would ever find the courage to express myself through actions and take responsibility for them. My identity is in abeyance as if I'm substance-less, between worlds, in a no-man's-land, crossing the line, and then retreating. I look to my mother. Her identity is defined by what she does. She works in houses, her pleasures are meeting with her friend Florence, writing home, going to the pictures and for walks, and serving Leonard. That is not all. Known as Ingrid in England, but Sophie in Germany, I know she hides Sophie in a dark place inside herself. It is Sophie that haunts me, it is she I want to know. I want to be close to Sophie. But I don't know how to find her. Questions are forbidden, particularly questions about her past. I listen and watch for clues. And so, we are like contrary twins, one made of fire, the other water, each hiding another person inside.

But despite all this doubleness, and the fire in me, I am

lonely. Sometimes, I miss Baby Pickles so much, I allow myself to recall how I once had him to myself. He was a sweet, attentive listener: 'Who cares if Bonnie and Paul go off together? We have each other, don't we?' I remember how he kicked his legs against his cotton blanket in glee. He was my little Buddha, my *confidant*, fat and assured under the sunshade in his sprung pram smiling like a sage, or more enigmatically like the Mona Lisa, yet sometimes flashing his two, lower pearly teeth. I needed two hearts to love him. When it rained we took shelter under the horse-chestnut tree at the bottom of the garden where he would lean back onto his pillow and let his eyes open and close like a puppy dog. His eyes held no malice or mistrust. He filled them with everything he saw. He relished the beauty of every moment. The olive-greens and dewy emeralds of the world deepened in the gentle rain dripping down from the leaves of the horse-chestnut.

'Baby Pickles,' I would say as he lay smiling in his dream, *'O more than moon*, I will always love you. Forever and forever, and I wish you were mine.' Then I would reach for a poetry book and read to him: *How bountiful the Dream-What Plenty—it would be. Had all my life but been Mistake—Just rectified—in Thee.*

Most days, since I lost my adopted family comprising Bonnie, Paul and Davy, I skate on the surface of things, but I feel an underlying pull towards a darker place. I'm exhausted and just want to lie down and close my eyes, and rest in eternal night, not by way of violence: not by knives, or pills or drowning, but gently, imperceptibly; inviting nothingness as easily as pulling the sheet over my head. People die of a broken heart, or give up on the world when they are tired of living. This destructive mood is powerful. I'm supposed to be happy, because I am young, and full of energy, and everyone says I have my life in front of me. I go to my room and lie still on the floor and stare at the ceiling. I close my eyes and listen to London cranking up its machinery in preparation for the rush hour: thousands of clanking wheels turning and turning, the mechanical motion of traffic and trains and footfalls—the monotony. My mother is in the bedroom lying down with nervous exhaustion. Leonard is working overtime so he will be late home. There's no point going to her. She will just turn her back to me. I take Willian Blake's words and mull them over: *Without contraries there can be no progression.* I try to understand what he means. What I begin to sense is that I'm never going to be English, however much I try. I'm tired of trying to fit in. God is laughing. I struggle to find another meaning. I'm not an existentialist, any more than I am a tree. I would like to be a tree in a safe place away from the saw threatening to cut me down. It is time to let events wash over me. To accept I'm not going to add up to much. To let go.

All the same, I continue with my ballet classes. I have taken a number of exams, which I manage to pass but not to the standards of some of the other dancers, many of whom have left. Now, a girl called Marion and I are the only pupils in Alexander's advanced class on Saturday morning. Marion and I warm up on the bar, while Miss Koval comes in her grey suit to sit and play the upright. 'I'm just warming up girls,' she always says, but never engages in conversation. When Alexander comes in we set to work. After an hour of practice without a break I am sweaty and sticky, but there's nowhere to shower so I catch the bus home feeling unclean and irritable. Marion normally gets a lift from her sister.

Then it all comes to an end. Several Saturday mornings just before the summer term, Marion fails to turn up. I hate this because it means Alexander focuses on me, and I become nervous, make mistakes. He's good-looking but unforgiving, and begins to shout, venting his frustration. On the second solitary lesson, he decided to lift me. He teaches me to leap into his arms and carries me half across the room. I have to let myself down gently, guided by his hands and strong arms. He tells me, the audience believes it is the male dancer who does the lifting, but much of it is the work of the principal female dancer so I need to lift without wings. We practise several times while Miss Koval daydreams, staring out of the window into the orchard. We don't need any music to practise these moves. It's while he is positioning himself to lift me, I feel his hand glide down from my waist to thighs and he strokes my private place. The shock of it, the sheer audacity sends blood rushing to my face, and my leap collapses. He breaks away and curses; then insists we do it again. I look over to Miss Koval. She is staring down at the piano keys. I become almost paralysed, my limbs refusing to work. After one or two clumsy leaps, Alexander ends the lesson. Afterwards I wondered if his touch was a mistake. I once had a little crush on him, but now I'm older, I see he's too much of a bully and I am losing respect. I have a sense I am no one in particular, just as Marion is no one in particular to him. We're marionettes to be made to dance to his tune and style. On my way home on the bus, I decide it was a mistake. Alexander had meant nothing by it beyond his insistence I learn to lift.

The following week, I decide to give him one more chance. I want his touch to have been a mistake so that he can reform in my mind as a teacher of integrity devoted to dance. Marion doesn't turn up again, and Miss Koval sets the rhythm on the piano playing a short piece and then once more she falls into reverie and leaves me in the hands of Alexander. This time his hands take full advantage again between my legs, and I squirm, my heart pounding. I wince as if in pain and ask to be excused. Alexander presumes I have to go to the toilet. He saunters to the piano presumably to talk to Miss Koval. In the changing room, I don't have time to take off my leotard. I dress over it, change my shoes and leave. I run across the road, not to the bus stop in case he decides to come outside and look for me. I take the road to the Heath, and run most of the way home, tearful and angry.

When I get to my room, Leonard wants to know why I was home so early. I tell him the lesson finished early as it was the end of term. My mother is out with Florence. I sob quietly. I sob because Alexander spoiled dancing for me. I wasn't asking much; I didn't ask him to make me into a famous ballerina. All I wanted was to be valued, however little, for being who I am, and someone who valued his talent and enjoyed dancing. He made everything ugly. He made me feel dirty, a low creature. The chance to enjoy dancing in the room of mirrors where I could forget everything was now denied me. Some might think I was silly and shouldn't let him dictate what I should do, and what I shouldn't do, that I ought to have told Miss Koval

302

at the piano, or told him not to do that, but he scared me. I didn't understand why a man should do such a thing. I no longer trusted him. I ran away.

Two weeks later Alexander had the temerity to write to my mother to ask why Susanna was no longer attending ballet classes. He wrote how promising I was (a lie), and how much I seemed to enjoy his tuition (another lie). He wrote that he was looking forward to my return and hoped I was well. I told my mother ballet is just for little girls and I was too grown up and too tall to be a ballerina. My mother looked genuinely sad. 'Oh dear, Susie, what a shame.'

The following month of June, something else happens to startle me out of my gloomy mood. When I get home from school, my satchel laden with homework, I pull the string through the letter-box and let myself in. I call out to my mother, but there is no answer.

On the kitchen table is a large, battered cardboard box. Lifting back the flaps, I find pungently scented, rosy apples saved from bruising as they lay among scrunched up newspaper. I can't imagine who might have sent this strange parcel. I take up a ball of newspaper and slowly open it. The print is in German. I put my face in the box, close to the layers of apples, close my eyes and breathe in the smell of a long-forgotten place and my heart contracts. Some of the apples have worm holes, and some have black indentations on their undersides as if bees have stung their flesh. I rummage further for a letter or card. There is nothing but old newspaper and apples, and the corpses of two wasps.

I'm so hungry I eat four apples in one go, consuming everything, the spicy flesh, the worm holes, grubs, and core and bitter pips. I can't stop eating the apples. I hear my mother returning from the shops. She is smiling and her face is radiant and alive.

'Susie, I see you have found the apples! Ach! You will make yourself sick.' My mother laughs. She puts down her shopping bag and sits beside me still wearing her best coat.

'Susie, listen.' I look into her face animated and glowing. Her eyes are full of light, and her voice holds an unusual rapture. 'These apples are a sign. They come from your grandfather Opa in Lüneburg, from our orchard. The apples are a sign we can go home.'

'Home?' I echo in a half stupor. A heavy lump lodges in my throat at the memory of a time when we wanted nothing more, but now after years of denial and separation, the word is painful. I'm too disturbed to ask why the apples are a sign that we were allowed home, and why it has never been explained to me that home has been denied.

'Oh, not for good. We have a home here now, but home Susie, *home*! My letters and parcels sent to my mother and father all these years have paid off. They want to see us. I know it. Oh, how I've waited and waited. I've been to the post office to take out all my savings. We have to get you a German passport, and I will write to Opa and tell him we can come as soon as you are sorted out. Oh, and we must take presents and buy new clothes for ourselves. We must look smart. It's so important in Germany…'

'A *German* passport?' This is stunning and frightening. A setback to my secret ambition to be more English than anyone I know. I have almost forgotten I am officially a

German. But my mother is intoxicated by the apples and can't afford to be concerned that I might have reservations. I hide my uncomfortable feelings behind a weak smile.

'And Len can write a letter to your school to tell them you will be away for the rest of September. I've told the Sterns. She said of course I must go, and they are both delighted for us.'

Her face opens into a ripple of generous smiles. I bite into another pungent apple, its flesh yellow and creamy. This time I taste a woody fragrance like the inside of my old pencil box. We carry the cardboard carton of apples into the hallway, and then I lay the table for dinner and help my mother prepare the food.

'But Susie,' she says. 'You must not tell anyone in Germany what I do.'

'What d'you mean, Mum?'

'Don't tell them I am a char woman.'

'No. Of course not. Don't worry, Mum.'

'I don't want them to know. They think I am a housewife and that I don't work. Did I tell you Frau Stern wants me to become housekeeper now Florence has retired? She will have to get another cleaner in to take my place.'

'That's good. But you should find something else. But don't worry, I won't say anything in Germany.'

'And best not to mention the Sterns. They are Jews you see.'

'Well, I won't, but the war is over now.'

'Ja but some people might still be a bit funny about the Jews.'

My heart beats irregularly. I know all about the

concentration camps now thanks to Alan Bullock and Theresa. 'Why? Were Oma and Opa against Jews?' My voice wavers, afraid of her answer. I notice her ebullience has faded. Her eyes lose their lustre.

'No. No! They were never against the Jews. Your grandfather smuggled a family across the border into Holland. They were good friends of ours. Maria was a good friend. The family planned to escape to England and then America. Many Germans helped Jews and hid them. But after the war with ex-Nazis still in power we kept our mouths shut.' We are standing opposite each other across the table. 'No, I don't remember anyone we knew who were against the Jews. Jews were good customers of ours, and good friends. Maria was at school with me. Her parents had a shoe shop in Bakerstrasse. Once when times were bad before the war, Opa exchanged a sack of potatoes for a pair of shoes for me.' Her voice drops. 'Later, people disappeared in the night. You learned not to have a loose tongue. Fear is still there, you know.'

'Don't worry, Mum. Honest. I won't say anything. Promise. Did your friend Maria and her family make it to America?'

'I don't know. Maria promised to send me a picture postcard of the Statue of Liberty. It never came.' Her voice drops. I look away. Given what I have read about Germany, I'm not sure I want to go, but I know I will have to go to Germany for my mother's sake.

When Leonard comes home, even before he has time to take his coat off, dismissing her most recent vendetta against him, my mother shows him the battered parcel of apples, and the German stamps on the front of the box, and her father's handwriting on the wrapping paper.

'Look, Len,' she says, 'A parcel from Germany. I can go home. I am forgiven.'

My heart pounds. I want to find out what bad thing my mother has done to find herself forgiven. But I daren't ask. I will try to find out when we go to Germany.

Leonard puts his arm around her waist and draws her to him. 'Forgiven? So you are, girl. So you are, I can see.' He kisses her lightly on her proffered cheek.

# Paris, April 1944

My dear Lotte,

I was so happy to hear from you at last. My mother sent your letter on, but it got waylaid somehow and was sent to Marseilles. I miss you so much. We mustn't let time and distance come between old friends. I hope you and baby Fabian are both well, and pray you will be reunited with Wolfgang, and have news of him soon from his base.

There are endless parties in the safe zones here (some areas we are forbidden to enter) but Liska, a friend I made in the training camp, likes to escape to the countryside when we have time off. We dress like local French girls in skimpy dresses and striped socks pulled to our knees and cycle into the peace of the fields, where we lie in the sun and eat our sandwiches and pretend there is no war. I get tired of all the singing and dancing in the bars. It's all so false. The Germans on the whole are well behaved but get too rowdy and in any case we are not supposed to fraternize with German service men. But it's all wrong that we are here. Paris is for the French. The Germans just don't fit in however much they try. (Not sure if this letter will be censored. Rumour has it there is slack censorship now.)

O dearest Lotte, I'm so troubled and unhappy. It is impossible to settle in here under the circumstances. Liska and I work at the M--- D--- situated close to the Rue S----- and we can sometimes make private calls. Erich's leave has been cancelled, which will upset my mother. I often call him where he is fighting and we have long chats, all for free. I can't say too much of course.

You ask how we are all finding this city. It is beautiful this time of year with crocuses in the parks and chestnut blossom dust falling over the boulevards. The cafés are bustling with Germans and French alike, and if it wasn't for the daily parades and trumpets down the Champ-Élysées and swastika flags everywhere, you would hardly know we are still at war. But it seems every serving man wants to enjoy leave here at least once, so the city is swarming with soldiers and airmen all through the seasons.

Klaus came for a few days to see me and wanted us to get married here, but I told him I prefer to get married in Lüneburg. The truth is, this was an excuse. I'm in an emotional mess. I have fallen in love with someone else called Hans, an officer serving here. Hans, like me, is engaged. He promised to marry his schoolgirl sweetheart waiting for him at home in Augsburg, so we are both promised to other people, and yet we are so much in love. I met him at work, and we instantly knew we were for each other. He takes my breath away. He is so quiet, thoughtful and considerate. I feel so safe in his arms. He is ten years older than I am. I think I still love Klaus, which seems to me impossible, but it is true. We're not supposed to love two men at the same time. But believe me Lotte, it is possible. If I had the courage, I would ask Hans, whom I love passionately, to break off his engagement with his sweetheart. He has left the decision to me, which upsets me as it looks like an act of cowardice on his part. If Hans really wants me, why ask *me* to make this choice for him? Poor Hans, like me he is torn. He is also very troubled the way things are going. He keeps talking about the end, and sometimes his mood is so dark I fear for him. We are not supposed to mix with other personnel, but really few can avoid it and I'm sick of all this skulduggery and hiding and waiting for the dark so that Hans and I can be together.

My life is further complicated. I can't break off my engagement to Klaus in any case because I think I am pregnant. Dr S--- at the M---- D---- refuses to help me. I begged him but he said I must leave here as soon as he gets all my papers sorted out with the authorities. We are not blind. Things are being run down here: personnel are packing up. Hans will be leaving next week. He wants me home too. I can just see us at the station saying goodbye. I can't bear the thought. But I know I want him, and I know I can't have him. He has to remain true to his childhood sweetheart. I would think less of him if not. I can't even confide in Liska, a very devout Catholic. Can you imagine what my mother will say and all the gossips? I had such hopes for my future, especially to get away from the work on the farm; you can see what it has done to my mother. I have always longed for city life. But now look at me? I've made a mess of everything. I'm not sure who the father of my baby is either, although I suspect it is Klaus. Still, it is nothing compared to the suffering some have to endure. Forgive me, dear Lotte, for all this sadness.

My best regards to your family. Soon we can meet again, and I can hold little Fabian in my arms. I hope you are both well and that you will hear from Wolfgang soon. If there is anything I can get you in Paris please write as soon as you can, and I will do my best.

My love to you all,
Sophie xxxx

# Lüneburg, Germany 1961

It has taken us almost fourteen difficult years to return home and I'm not myself. There's so much going on in my heart and head, I'm dumbstruck. My eyes fix on a teenage boy standing with hands behind his back, totally at ease, while his mother, Lotte, runs across the grass towards my mother with open arms, and embraces her long lost friend. They make a little bee dance on the spot joined together as they bob with joy, and everyone laughs to share their pleasure.

I allow myself to study the beautiful boy, my heart racing. He wears loose trousers and a denim shirt open at the neck. His dark blond hair is short at the sides, but longer on the top and his eyes are screwed up against the sunlight. On his lips a bemused smile lingers. His skin is tanned and unblemished. His eyes shielded by his raised hand shift from the noisy reunion and slide across to look at me. Painfully self-conscious, I want to look away, but his eyes inform me of a recognition, and it is so intensely powerful, I can't avert my eyes. My heart gallops so fast just beneath my blouse I'm afraid everyone will notice its palpitations. I lift my hand to my face, breathless and faint.

'Come Fabian,' says Opa, my grandpa, gesturing to the boy, 'and you, too, Heike, come and sit at the table with us.'

Here in Germany, I am Heike, the long-lost granddaughter, the daughter of Sophie, who was once sister to Erich who never came home from the war, leaving a widow Helga and a baby son. I am Heike who as a small child played and slept with Fabian, the son of my mother's best friend Lotte, who waited for her husband Wolfgang to come home from the Eastern Front but who remains a widow ever since.

A gentle southerly wind wafts over the two tables placed end to end in my grandparents' cottage garden. The table is laden with apple-cake, chocolate tart, salad, cold meats and freshly baked rye bread. The late summer air mixes the smell of apple and pear windfalls, and the loamy aroma of earth and pine needles mingle with wood smoke from the aga chimney blowing in short gusts just over our heads.

Fabian sits further down the table, next to Oma wearing her blue serge apron over her shift dress, her head nodding in assent to snippets of conversations caught from guests close to her at the table. Fabian is engaged in conversation with Frau Kurtis's granddaughter, Ilse, who cradles a baby in one arm, and uses a fork in another. Frau Kurtis is a widow with skin like crepe and sits next to me in her wide-brimmed, straw hat with plastic cherries, holding a kitten she places into a picnic basket under the table from time to time when it is tired of petting and tries to jump from her lap. Its frequent mewling persuades her to lift the lid and let it out again for more fondling. She lives in a ramshackle cottage down the lane. When she was younger she worked the fields for Opa and Oma with other workers. She knew my mother when she was a small child and remembers me as a baby. She keeps chickens and supplies locals with eggs. She is warm and familiar with me, touching and nudging. But she is a stranger after all this time.

A band of young children play chase close to the flower fields. These are the children of women from neighbouring farms who make up the workforce, sitting at the tables all talking at once, and helping themselves to the food. My eyes roam from person to person absorbed either in eating or talking, bathed in the mellow light of an Indian summer. Behind them, the seared leaves of the lilac trees, the stretch of white grass and grandpa Opa's flower fields, but I am uneasy, uncertain.

I am happy, I think. How best to describe it? A mass of contraries: joy mingled with sadness; a peacefulness disturbed by waves of agitation. It's a guilty secret: I am happy in Germany, the land of the enemy. How can this be? I'm mesmerized by the mouths of those around the table, the sounds of their speech, their warm eyes and smiles, which lift my heart, but I feel it's wrong to enjoy and indulge in their welcome as I have given nothing. I can barely confess all this to myself. There is a niggling resentment. How dare everyone sit at the table enjoying themselves. It seems wrong. I think back to when we said goodbye to Leonard, the prospect of visiting Germany, that strange, remote homeland was not promising. Clutching my German passport and having it stamped at the border in Dover, I felt as if I was made to wear my coat inside out.

I was British but considered German by officials. Once we reached the northern stretches of Germany by train, I felt even more alienated. The landscape was dreary and disappointing. Fallow, dun fields spun off into the distance, flat and featureless, with only telephone poles and electricity pylons like the skeletons of gigantic birds to relieve the uniformity.

I was on the lookout for the bull-necked enemy, but it was difficult to scrutinize them as they slipped silently in and out of the carriage at night like shadows, and in the morning the train creaked under the weight of hundreds of American GIs, some of whom crowded on the train, falling asleep as soon as their heads rested against the wooden frame.

In Hamburg, we changed trains, and took the little chuff-chuffing train, rocking its way to Lüneburg, the window framing little country gardens with honeysuckle running wild over sheds, and potted red geraniums on the windowsills. When the train chugged slowly round a sharp bend, I looked across at my mother in her best grey suit, her face composed but strangely expressionless, and then Lüneburg came into view. I was enchanted. Waves of red higgledy-piggledy roofs supporting tall steeples and onion domes made of pea-green shingles like scaly dragon skin glowed in the sunlight. I was amazed I couldn't remember this fairy-tale place; it was difficult to believe my early roots were nurtured here and spread all the way to The Horseshoe and Ida's house and Mrs. Bailey's hallway sucking up the liquid ordure of the Thames nourishing my green-stick bones.

Opa, my German grandpa, is a huge, formidable man. He wears thick cotton shirts and his trousers are tucked into his long boots, which he leaves outside the back door under a bench before entering the house. He has blue eyes, closely cropped, slate-grey hair, and an open broad face. He is gap-toothed, which gives him a clownish look when he smiles. He seems sanguine and untroubled. But when brooding over his account books, which he consults every evening at the end of the long kitchen table, I detect concern in his concentration.

'My real passion is still flowers,' he told my mother in the truck from the station, 'but there's not enough money in it. So I stick to the fruit and vegetable business. I still have a market stall. Remember how you used to help me? I always knew you gave your friends a cut price!'

My mother laughed and pretended to be mortified he knew her little game all along. We passed the town square, broad and flanked by trees, presided over by the Town Hall looking in need of paint, but in the forecourt is the Luna fountain bearing the goddess of hunting crowned by a half moon. I later learn this is the goddess Diana.

They continued their conversation through the cobbled streets of town, and Grandpa has to slow over a little bridge taking the road south towards Lüneburg Heath.

'How I cycled through these streets at top speed!' my mother exclaimed to herself.

Opa said, 'You made the deliveries of flowers.'

'I know but I didn't want the boys I liked to see me and sometimes I would hide down a side street!'

Then I lost the thread of their conversation, taken in by the tall houses that looked like steps and as if they might topple. I listened again and heard snippets about Uncle Erich's death.

'I remember that sad time,' said my mother, leaning into her father as the car turns down a stony track.

'We had a visit from a witness, a Sergeant Frey. He told us Erich was shot by a sniper in the back leading his men out of the Balkans in retreat. Could have been a Partisan or a Chetnik. The horse bolted. We don't know where he is buried. What made it worse was that the war was over, but not to the Yugoslavs. We feel his absence every day. It was good of the man to find us and tell us about Erich.'

They spoke in German, and I could only understand snippets, but my mother told me all this later when we are alone in her bedroom.

On our arrival, Grandma Oma waited at the back door. The small house, with its tiny windows, low eaves and green front door, has no fence or obvious boundaries. There is a modest attempt at a front garden full of sunflowers with heavy down-turned heads. A path at the side of the house, creating an intersection between the house and flower fields, leads to a cottage garden of tussock grass and lilac trees that grows wilder further from the house, and merges into potato and other vegetable fields shielded by tall elms and poplars. Close to the house in the adjacent fields, Opa has planted row upon row of flowers, long regimental and parallel lines stretching into the distance of gladioli, blue daisies, white daisies, and sunflowers. Adjacent to the house on the eastern side are extensive outhouses for storage, and a wide path leading to apple and pear orchards sloping downhill, their tops uncrowned, shaped by the winds.

Oma, a diminutive figure, remained very still in the frame of the doorway, her head tilted back a little as we walk towards her. She wore a blue linen dress that looks too big for her, and her grey hair is drawn up into an untidy bun. She embraced my mother loosely.

Neither spoke but then my mother turned to Oma and told her she had brought Heike to Germany. My mother took my arm and guided me towards Oma, who briefly embraced me. She felt fragile, bony and I was glad to be released.

It didn't take long for me to understand Oma is blind. No one had told me this and I'm hurt to learn it now. It spoils the evening for me that my mother didn't think of telling me. Later, when we were alone walking down to the orchards, my mother told me Oma's story. Blindness struck when Oma received the news of her son's death in May 1945, when war was officially over. It was such a shock and ironic that, Uncle Erich, my mother's brother, had survived the war, only to be shot dead in peace time. That day in 1945, Oma made her way to the fields and screamed his name to the setting sun; she has never regained her sight.

Later Oma explained to us that she is not in total darkness as people imagine. 'I can see different shades of grey and black and sometimes these are moving like the river flowing at night when it's black and has some surface light, you know? But it doesn't stay like that. I can make out the outline of things, especially outside. So I can still work and cook and clean. But at night it is all black and then my dreams come to me in vivid colour.' Oma paused for a while and stroked the tablecloth with her hand.

'I never dream in colour,' said my mother regretfully.

'Mostly I see a grainy grey, like coarse cloth, but when someone I love comes close to me, I can see the lovely whiteness, shining you know, like silk and I remember what the sunlight is like.'

'That is beautiful,' said my mother. She smiled and rested her hand on the tablecloth close to her mother's hand, but I noticed they did not touch.

'And you *Heikelein*,' said Oma, maybe looking wistfully

at a picture in her mind of the little child locked in her memory, sitting on her mother's knee, with her long boots and pigtails. 'What are your dreams?'

'Oh, she dreams of books. At least her head is always in one.' My mother laughs, answering for me in German. I understand more German than I allow myself to speak. I know at home it is forbidden and much of my ability to speak German is lost. It is strange and liberating to hear it spoken as natural. It is lyrical and soft. It doesn't sound as bad as I have seen in films when the brutal Nazis are always screaming and shouting and spitting.

Despite this initial intimacy, Oma remains a silent, shadowy figure during our visit. I try to keep out of her way, to allow her the space I imagine she needs in her shadowy home. She frightens me a little and makes me shiver. I don't know why. Oma is so unlike the bold and forthright Grandmother at The Horseshoe. Oma is gentle and unassuming and yet I'm afraid of her. She knows bad things she will never tell. The kitchen, her domain, remains as it was in 1945 so that she knows exactly where everything is, the black fire range fed by kindle, the old-fashioned blue enamel coffee pot brewing on the warm top plate, the dresser with plates, opposite the sink. The kitchen is dominated by a large, long table with a cloth and four chairs each side and Opa's chair at the end near a bench and high shelf with a radio. A door leads straight through to a tiny hall, the front door hidden behind a curtain. To the right are two bedrooms, the one my mother occupies, and another Oma and Opa occupy, both looking out beyond the side path over to flower fields. To the left a staircase leads to the attic room, where I sleep, and I imagine my mother's brother slept. Further along the hall is the sitting room, always shut away. I ventured inside once. It has a curious, half-glass door with a net curtain. Inside there is a strong smell of damp, overturned earth as if a moles and earthworms live there. Heavy baroque furniture, a sofa, side tables, a piano, and a large clock on the mantelpiece. The little light coming from the low window makes it a grim, unwelcoming room. I wonder if this is how Oma sees the world, remembering how her world was full of shadows, rather than total darkness. I don't know if her impaired sight is a barrier between us. If I find her in the kitchen or along the garden path alone, I don't know what to say or do so I hide by standing still or tiptoe a retreat.

It's as if we can't find each other, that any thread or link that bound us was broken and lost. Although she appears frail, there is something about her I later sense is indomitable, steely. I feel she doesn't like me. That she knows my subterfuge, my cowardice in avoiding her. The last time Oma saw her *Heikelein* was in the late summer of 1945 just before darkness fell across her eyes, when I settled happily on her lap and she plaited my hair. Now, she is no more my grandmother than the clouds and seems to have no interest in addressing or touching me, in resuming our easy intimacy. She is in her world. I can't help being sad that once, this house was a home where I learned to walk from chair to chair, and that the inanimate world of her kitchen recognized and protected me. But now for a reason I can't fathom, the house refuses its occupants and visitors comfort or love. It eschews the present and light. It is as if the house is Oma herself, her stone carapace, the extension of her pain.

But on this particular afternoon, I'm like a girl suffering amnesia, thrust among strangers who know and probably feel some affection for us. It is lonely. Yet now, one look from a boy and I feel a pleasurable lightness, my brain full of feathers, my eyes failing to focus. I have to listen and watch for clues to link them to me, but the more I'm kept in the dark of irretrievable memories, the more distanced this newly discovered family becomes.

It's difficult to hang on to the distorted voices around the table. Lotte and my mother's friend Tia want to practise speaking English with my mother. '*Also Sophie*, tell me vat are the English ladies like?' Tia insists.

'Oh, the women! Well, they're not chic like the French,' says my mother, 'they often don't care what they look like.'

'*Wirklich*… really? How interested.' Lotte looks pleased with her first English utterance.

'But not caring how you look is *the look*. There's quite an art to it. You mix up colours and styles. It is hard. Everything is so expensive. Some women really don't care much. They go shopping in hair-curlers and slippers. Nobody minds,' says my mother with authority.

'*Ach*… tut… tut… Not like here. You must look smart from the house otherwise everyone says you are bad.'

'It's good in England because you can look how you like, so it's much cheaper. You can wear the same season's clothes every year. No one buys a new coat every winter! They make do with the old one till it is threadbare,' explains my mother.

'Ach! That is very good,' says Lotte, wrinkling her nose. 'But how do you say, but *langweilig*?'

'Yes, very boring. The English women want to be free from the house. They don't like housework much. They want the same as men. They want to go to work and not be slaves in their own home. I admire them. They are strong women and joke. They make fun of men and laugh even when they are miserable.'

I'm impressed by my mother's observations, which she has never shared with me.

'Mmm, ja so tells us about the men!'

'In England,' says my mother with a wry smile, 'the men like sport and pubs and dogs. They are not very romantic, but *praktisch*.' Everyone laughs. My mother is not being entirely truthful and speaks for effect to impress her friends. Maybe in private the conversation takes on a different tone between the women. Lotte is plump and homely, with short brown hair, a widow and her son Fabian is without a father; he was killed in the war, like my father. Tia is extraordinarily beautiful. She is tall, blonde, expensively dressed and also a widow. She wears a white silk blouse, a pencil skirt, and crosses her long, beautiful legs. She sits back with an ironic smile.

Opa wants to know what the ladies are talking about in English. When Tia offers a summary, Opa makes critical remarks about the Germans, how they focus too much on perfection and take themselves too seriously.

'Robert. Robert. Not now. The ladies don't want to listen to your old-fashioned opinions.' Oma raps the table with a spoon. But he ignores her.

'The Germans do nothing but work,' says Opa. 'We

should look to the Americans who know how to do things. They have a good mix of culture, films, and music. They embrace the new. They know how to live, the Americans. We only know how to exist. The Germans should all be more like the Americans, then we'd make real progress in the world.'

'Oh Robert, please, no more,' begs Oma.

Ilse begins singing *Che Sera Sera, whatever will be will be…* The children join. Oma looks up. Her eyes a milky blue, paler than the evening sky.

'Yes, you can sing!' mocks Opa. 'But listen to me, the Germans are finished. The Germans in America are the new Germans who will become proud people again by intermarriage with others.'

'*Ja, Ja*, everything American is good,' rejoins Frau Kurtis, shifting her hat back on her head. 'Do you think integration will dilute us?' Everyone ignores her comment. It is a serious breach in the social event that must be smoothed over. A distraction is called for.

'Susie, go to the kitchen and fetch Oma's cake. Bring out the strawberry one,' says my mother in English, clearing the table of dirty plates. I notice she doesn't call me Heike.

Adjusting to the darkness of the kitchen, I lean for a moment against the table and I have a sad thought about Leonard making his own dinner, and putting on a 78 on the radiogram full blast, his blue cigarette smoke curling from the ashtray as Caruso sings from *Pagliacci*, 'Recitar! Vestila giubba…' I don't want to think about him, or imagine him, but I can't help my thoughts turning to him alone in the house without us. It makes me guilty we are having a good time. Suddenly, I am homesick for London, and I don't like Leonard being alone. I find all this upsetting and confusing. For years I have kept Leonard at arms-length, managed to live with him as if he were not present, as he has managed to live with me in the same way. I feel ashamed for blocking him out, and find I have feelings for him surfacing. I stifle a sob. I'm confused. I am angry and miserable.

'Susie! What are you doing? We are waiting and waiting for the cake!'

My mother roughly shoulders me out of the way as she takes up the plate with the magnificent lemon cake. 'Bring the cream. What is the matter with you!'

My mother's second cousin, Irena, is the last guest to arrive, lingering by the kitchen door with Otto, a boy of ten with a mental age of four, who according to Oma took too long to come into this world, and left part of himself behind. My mother, cake in hand, greets them both and introduces me.

'Ach, the baby Heike,' Irena says, taking my face into both hands and kissing me on the forehead. 'Otto, look. Here is your cousin, Heike from London. So grown up and pretty!' I blush crimson. No one has called me pretty before. I know it is a mistake.

Otto hides behind his mother's skirt, his white mass of hair making his head look too big for his shoulders. I follow them both with the jug of cream. Everyone has to shift up at the table to make room for Cousin Irena and Otto who wants to sit on her lap.

'Ah Frau Beck! The cake is divine!' compliments Frau Kurtis with her mouth full.

'Mmm, one of your best, Gustchen,' exclaims Grandpa with cream on his upper lip.

'Your mother is still famous for her cakes!' says Lotte, satisfied and pleased.

Fabian sucks on strawberries, his eyes wide.

'Eat up,' says Tia, nodding towards my plate. Otto begins to cry.

I leave the table and lead Otto to the basket under Frau Kurtis's chair to show him the kitten. He lets out a deep hollow sound as if he has been thrown into a well. Fabian asks to leave the table and takes Otto's hand.

Soon all the children ask to leave the table, and we gather down the lane with Fabian walking alongside an old bicycle he found leaning against one of the outhouses. He hitches Otto up onto the crossbar and moves off slowly over the gravel path with a grinding noise, pierced by Otto's shrill, unearthly song of glee echoing through the pines. We all run after them calling and laughing as Fabian wobbles down the path.

# Lüneburg, 1945

13th February fell on a Tuesday. The RAF together with the US 8th Air Force wiped out the city of Dresden. There were fire storms and gas explosions and the smell of burning flesh hung over the city for days. The Germans resigned themselves to these acts of retribution. No one expected mercy. Hamburg and Berlin were repeatedly bombed. At night, the sky was permanently red, and the moon caught fire through the pine trees.

On this day, Sophie walked down Feldstrasse in the fur coat she had bought in Paris looking a little less glossy and worse for wear. She held her baby close swaddled in a shawl, which she'd pulled over her face to protect her from the cold wind coming off the icy waters of the river Ilmenau. Sophie was on her way to the clinic to have the baby's weight and health checked.

The clinic was held in an annex of the small hospital. The side door led immediately into a hallway with wooden seats along one side, and at the far end a series of several screens end to end, behind which the nurse or doctor attended to the infants. The room was cold; the whiteness of the old, tiled walls, the single harsh ceiling light, and draughty windows accentuated the general atmosphere of severity and impoverishment. Sophie sat among coughing mothers and squalling babies. Country girls from the surrounding hamlets rocked their unsettled infants. Sophie did not want to engage in conversation with other mothers. She was depressed and didn't feel like engaging in mother-talk, or war-talk, or missing lovers, fathers, brothers-talk and hunger talk. In any case her hands hurt raw from scrubbing soiled nappies in cold water without soap, and the cuts and bruises stinging from topping swedes and gathering potatoes. The other mothers averted their eyes when Sophie sat with her baby; some threw her hostile looks. They were suspicious and saw her as an outsider who may have once worked on the land like them, but was now a stuck up city girl fallen on bad times. They could almost smell her misfortune brought upon herself as result of moral dissolution. They defined her in a way she couldn't defend except by remaining silent, and distantly dignified. But the women were suffering from bad faith. They were all in the same boat. The constant terror at the back of their minds could only be alleviated by assurances the Russians would never get so far, and the Allies were surely closer, so they prayed the English and Americans would arrive first. Even so they had plenty of imagination to know what they might be in for. Older mothers advised young women and girls to make themselves look as ugly as possible to save themselves from being raped. But Sophie wasn't thinking about these things. She felt superior to these peasant girls known to be crude, lacking in social finesse. The truth is they didn't really concern her. The state of the nation was no longer a priority. When the world is shattered, the mind saves itself from madness and narrows to focus on the basics of survival. Sophie was worried about the baby. She had nothing to give her. Her milk had dried up and cows' milk was hard to come by. Shadows seemed thick with substances denied her. My poor fatherless little baby, she thought, what is to become of us? Suddenly from behind the screen, an old nurse appeared, 'Fräulein Chmieloviec?'

Sophie rose and carried her baby behind the screens to a small space with table and scales, hot with embarrassment for being publicly announced as an unmarried mother with a distinctly foreign name. First, there was a form to fill in giving personal details. Everything could be heard from behind the screen. Then the baby began to fret. The nurse told Sophie to undress the baby, but underclothes had to remain. 'There's no heating and I have no assistant,' complained the nurse. Sophie unwrapped the baby from the shawl. She was nervous, all sore fingers and thumbs. The nurse looked down at the baby's wasted limbs and pot belly. The sight of undernourished babies, some worse than others, was becoming familiar. As the nurse lifted a woollen vest, she cast her eyes over the dehydrated folds of skin around the baby's thighs. The nurse lifted the baby onto the scales and made a note of the weight. 'This is serious,' said the nurse. 'Your baby is underweight and in terrible condition. She is badly dehydrated.'

Sophie frowned at her baby, defeated.

The nurse continued, 'Give her plenty of sugar water. Are you still breastfeeding?'

'Yes,' said Sophie, 'but my milk supply is not very good.'

'I understand. Give her supplementary cow's milk if you can. Carry on breastfeeding as that is best for baby. But most important is your own health. I know it's hard. It's the same for us all.' She threw the young mother a habitual smile of dismissal, before turning her back and washing her hands.

Sophie managed to dress the baby; the baby whimpered

listlessly and fell asleep again.

'Give your baby daily baths to soften all the dry skin and then bring her back in a month. I hope to see some improvement. I don't want to have to report you to the authorities.'

Sophie dressed her baby, put on her gloves, and braced herself to walk from behind the screens knowing the other mothers were witness to every moment of her humiliation and shame. She could imagine their whisperings: Look at her all dolled up in a fur coat. The war is no excuse. What kind of mother is she? She thinks of nothing but herself.

The following day, Sophie put the baby wrapped in a shawl in the wicker basket at the back of the bicycle and cycled to Heim Farm for milk. Her mother and father were in the fields harvesting potatoes. The frost was thick on the hedgerows and the fields glistening with mud-rutted grooves encased in blue ice. The February sky was sharply blue and cloudless. In the pine forest nothing stirred. Sophie heard only the whoosh of cold air rush past her face and began to hum.

She became aware of the darkness falling across a yellow shaft and a distant, familiar drone as the shadow took the shape of an aircraft losing height. She recognized the Allied plane and leapt off the bicycle, dragging it to the side and throwing herself over the baby in the basket. In an instant her back would be pelted with bullets as the guns rattled. Then she heard the plane rise, circle and swoop again. She repeated: Please God. Please God, not the baby, hundreds of times. In a split second, she arched her body over the baby basket, aware that when she was shot she would slump and her body suffocate the baby. She knew

328

that when her back was riddled with bullets, she must fall away to the side, face up.

Looking up she could see the face of the pilot smiling. Then the roar of the plane became distant as it climbed into a sky grown pale, almost white. Shaking, she remained arched over the baby for some time, until daring to look. She watched the plane disappearing far into the distance like a migrant bird and began to violently tremble.

This experience did not stop Sophie's regular visits to the Heim farm. The large house nuzzled into the low hillside just before the heathland proper covered in springtime purple and pink heather spread south. Milk wasn't always available for the whole Beck family, but Frau Heim would save some for the baby Heike.

'Welcome. I have only a small canister today, Sophie. The cows are not producing much again. Hamburg is getting it bad.' Frau Heim tucked stray hair under her cap. She had four sons away, fighting for the Fatherland. 'Did you see the raid yesterday evening? I thought it was thunder. They came in their thousands. We ran into the woods. There were so many planes the sky went black.'

'Where is everyone?' Sophie asked holding baby Heike in her arms and looking round the farmyard kitchen and then beyond into the fields through the tall window.

'Johan and his mates are over at the Dosch's place. Their machinery is in a bad state. Johan likes a change of scenery and tinkering with a tractor or two. I told him not to leave me too long. I've heard rumours about bad types, you know like deserters, living in hovels in the woods. Sit down. Have some bread. It should be ready by now.' She bent over the oven and opened the door to have a look.

'Do you mind if I give Heike a little feed before I set off again?' Sophie was reluctant to leave the warm farmhouse kitchen with its enticing smell of baking bread. She opened her blouse and put the baby to her breast.

'Carry on. Ach. Look at that. My loaves have hardly risen.' Frau Heim lifted the baking tray from the oven and put it on the table. 'Still, with a little butter, it should taste good. Better to let it cool or it won't cut evenly.'

At that precise moment, a motorbike engine stuttered down the track at the back and silence fell. Sophie and Frau Heim's eyes locked. They both kept perfectly still as if the air would give them away. 'The side-door is locked,' whispered Frau Heim. She moved over to the window. Two dirty soldiers appeared. Sophie recognized the uniform from her training in Lübeck.

'Russians,' she whispered.

'Quick, take the baby into the back room. Hide the baby behind the sofa. There's a fire on so she won't be cold. You stay there too.'

Frau Heim knew that soldiers in a foul temper could break the door down in seconds so she went to the door to turn the key and let the men in. Sophie left the baby in the corner on the floor behind the sofa, wrapped in a blanket with a cushion under her small head in the small back parlour. She closed the door.

Then she returned to the kitchen. If possible, she would distract the Russians from going into the parlour, and in any case she couldn't leave Frau Heim to fend for herself.

Both women sat at the table as if to begin a meal, waiting for the invaders to enter the kitchen. The two men walked in; they pretended to disregard the two women and helped themselves to the freshly baked loaves, stuffing them in their army coat pockets, tearing at the bread from time to time with their teeth as they rifled through the cupboards and drawers, making a small grocery pile on the kitchen table. They were hefty men, clumsy in layers of clothing that made their bodies bulkier. Unshaven and dirty, they exchanged comments, grinning and grimacing, ignoring the two women who watched them like captured animals. One opened the door to the hall and continued his exploration of the house. They could hear him kicking open doors, drawers being thrown down. In a short while he returned with contraband to steal and sell. Thank God, thought Sophie, he hasn't found the baby. The soldier, by now ruddy and hot in the kitchen warmth, pointed to Frau Heim's watch. Trembling she removed it and dropped it into his hand. He was delighted. Like a child, he held it to his ear, and laughed. Then for no reason, the other soldier lashed out and hit her across the face while the other looked on biting into the bread. Sophie stood up to comfort the poor woman who was sobbing quietly and had fallen to her knees, her hands cradling her face.

Sophie's eyes met the soldier's eyes. He lurched towards her and dragged her by her arm into the small parlour while the other soldier remained in the kitchen for a while to kick the old woman he had thrown to the floor. Then he mimed he wanted a drink. Frau Heim had nothing to offer, apart from water and the baby's small bottle of milk, and for this he kicked her again. She sobbed and filled the silence with prayer. The soldier then spat at her and left the kitchen to join his comrade.

Frau Heim pulled herself up from the floor with her hand on the kitchen sink. She looked out of the window at the desolate road winding down into the woods. She feared what they were doing to Sophie.

The door banged open, and the soldiers entered the kitchen again. They sauntered to the table to fill their capacious pockets, grown lumpy with purloined tins and bread. Only when she watched them mount the bike, and pump the engine, and roar down the road, did she run to the other room calling, 'Sophie! Sophie!'

She found Sophie lifting the baby crying in her arms. 'Oh look Frau Heim, the baby crawled to the fire, and she has burned her leg. A burning stick must have fallen out of the grate and she didn't cry.'

'Ach, no. Look at the blood on your skirt. So much blood.' Frau Heim stood back in horror, her hand to her face.

'Don't worry Frau Heim.'

'Here, lie down Sophie. Keep still. Give me the baby. I'll put some goose fat on her burn. Let me cut up some rags. You can't cycle home in this state. Herr Heim will be back soon and he can take you back in the car. I'll boil water so you can clean yourself. I will find another skirt for you. We can burn this one. *Reinheit macht frei.*'

'Please,' said Sophie weakly, 'I don't want to cause you more trouble. What about you?'

'I'll survive,' she sobbed. To the baby: 'Hush now, there-there. We'll soon have that nasty burn seen to. Hold her for a minute while I put the hot water on.'

'I must go back in the room and wipe the floor. Do you have a mop?' Sophie looked around the kitchen and then went into the outhouse.'

'Come out of there! Now you just go and see to yourself. The water has nearly boiled. I'll get some clean rags and a new towel for you.'

'Burn my skirt please, Frau Heim, I never want to see it again. Do you have one I can borrow?'

'Give me the baby. Look she's smiling. The burn on her little leg will soon fade. I'll see to everything else. Don't worry about me. I'm tough as old boots. *Gott Sei Dank* we're saved. Don't worry, now. I won't tell a soul what happened to you. Let's hope the Americans and the Tommies come to save us from those pigs. But from now on, that bastard husband of mine can leave me his shotgun.'

# Lüneburg 1961

The children run deeper into the shadowy woods, shrieking and whooping. Fabian leans his bicycle against a pine and lifts Otto from the crossbar to chase the others. Fabian and I follow the children, pine needles crunching under foot, emitting their strong scents trapped by the tall spires overlapping above. The light is lemony and green and the air tastes sweet. Fabian catches up with me. We glance at each other and grin as if sharing a private thought. Hysterical laughter bubbles up inside me every time our eyes meet.

Sometimes Fabian pretends to stumble. I laugh. I know it's silly. I'd prefer to appear deep, enigmatic and tragic, but somehow as if he is well aware of my aspirations, he doesn't allow it. His eyes dart over my face. They shine with mischief while I try to think of something to say in German, but the grammar won't conjugate. The rules of my German textbook dance before my eyes. But I can't remember a suitable phrase. My tongue and body burn, while my eyes keep sight of the children frolicking in a sunlit mossy hollow, chattering and tumbling like fox cubs, unaware of a drama unfolding among them.

As we walk side by side, I bask in this boy's heat and imagine that if I touch him, I would catch alight and the whole forest would go up in a blaze. We sit some distance apart and yet we are close, as if we held each other. I love the smell of him; the shape of him. My head empties of feathers. It's so lovely to be like this. It's like a love letter pulsating down from the sun, streaming with words of light and affection. I want to cry. I want to hurt *for* him so he will never suffer. Soon the children find us and come running over, but the magic of him is not destroyed. He wrestles with them in the grass and we all laugh.

Darkness rises up from the earth early in the forest. Then, when we leave it, the track home blazes white and the outside world hurts our eyes. The children chase us back to the cottage-house. Some guests have already left and Oma has gone to her bedroom for a rest. We wave Lotte and Fabian away down the lane. They turn several times, reluctant to lose sight of us. But even when Fabian finally disappears, and the lane is empty of him, his image is fixed on my eyes and wherever I look—on the path, in the dusky windows of the house and in the gathering clouds—his image clearly comes into focus like an afterlife.

The world has changed. It's newly found magic leaves me heavy, aching for the next moment when I will see him again.

The next few weeks of our stay, I'm lucky enough to see Fabian often because my mother and Lotte want to make up for lost time. They drag me and Fabian along, silent and infatuated, snatching moments of touch in the cinema when our knees nudge, or when we climb the hill outside the town to view the town from the ruins of the mediaeval watch tower, allowing our hands to brush as we walk. We are shy and awkward in the presence of our mothers, doing our best to disguise our feelings.

Other days, my mother is duty bound to visit all her close and distant relatives, and friends of my grandparents. It seems everyone wants to have a good look at us and refer to us with a smile as the London Germans, a fortunate and gifted race apart.

Meeting them all entails dressing up so as not to disappoint them, my mother clattering on her high heels on the cobble stones in her best suit, armed with a white cardboard box of delicate cakes or expensive flowers and then finding ourselves sitting upright in the best room with the lace roller blinds half drawn, tall yellow gladioli in cut glass vases on the upright piano like blood-stained spears, and dusty antimacassars draped over faded chairs.

We sit perched forward so as not to dent the cushions, admiring the contents of aunts' wardrobes, and chests and cupboards: the embroidered tablecloths, the napkins in cross-stitch and handkerchiefs, making up the sum of their spinster evening industry or *Halbkünste*. Afterwards we sip coffee and there's chocolate cake glued to my teeth.

During these visits, I have moments of frightening disassociation. Who am I? Surely I don't deserve this lavish affection given unconditionally and so spontaneously? It seems fraudulent to accept it, as if I were stealing love meant for someone else. I'm open to temptations and superficialities, gobbling up love like some wretched turncoat or changeling. How can I find that large tap root of place and self, in this tangle of roots, a dilemma compounded by a new obsession, my love for Fabian?

I see Fabian everywhere: in the narrow streets of the old town with the stepped facades of the tall houses of Am Sande; he's there in the tiny port that presides over the old salt warehouses, and beside the ancient crane poised like a giant heron on the water's edge, and again beneath the glockenspiel of Meissen china set in the sandstone of the

Town Hall with its gracious stone statues painted gold. Like an obsessive thought, he stalks my head. Only when I find myself helping Oma lay the table for supper, and when Opa calls me outside to help him off with his muddy boots, does the image of Fabian fade and I can be separate from him again.

And there's the little brown wireless on the shelf high on the wall, and the thick twisted cable hanging down just as I used to remember it as I lay in the cold bed in The Horseshoe, and now the newsreader's crystal-clear German is like a mountain stream and it is so wonderful to me that the sounds of the language I first heard, is not forbidden here. I manage to understand that in East Berlin Walter Ulbricht has become head of state. Nixon and Kennedy thrash out their differences on US television just when Oma turns the sound down, because she is ready to dish up a stew of vegetables and Bratwurst, but as soon as her back is turned, Opa turns it up again. My mother hands out the full plates and we eat without speaking while the weather forecast plays out at full blast.

Afterwards, I excuse myself from the table explaining I have schoolwork to do in the attic. I lie on the bed and imagine the sounds of London to fill the drumming silence; the hum of traffic up Putney Hill, the distant clickety click of tube trains from Edgware Road to Wimbledon, and the piercing song of a blackbird in the hawthorn outside my bedroom. I think about how it would feel never to return to London. Strange how I have always doubted my mother, for her unpredictability, secretive nature, depression and tears, and yet here I have watched her become someone else I barely recognize. I'm worried for her. When we return home I'm afraid she will become her old self, distracted, and off to the doctor's for antidepressant pills.

I look around the room, stripped of personal photographs, the forlorn chest of drawers rattling its emptiness when you walked across the floor, the narrow bed by the wall under the slope of ceiling, and I imagine with trepidation that this was in all likelihood Uncle Erich's room where he hung up his Hitler Youth shirt and later his Wehrmacht uniform on the back of the door, and opened the window under the eaves to let the honeysuckle scent drift over him before going off to war.

There are raised voices downstairs. My mother and Oma talk animatedly, and I tiptoe and open the bedroom door a crack to listen. Then as they lower their voices, I catch snippets about how Berliners are all the same, and why didn't my mother choose a nice boy from home. My mother replies softly that everyone knows you can't choose the one you love. It was a war romance and a mistake, but it is all finished now. But Oma won't let go. She asks my mother if that selfish swine ever sent money for his daughter Heike, and my mother says no, she never wanted money from him. All Klaus asks that he receives regular news of Heike and photographs. Len is Heike's father now, even though he doesn't fully provide for her, and Klaus should keep out of it. Opa is of the opinion my mother is a fool to take the burden of a child upon herself, but then Oma says maybe it is best this way, for Heike's sake. We have Len, says my mother. Len is good to us.

I close the door slowly, release the doorknob spring carefully, and once it softly clicks into place, I press my whole weight against the back of the door. I can hear my mother's voice as if it comes from an echo chamber, telling me my father was killed in the war. The sword and flag in the black suitcase, which I used to curl beside in an attempt to relieve homesickness and his absence, I believed was proof of his death.

But this very evening, it doesn't take me long to understand that my father is alive. Instantly, the weight of his death in life takes on a different meaning. He did not die for the Fatherland. He slunk away from Mister Death like a criminal, or a monster, and set himself up in Berlin. Now that he is resurrected, I am in shock. I sit on the narrow bed and look at my feet. My father lives. He wants to hear news about me, wants my mother to send photographs of me. Joy is infused with fear and horror. Push. Pull. Without contraries there is no progression. If my mother secretly sends word what does he think of our news? Where is he? Does he have another family? Does he love me? I want to meet him. No. Oma called him a swine. First, there's Leonard's secret daughter, Chrissie. Now this. All these lies. Lies at the core of silence, feeding on the silence. I remember the sands on holiday with Bonnie and Davy, when we stood on the shore and the sand from our feet got sucked back by the waves and we almost toppled. I am toppling now. I sit on the bed opposite the small attic window. The blue sky is oppressive, and you can just make out the tips of trees, still on an airless evening just before sunset.

Irrationally, I want Grandmother: her presence, firm,

and resolute. I want her to button up my coat and pull it down sharply so it hangs right without a wrinkle. I want her to wind the scratchy plaid scarf around my chest tightly to keep me whole and tie a knot at my back, and slip my pixie hat on, as I stand beside the grandfather clock with its swinging pendulum and powerful, intimidating tick-tock. I want her to take my hand, and briskly walk through the open front door into the cold, clean air and down to the High Street.

# Lüneburg November 1946

There was a gentle tap on the door. Sophie stood straight from the table to listen. She kept perfectly still, afraid to move. There it was again. Tiptoeing to the door, she listened attentively. Captain Saunders always knocked firmly, three times and then gave a little embarrassed cough. This was more of a tentative tap-tap, so it probably wasn't the English captain. The small children, Heike and Fabian, were asleep in the next room, and she didn't want to disturb them; they had taken time to settle, and she was tired. But it was as if the door were transparent, and the person could see her.

'Who is it?' She spoke quietly but impatient, memories of the Gestapo night raids quickening her heart. It was then she recognized the voice of her husband Klaus and with trepidation her most recent past came flooding into her head, a past she tried not to think about any more. The future is all that mattered, and the everyday minutiae of survival.

She and Klaus had married in March 1945. The baby was born in the previous year, December 1944. Klaus, presuming he was the father—although there was little doubt in his mind—did the honest thing. Now, he didn't know how he felt about Sophie. He had no feelings anymore. His emotions were spent. All that remained were the memories of the love he had for her, and for members of his family, his parents and brother, who for all he knew were dead in the heavily bombed Charlottenburg district of Berlin. But Sophie had no certain idea who was the father of her baby: it was most likely Klaus's child, but baby Heike could be her lover's child with whom she had an affair in Paris while engaged to Klaus. However, Hans after a brief affair with Sophie while serving in Paris, returned to his hometown to marry his childhood sweetheart, and Sophie returned to Lüneburg. Heartbroken about Hans, Sophie wasn't sure about Klaus any more, but still felt affectionate towards him. He married her as soon as he could get leave. Life would have been so much simpler if she hadn't got pregnant, and if Hans had abandoned his fiancée waiting for him at home, she would be married to him now. It was difficult to be with Klaus and hide her broken heart. Once home again in Lüneburg, dismissed from her duties in Paris, Sophie swam in the freezing cold river, hoping maybe she was mistaken about being pregnant. She tried gin and a hot bath. Her mother seemed to have a look of *I told you so* fixed on her face. But what did having an illegitimate baby matter anymore? The war changed everything. The Führer himself forgave unmarried mothers. It was announced in the press. Germany's losses in war meant more babies must be brought into the world to replenish the depleting Fatherland. Yet still the prewar mores survived, making it hard to keep one's head high knowing that behind net curtains tongues wagged.

Once it became obvious she was pregnant, Klaus did the right thing, secured a few days' leave by the time Heike was a year old and married her. He insisted the baby should have an addition to her name Heike, and gave her his mother's name Hedwig who was Dutch by birth. Sophie chose Maria too after her best friend who escaped from the Nazis and hoped to flee to England, and then America.

After the wedding, Klaus had to return to duties in Berlin; he was still serving in the Luftwaffe but grounded. Then after the German defeat, she lost contact with him. He did not telephone the post office. There were no letters. Europe was full of refugees, and the captured Germans were likely to be shot or beaten, starved and flung into camps. Neither she nor Lotte, with whom she shared a flat, knew where their husbands Klaus or Wolfgang were, whether they were dead or alive, whether they would ever return. It seemed unlikely the men would ever be seen again. And now, the knock at the door.

Sophie unbolted it, her hands shaking. She saw a man older than his years. The handsome man she had met in Gütersloh had disappeared, but she still recognized him. His once glossy hair was cut close to his head, but he hadn't shaved for weeks. His upright stature was gone, he stood with his shoulders bent. And yet his eyes shone with affection and didn't betray what he thought when he saw before him a thin, tired woman with her hair in disarray, wearing a shabby apron. Her face wore a mournful look, pitiful, her mouth turned down, and her eyes without light.

'Ah, Klaus,' was all she could manage, stepping aside to let him into the room. Her eyes filled with tears. They moved closer hesitantly and embraced a little against their inclinations; they didn't want to hurt each other. Each looked fragile and unsure.

'Ach, look at you,' she spoke as if to a child. 'I will boil up some water so you can wash. I have no soap or razors.' She opened her hands in despair. He looked around him in the cramped room at the two single beds against the wall, the table and chairs beside the sink, and the cupboard under the window.

'Let me take your jacket.'

He took off his threadbare jacket. It felt grimy and damp. His eyes searched the room again. Before he made any judgement, she found herself explaining her new situation.

'We're living with Lotte. I look after the children while she works in the Naafi in the evenings. During the day, I go home to help my parents and Lotte looks after Heike.' She was aware she sounded apologetic as if her new life without him was shameful. It felt shameful. They were poor and hungry. Everyone was in the same boat.

'I went to find you at home. Your mother gave me this address.'

Klaus looked across at the Naafi coffee, sugar and tins of processed meat lined on the top of the cupboard. He understood what was going on before he realised, or admitted it to himself. Then he lifted his head towards the door to the room where Heike lay asleep near Lotte's young son Fabian. She put her finger to her lips. He walked to the room and quietly opened the door. Sophie left him looking down at his sleeping daughter and boiled a large saucepan of water on the electric ring waiting for him to return.

His face softened. 'She sucks her thumb. Her hair is almost white. Is she good?'

'Yes, she is very good,' said Sophie, remembering the time at Frau Heim's how she hadn't cried out when the fire burned her leg as if she knew it was dangerous with

Russians in the farmhouse. 'She's a quiet child.'

Klaus smiled, satisfied. 'Is there something to eat?'

Sophie poached him an egg in boiling water and served it on dry rye bread. She watched him eat and sat with him because she knew it wasn't polite to allow him to eat alone.

'I have no change of clothes for you,' she said, 'but maybe Lotte's husband wouldn't mind if I looked in the wardrobe.' She daren't tell Klaus she had sold his clothes months ago for cigarettes. He didn't question the fact his civilian clothes were missing. It hardly mattered. There was too much or rather too little on his mind.

'Have you heard from Wolfgang? Is he coming home?' Klaus asked, watching her carefully as if he had almost forgotten all about her.

'There's no news. We think he's being held by the Soviets.' Sophie rummaged in the wardrobe and found him a clean shirt, trousers and a coat.

'I hope these will fit. I'll boil up more water if you want to wash.'

'Thank you,' he said taking the clothes. 'I will return them.'

'What about your family, your mother and father and brother in Berlin?' she asked.

'I haven't heard. Where are all the letters we sent to each other? There's no post. When there is news, we will be old.' He stood and watched her uneasily.

'Everyone is missing,' she said as he undressed. She turned, embarrassed as he discarded his dirty clothes and left them on the floor. She thought it was bad mannered.

'Everyone is missing or dead,' he said. 'I was held by the British in a camp. My job was collecting dead bodies in the camp huts.' She listened without a word. 'They were the bodies of Jews, women, children and enemies who perished. Starved in the camp. Some were very sick. The camp commanders are all sentenced to hang. The British let many of us go last month when they ran out of food and the job of mass burials was finished.'

'The Law Courts have been busy here too,' she added. She didn't want him to think she was brainless or insensitive. She could feel his shame; there was her own shame to deal with too. It was meant to be. It was impossible to go to the cinema without the newsreels of Nazi atrocities. At first everyone thought it was Allied propaganda to excuse the harsh treatment of the Germans, but it had to be accepted as truth. A truth so awful it was difficult to believe, to comprehend what monsters the Nazis were. Soldiers would never be heroes in this land.

Klaus sat on the bed with Wolfgang's shirt unbuttoned. He had to tell her about cleaning up the camp. But he felt he defiled her by doing so. He too was defiled. He was not fully dressed and stared at his wife. He wanted her to make him feel clean again; in contrast to his own self-disgust, she appeared pure, innocent. He wanted to be redeemed by his love for her and his daughter. She was standing with her back against the sink, watching him now, her hand on the table where his plate had grown cold, and spots of egg yolk had congealed. He patted the space beside him and held out his hand. His imploring eyes were so pitiful, it was horrible. She knew what he wanted. Her legs would not take her to him. She let out a small protest that didn't sound like a word. Then she covered her mouth with her hand and began to cry without a sound.

Klaus stared across at her. Of course, he should have known. He had heard about what was happening to German women by the Russians and Americans. How insensitive he was to her life, her suffering. The women were all left unprotected. She was frightened so he had his suspicions. He didn't know this woman. She was the mother of his child, but he no longer recognized the young girl he fell in love with at Gütersloh, and again the lovely girl he made love to on leave in Paris. He put his head in his hands and then with resolution he looked up without looking at her and said, 'I'm going back to Berlin. It's for the best.'

'Maybe my parents could put you up for a while.' She panicked a little. His return was a shock, but for him to suddenly leave seemed a failure. Yet in her relief she wanted to make it up to him somehow now that he was going. She felt a pang of guilt. Klaus deserved more from her. She had loved him once.

'Has it been bad?' he asked. 'You know… I don't mean without me…'

She knew what he meant. She wanted him to leave. Klaus looked grey and drawn. He stared at her and wanted to hold out his hand for her to take so he could draw her to him to comfort her. His body froze knowing she would recoil if he touched her again. It wasn't blame, or anger or even pity in their hearts; it was simply a strong awareness of their defeat and more: an acceptance of defeat. He was impotent. The burning desire deep inside to avenge her suffering was a small flame starved of oxygen, of will. Maybe he was grateful she kept her distance. He understood in his infinite sadness this was the end. There was truly little more to be said. Taking another man's trousers, a man who had not yet returned from the Eastern front, Klaus got dressed. The clothes were too big for him. It made him look like a vagabond, a refugee. He had to face the facts. He was nothing else but a vagabond, and a refugee who had nothing to offer his wife whose suffering he couldn't bear. There was no life for him here. There was nothing he could do for her. He had upset her arrangement with Lotte who was saving them, and his child from starvation. It was not his business how Lotte earned the food. He didn't want to know about betrayals. They were necessary and he was not lily white himself. But he had nothing to give Sophie, or little Heike, to keep them alive, other than love. And love is not enough. He was no fool. He stood for a moment under the light. His hair, once so abundant with auburn tints, was now thinner and coarse.

'I don't suppose, you've got a spare cigarette?' he heard himself ask.

She took an English packet of twenty *Players Navy Cut* from her apron pocket and gave it to him. He looked at the packet for a moment in his hand, took a couple of cigarettes and put them in his pocket. He looked up and caught her eyes. Sophie looked away. He threw the packet of *Players* on the table and drew up his shoulders with a deep intake of breath. She wanted to say keep the packet, but that would have seemed cheap.

He walked across to the room where Heike and the boy lay asleep. After a while, he reappeared from the room, his face stony.

'Write to me. I'll send you my address in Berlin if it's changed. Write to me with news of Heike. Don't forget. I will do what I can.'

She nodded but couldn't look at him, couldn't ask him to stay. It was understandable. How could he find her attractive after what had happened to her? They had both been honest. It was for the best. They were not the same people who fell in love when they were attractive young things on the brink of a young adult life; their circumstances made reconciliation impossible. He turned and left, closing the door gently so the children wouldn't wake up.

Sophie went to the window. She remembered how she used to watch Hans stride across the courtyard below in Paris. They were deeply in love, but both engaged to others. Waiting for him in his hometown was Hans's childhood sweetheart. Both knew they had to come to a mutual decision either to continue in their present relationship with their respective fiancées or abandon them and run away together. But the sense of Nazi victory in Paris was tainted by the threat of the Allied invasion that was becoming more and more a certainty. The Nazis were disbanding, slowly and discreetly. Sophie was being sent home, and Hans was closing down the communications network he had been responsible for some years earlier. He had met Sophie at her work on the telephone exchange and was struck by her. She was impossible to resist, and he asked her out even though she was ten years younger, and engaged to someone else, plain, less exciting but homely. He never felt at home in Paris. The occupation was wrong. He felt it strongly. Although the Germans enjoyed the high life, the free-love, Avant-garde atmosphere, they behaved like immature lads on holiday: brash, loud, and embarrassing. Despite her striking good looks, she was reserved, quiet, and shy. At the same time, she was often sophisticated in her manner, the way she sat, crossed her legs, walked, and spoke. She was undoubtedly well brought up and from a good family. He didn't know what to do. He didn't know if this romance was a mere war-time fling in Paris, a city that lent itself to love, or the affair of a lifetime, one he might regret not acting. As her departure neared, he still couldn't decide.

For her part Sophie wanted him. But she was careful to make sure he knew whom he wanted. She felt for his childhood sweetheart. He would find it difficult to return home having jilted her. And should Sophie have her way, she would never be accepted by his family and friends as his legitimate wife, but the one who caused Hans's girl terrible pain and misfortune. Sophie was prepared to risk it, but only if Hans was brave enough to take the first step. She still had feelings for Klaus, but he was often showy and boisterous despite always being so kind and considerate to her. To complicate matters, she discovered she was pregnant but kept this from Hans as it might prejudice his judgement.

Nothing was decided in May 1944 when Sophie was at the railway station ready to return home from Paris with a number of her colleagues. Finally, Hans arrived and found her at the train window, wide open as she leaned out looking for him. Immediately, he begged her to decide. He promised whatever she decided, he would go by it. Sophie had the wisdom to understand that this was not good news. He had cowardly put her into a position that would be forever untenable. She knew the decision could not be hers alone and in suggesting this she saw him as weak and uncommitted. She remembers the sounds of the station fading, her heart breaking. She couldn't even leave him a smile, or a gesture of comfort. The train began its movement, and she stepped from the window afraid she might faint.

This time she moved to the window. She remembered how often she would watch Hans leave the Paris flat from the balcony window. Her husband's slow, defeated walk along the street now would stay in her memory. She would remain connected to them, the men she loved; the men she allowed to walk away.

# Lüneburg 1961

There are only a few days left of our visit. My mother has taken the liberty of going on secret assignations. At least that's what I think. She doesn't tell me where she is going or whom she is about to meet. Instead, she seems to be enjoying her new life, or is it her old life? After a morning with me and her parents at home, or meeting up with Lotte and Fabian, she returns here to change into her best clothes and then calls goodbye and disappears during late afternoon and evenings. I help Oma shell peas, spoon out cake mixture into tins, and peel potatoes in between going for walks and talking to myself. I still feel uncomfortable with Oma, but I do what I can to help. My mother's absence makes Oma and Opa sad. I hate to see them downhearted. We listen to the evening news during supper, and afterwards Oma sits at the table with her eyes closed, while Opa pours over his accounts book; you can hear flies buzzing around the lampshade. The atmosphere reminds me of The Horseshoe, that oppressive censorious taste of disapproval with every breath, and Grandmother's stubborn insistence not to open the windows in mid-summer in case the flies shot in.

Here the flies were *in* all right, feeding from crumbs and scraps on the dresser, thumping the windowpane and rubbing together their little hairy legs on warm newspaper. But they know their place. I watch them. Not one lands on our skin or the food on our dinner plates. I want to put my arms around Oma and Opa or compensate somehow for my mother's absence. But their sadness creates a forbidden, familiar aura, so like the flies, I keep to my allotted place too.

Despite the disappointment and embarrassment about my mother's lack of manners, I nurture a hope she might be meeting Klaus the Berliner, my father, and excitement surfaces as I entertain the possibility they could be arranging a surprise visit when I will have the opportunity to meet him. I daydream my Berliner is taking me in his arms in the morning mist over the heathland, or maybe in the dying rays of the sun, his handsome face glowing with love and atonement. But these are only fleeting images taken from schmaltzy old Hollywood films, so I dismiss them, having wrung out as much pleasure and comfort from them as I can.

But as the day of our departure to London grows closer, the intense sadness of separation can't find expression and the dream of seeing my father who *lives*, melts into nothingness. I don't know any longer what would satisfy me, except I'm guiltily excited about going back home to London. The morning air already grows cold and crisp and the forest from my little attic window grows darker and ragged in the wind. Then something horrible and wonderful happens all on the same day.

Just before the workforce arrives, Oma and Opa rise at five-thirty as usual. It's the time of the onion harvest. You can hear the boots of the women shuffling over the dirt track and finally their chatter as they gather round the table in the kitchen for coffee and breakfast cake. When the troupe departs, and it is quiet again, I hear my mother rise and the pipes crank and bang inside the walls as she uses the bathroom. I indulge in a little reading of *Hamlet* for my

English studies, appalled to learn that Ophelia drowned. I let the text fall from my hand to take it all in, and then my mother taps on the door.

'Susie, we must pack today. Come and help me wash my hair. I want it nice for London. Let me see yours.' She rubs my scalp. 'Yours is all right. It doesn't need a wash.'

'I'll get dressed. I'll be down in a minute, Mum. Are you going out again today?'

'This afternoon Lotte and I are going to meet up with Tia and some other friends.'

I look glum. I haven't seen Fabian for three days.

'Ah hah,' said my mother smiling. 'You are missing him, nah? You like Fabian?'

Furious with myself for being so transparent, I frown and my face flares up. 'No,' was all I could muster to try and protect my precious secret; clearly no longer a secret.

Downstairs my mother stands grimly in her bra and petticoat; her mood instantly changes. 'Come with me a minute,' she says, leading me by the hand into Oma and Opa's bedroom. Facing north it has little sunlight, only a grey, shadowy tone as the rays attempt to penetrate the thick lace curtains. Beside the iron bedstead are the open drawers of a tall-boy and the smell of camphor floods the crowded room filled with furniture belonging to a larger, grander abode.

'Look. Just look at this!'

I stare down into the drawers. Piles of new clothes in tissue paper are neatly arranged. I don't understand what I should be looking at.

'Look, all the presents I sent Oma and Opa. Untouched. Look, still in the wrapping paper. I saved and saved but look. Just look, Susie! Good clothes wasted while we went without.' She flings up her arms and then falls down on the bed and begins to sob.

'Oh Mum. Don't. Please. I expect Oma wanted to save them for a special time or something...' my voice trails. I want happiness for Mum and not a visit disturbed by mortification and pain.

'It's silly. I shouldn't have snooped.' She sniffs. 'I was looking for photographs to take back to England. But I can't find any Oma might have hidden away. But anyway, after the war we had to burn all the photos of men in uniforms. Close the drawers. I'll just smooth the bed over and I'll get a handkerchief to blow my nose. Come, help me wash my hair.'

Because hot water from the wood range is always immediately available, my mother washes her hair in the sink. While I'm massaging my mother's scalp, watching the lather froth between my fingers, I feel something stir in me. Empowered, not by a show of hurt on my mother's part, but by something else I sense about her, something I cannot identify. My mother is bent over the sink, so I take my chance because I reason she can't control or silence me with one of her admonishing looks. My mouth feels a kind of paralysis creeping from its corners.

'Mum?' I could feel her double crown like my own under my working fingertips.

'Mmm. What?' comes her muffled reply.

'I was thinking last night,' I say, lifting the jug of water to rinse her hair from the draining board, 'I was wondering about everyone. Were you all Nazis?'

A flicker of silence first, the way the world can go

deathly quiet before a natural catastrophe, and then my mother's scream. She raises her head bedraggled and dripping above the sink. The chaos in her whole body drains the blood from her face. She moves forward, bent like an old woman with her dripping hair hanging down in thick strands falling over her glistening face. Burning with guilt, I stand back, the empty tin jug in my hand, certain she is about to strike me.

'Stupid. Stupid!' she cries, moving after me and snatching the jug, which she throws down on the table. 'The water is boiling. You burnt my neck and head!' She lunges forward, turns on the tap and immerses her scalded scalp in the jet of cold water for a long time. I stand beside her, outside myself, witnessing my own remorse. I never in the world would want to hurt her. There's an explosion going off at the base of my skull. My mother finally raises her head and wraps her wet hair in a towel. Without a glance in my direction, she walks to her room with dignity and very quietly closes the door.

Disregarding me, the bluebottles take advantage of the empty room. They dive from the light shade and zigzag over the tablecloth, crawling around the jug that has rebounded and lies on its side. I stand perfectly still.

I don't want to be German. It is too dangerous.

I want to be free; free from those who ignore past sins, pretend to be guiltless, and claim to be happy without happiness.

I turn from the desolate scene and run outside through the pear orchard, where the ground is littered with syrupy windfalls, where wasps burrow into the bruised fruit. The wind blasts from the fields. I can just make out the onion harvesters in the lower field and then I run back towards the house, my eyes welling up, but nothing in the world makes me want to go back inside. I take Opa's bicycle leaning against one of the outhouses, and cycle past the field of yellowing fennel onto the track leading towards the forest. The sky and an on-coming flock of crows herald a change in the weather. A mass of purple clouds threaten heavy rain. I push down hard on the pedals to give vent to my torment.

Soon I hear someone calling, 'Heike!' I turn to catch sight of Fabian and wobble on the stony track, reducing my speed. He overtakes me as I lumber behind the old rattle of a bike he rides. I follow his blurred shape for a good mile until I run out of tears.

In the forest the light is thick with pine dust and the air tastes of wild thyme. We lay our bicycles just off the track and I follow Fabian into the woods. I trust him. I don't want him to see my face all puffed up and my piggy eyes red from crying. We walk deeper and deeper in, the sounds of the modern world, the distant drone of aircraft and traffic can barely be heard. When we reach a sunlit oasis of tall grass, a deer leaps away and disappears into the shadows and the air barely stirs as if a sudden indolence takes hold.

Then Fabian vanishes. My heart skips a beat. I spin round several times and sink to my knees into the tufty grass, and he jumps out at me from behind a spruce. I give out a small scream. He kneels beside me. My heart's beating so fast it threatens to burst. I pull at the grass. My mouth feels swollen from crying. Fabian lies before me on his back, his arms behind his head. He closes his eyes and lifts his face to the sun. I lie beside him on my stomach my head turned towards him, and draw an imaginary outline of his profile with my eyes. I want to remember it, always. I like his freckled skin, and the way his fair eyelashes are dark at the root. A horse-drawn carriage passes by on the distant track. You can feel the vibrations of their hooves on the ground as the horses trot on, and hundreds of bells on their halters tinkling and jangling fade away. I roll on my back to feel the warmth of the healing sun on my face. Fabian sits up, leans over and lightly kisses me. I open my eyes and his gaze goes straight inside me like a single arrow of light, and then he nudges his nose against my cheek. 'Say after me, Heike, *ich liebe dich*,' he whispers.

I open my mouth to speak, but I can't speak German to him. I love you, I mouth.

'No, no.' He smiles. 'You English think you can get away with everything.' He laughs. 'Come on, sit up and say after me.' Taking my hand he hauls me up to the sitting position. 'Ready? So, we must begin. Do you understand me?'

I know I must try so as not to offend him, but I feel shy and uncomfortable as if I have an insurmountable barrier to overcome. Then he kisses me on the nose.

'Heike, you are not trying. Okay, let's begin with *ich*…so say *ich*.'

This time I open my mouth. Nothing. I fill my chest with air in preparation. Finally, *ich* is spoken. 'Bravo!' he says. 'Now, *liebe*. That's not difficult.'

At last, we come to *dich*. At an end of the exercise, I say it fast and then faster until we roll about laughing and I'm hopelessly tongue-tied and muddled. And then we kiss more, and tears came to my eyes that I didn't want him to see. I turn away, looking up at the sky curdling with cloud.

But it doesn't rain. In each other's arms, listening to the fast beat of our hearts slowing, we fall into a light sleep, woken by the faint cawing of distant crows, clamouring at the imaginary glass walls of our enclave, a reminder of the past and the world beyond. Our mood has changed. We make our way back to the track and cycle to Oma and Opa's house. I'm nervous. We have been out virtually all day without food or drink, and now it is late afternoon. I'm afraid Oma and Opa will be angry with me.

I wait for Fabian to turn to wave at the bend in the track just before Frau Kurtis's house. I wait for him to appear against the gloomy sky, my face raw from his kisses. A snapshot: the whiteness of his shirt against the rising darkness. A flock of geese flies over the house to distract me. I turn and push the bicycle to the back of the house, its little windows looking black and empty. My mother waits for me at the back door with a worried expression, melting to one of relief. Without a word she takes the bicycle from me and returns it to the outhouse. Oma and Opa are still working in the fields.

My mother says she is going out and will be back late. I go up to the attic room and try to continue my study of *Hamlet*, but I am gripped by love and longing. Oma and I later prepare supper while Opa goes to the outhouses and fills crates of onions for the market in Hamburg. Oma takes a bath and retires and Opa sits listening to the wireless turned down low. I say goodnight and go to the attic room. I can't settle. Tomorrow we will go home. My little red suitcase is packed. My feelings are in turmoil. I open the window wide and wait in the dark for my mother to come home. Close to midnight, car headlights follow the track and light up Frau Kurtis's cottage and then the bedroom wall. I duck for a moment, and the car turns; the lights are switched off. I can see an outline of a person at the wheel, and guess it is a man, thickset shoulders and a large head. My heart pounds. Eventually, my mother gets out of the passenger seat, and shuts the car door carefully. She hurries along the path into the house on tiptoe. The car drives slowly back to the main road and disappears in the darkness towards Lüneburg.

On the last day of our visit, Oma sets the table for a farewell party. We are presented with going away gifts. Tante Minnie, gives us a squat, elaborately painted Chinese pot; Lotte gives me a red diary to record my secret thoughts with a tiny brass key. Tia presents us with a box of chocolate marzipan and Frau Kurtis has baked cupcakes for our journey. The children give me cards they have made with drawings of Opa's sunflowers in thick wax crayons. I'm touched by their gifts. *Ach Danke schön! Danke. Viele Dank* I murmur and kiss everyone. So much kissing and hugging. No one seems able to stop.

We assemble around two long tables placed end to end in the kitchen and eat *Apfelkuche* with clotted cream and Oma has made a beautiful shortbread raspberry cake everyone admires saying it was too stupendous to cut, but cut she does. Our visit begins and ends with a party. In the midst of all this chatter and laughter, my heart stops. A shadow crosses the window. I freeze. This has to be my father, Klaus, come to see me after all this time. Can it be true, is this reunion the outcome of my mother's secret meetings? Maybe this will lead to more visits, trips to

Berlin, to meet my brothers and sisters, his second wife, his brothers who are my unknown uncles, and my paternal grandparents. The door opens wide. Everyone looks up from the table. The light comes flooding in and the figure is a dark shadow in the midst of it. I forget to breathe. I wait, full of hope and expectation.

'Hello, you rascal. Where have you been. Come and join us. Heike, move up a seat.'

It is Fabian. Fabian explains he has been in town to buy a pair of shoes and he shows them off to us in his shorts, which makes us all laugh. He sits next to me, and we clasp hands under the table while our thighs and naked legs caress each other.

I look across at my mother. *Heimat*—being at home has intensified her beauty. I'm so proud and happy for her. Her forget-me-not flowered dress matches the colour of her eyes lighting up as she listens to Lotte's future plans for Fabian, how he will go to college or university and study engineering. 'Ach, Mother, please. You are embarrassing me! I might not manage all your ambitions,' Fabian protests.

'He was a plump baby,' says Oma. We all laugh. 'It is true. I remember the deep dimples on his chin when he came to supper, and we ate rabbit stew.'

'Ah yes,' says Lotte, 'he liked playing with baby Heike even then!' Fabian and I laugh and blush with embarrassment. With Fabian at my side, my disappointment about my father fades.

Everyone is sadly jovial, and I'm overcome, dreading the departure and unable to enjoy the last family gathering, knowing my suitcase is packed upstairs and we have to say goodbye. But there is still hope. My father will be waiting for us on the station platform, or maybe if the train is not on time, he will go on to Hamburg and surprise us there. I will run into his arms and forgive everything. I feel perverse when I remember only yesterday I hadn't wanted to be German.

I remember the small band of people on Lüneburg station platform. Not bothered about the warm rain, they spread out, waving and calling 'Auf wiedersehen' as we find our seats, the train curling around the bend, taking us away to Hamburg and then to England. Lotte threatens to visit us the following year with Fabian, and Oma thrust into my hand a little brown bag of doughnuts she made at dawn, which I clutch as I lean out of the train window, reluctant to lose sight of the leaving party.

Tia in a wide-brimmed straw hat stands among my mother's aunts and cousins. Tante Minnie holds Otto's hand as he jumps up and down. Ilse leans against Frau Kurtis, holding the baby, her great grandchild, and Lotte links arms with Oma waving. Opa looks grim, not waving but standing close to Oma who seems to sway under her white umbrella.

Fabian is there. The beautiful boy. He stands apart from the small band, hands in his trouser pockets, frowning and bareheaded in the rain. Aware of everyone's eyes on us, we only dare shake hands to say goodbye, our faces flushed with the pleasure of touch and longing.

From the open window of our carriage, I catch sight of Heike, now the same age as me, standing on the platform beside Opa. Electing to stay, she sidles away, and I lose sight of her in the rain-mist. My mother and I lean out of the train window as far as we dare, waving at the ever-diminishing figures. There is no sign of my father from Berlin. He must have forgotten, I tell myself, or maybe he did see me but kept himself hidden believing he must maintain my mother's lie that he had been killed in the war. One day, Heike and I will find him. Meanwhile, I am Susanna going home to London. Tia flutters a white handkerchief, and they are gone.

3

# Putney 1961

On our immediate return to Putney my mother has a terrible shock. She has to face the possibility of losing Leonard. He and my mother taunt each other as if in a strange dance choreographed by a malign force. I listen to them quarrelling from the other side of the bedroom wall. I can't understand what is going on. Maybe my mother did meet my father in Lüneburg. Maybe she is planning to return; but where do I figure in this plan of hers? Leonard might be protesting he doesn't want to look after me, to attend to my education. I can't untangle their words to find meaning in their private language. I might as well not exist. Their pain locks them inside themselves. My mother has returned to the person she was before we left; overwrought, anxious, and weepy. I can do nothing to help her. It's almost as if she must now be punished for her happiness in Germany. She causes me worry and pain, and yet because of my helplessness, I'm pleased to be back at school and distracted by my studies. All this distracts me from thinking of Fabian.

A few weeks later, I come home from school, and notice to my horror, Leonard's suitcase standing in the hall packed to capacity. My mother isn't talking to anyone and doesn't mention it. Leonard comes home from the office and doesn't mention it either. Their differences have entered the next level: a silence reigns over them. The atmosphere is so volatile; I daren't ask any questions fearing an eruption of violent quarrelling and tears. My mother is inviolable. She is made of metal. She has dammed up her tears. Everything about her is steely, remote. She ignores me as if I am the centre of her pain. Each day as I return from school, Leonard's suitcase occupies the hall like a loyal, battered dog. Is Leonard preparing to leave us, or is my mother pushing him out? I'm emotionally torn: part of me wants the suitcase to disappear, for Leonard to disappear; but then another part of me fears he will leave us. I remember as a small girl I mistrusted him, disliked him. I have always kept my distance, always rejected his advances until his attempt to befriend me disappeared altogether. We live together in a spacious truce.

On the other hand, my mother is not fit to fend for herself. She doesn't have the means or capacity to cope with desertion. I wonder that she loves him. My mother takes to her bed in the afternoons and rises in evenings to cook a simple dish. We eat in silence. Nothing progresses or changes. Once more, I'm locked in their prison of unhappiness, which commits us to an isolation made poignant by our presence. I don't know what is happening. They tell me nothing. I am the useless witness to their cruel end. I can't desert their silence.

It is Theresa who enlightens me. It would be her, the one who knows everything. She catches up with me walking to school and I refuse to appease her by faking pleasure in her company, so I stride on feeling once more the victim. She delights in stepping into my fast stride.

'Well, who would have thought it. You and me are to become sisters!'

I slow down and face her. 'Sisters?' I am contemptuous.

'What are you talking about?' Not waiting for an answer, I carry on walking away. I loathe her and she frightens me with her truths. Maybe I should be grateful to her for helping me face my mother's past, but at this moment I can't find any kindness to give.

'You and me are to be sisters, now that your Daddy is coming to live with us,' she says.

I stop dead. 'You and me are going to be sisters! You could at least speak grammatically! Don't they teach you anything in that Convent of yours? And for your information, you know nothing about my father, even if you think you do!' I had to upstage her. If not, she would get the better of me again.

'Oh, so you don't know your Daddy and my Mummy are in love and he is coming to live with us. They are having an affair. I believe that's what it is called.'

I continue walking quickly. I am in a panic. The information begins to sink in. I look down at the pavement and concentrate on side-stepping cracks. Soon Theresa and I have to part. I hurry along, dreading sordid details or further unpleasant revelations that might spill from her lovely but poisonous rose-bud mouth. Then at the top of Cambalt Road, I stop to look at her. She is just as lovely as I remembered, and I can't help feeling envious, and wishing she liked me a little and could find it in herself to be a friend.

She shakes her head to question me, to show her impatience. She wants a magnificent, devastating response. I open my arms wide, and she steps back thinking I might hit her. I want to hit her. I tighten my fist ready to punch her in the mouth: her dirty, nasty little mouth, worse for looking so perfectly pink and bow shaped. I can't comment on her latest revelation. I am too appalled to think of Theresa's mother with her black hair and red fingernails taking Leonard away. The audacity of it. Leonard belongs to us.

'You always did say filthy things. The nuns haven't managed to teach you how to be nice!' Then overcome with mounting rage, unable to think up a parting shot to hurt her and restore my shaken dignity and self-esteem, I hear myself speak: 'I like your shoes.' And we both stare down at them dumbfounded.

Despite my lack of emotional ties to Leonard, I am angry and jealous. As I walk on to school I admit to myself I don't want Theresa to have him. I feel a surge of possessiveness. He is ours. He belongs to us. Beneath my anger and self-loathing for allowing her to crush me again, I am deeply hurt by Leonard's affair. It's incomprehensible to me that Leonard would prefer Theresa's mother to my own, that he would consider taking on Theresa as his daughter. Why is he so greedy for daughters? I seethe during the fearful silence at home and try to support my mother in every way she allows. I dust, clean the kitchen floor, bake a Victoria sponge cake, go on shopping expeditions to the hardware shop and Lipton's. And still Leonard's suitcase remains in the hall. After weeks of this torment, I want to shout at him to go, to leave us alone. He has brought us nothing but misery.

After several more weeks, Theresa and her mother vanish during the day when everyone is out, and we never set eyes on them again. It's extraordinary. The attic flat remains empty. Leonard unpacks his suitcase and puts it back on top of our black suitcase with the brass lock stacked on the wardrobe, and my mother is quietly content because even though he might have fallen in love with Theresa's mother, she remains undefeated. He has chosen us and they have been driven away.

I have different feelings for Leonard, though. A solid tolerance and fondness has weakened almost to indifference. I am distrustful. I don't try to like him anymore. All guilt about not loving him has gone. We barely acknowledge each other. The only time he speaks to me is to criticize me when we sit for the evening meal. I eat too fast. I should chew my food. I say nothing. I am not interested in what he thinks. He is a mystery. I don't know this man who was once planning to abandon us. It is enough that he makes my mother happy, or at least, less unhappy.

At last, with their crisis over, I can concentrate on schoolwork, but a nuclear blast is imminent. President Kennedy is leading us towards the annihilation of the human race. Germany is a tamed beast and nothing to worry about. It's the bald-headed vulture Khrushchev who threatens the democratic western world. Both he and Kennedy have been stockpiling nuclear warheads, while missiles have been blatantly transported from the USSR to the communist island of Cuba. Kennedy doesn't much fancy having missiles pointing his way and warns Kruschev to send back the weapons or else the United States will strike.

You'd think we would be safe enough in London from

all the posturing, political rhetoric and threats. Not a bit of it. After all, although we're just a group of seventeen year olds languishing in the Prefects' Common Room, determined not to play hockey, we can't stop world affairs seeping in like polluted water. Staff are forbidden to enter our sanctuary, which means if there is a knock, we know it's either a winsome first year pupil suffering from a crush on one of the prefects, or a teacher. The elect just burst in—as is their right. But world affairs are another matter.

Sometimes we open the door to the sound of knocking and sometimes we don't. It depends on our moods which fluctuate like the tides and phases of the moon. At seventeen, we've become increasingly anarchic in our own little ways; the minor ripples in the shockwave of a changing world threatening our sense of security and well-being, are welcome and exciting all the same. This sense of impending anarchy means we can live outside the rules: enjoy the squalor, reuse old crusty coffee cups, skive from boring classes to finish prep, and smoke foul dog-ends out of the windows.

It's here curled up in one of the misshapen, capacious armchairs, I write endless love letters to Fabian, which I never send in case Lotte reads them, so I hide them in my English folder. During lessons, I read them only to embarrass myself because my love and adoration are not as eloquently expressed as I would wish. The language of love eludes me. Yet how that treasured feeling of guarded secret intensifies the passion of an aching heart, the price we must pay for perpetuating its mystery. I sigh, and then I cross my legs over and sigh again. I chew on my pencil, bitter graphite grit on my tongue. Sooner or later, I'm going to die of lead poisoning, unrequited love, or a nuclear blast.

And then there's the insistent knocking at the door. The hockey mistress sounds rather frantic, 'Girls, time for the game!' she calls. One or two girls hide in the sports cupboard, more like an annex, but the brazen ones simply shrug and puff their smoke out of the sash windows, kept raised in all seasons, and look down on the prefect's lawn studded with frozen yellow leaves.

Let the sad old sports mistress, an ancient twenty-five years old, beg at the door while the world ends and we lounge in armchairs deep as boats and turn to ash. We know the score. The sirens are whooping all over London. We have four minutes to complete the drill issued by the bizarre government pamphlets. We must whitewash the windows to prevent us from being blinded by the nuclear light. Then we have to leap across the room, rip the door off its hinges and rest it against a wall to cower underneath with food supplies. Unfortunately, Miss Kent, the headmistress, has not supplied us with buckets of whitewash and paint brushes.

I turn my head in slow motion towards a granulated sky. The air-raid sirens cut through the softening, muffled sound of the stupefied city. One or two girls have gaping mouths and eyes wide staring up at the ceiling. We freeze waiting for the sequence of events outlined in the pamphlet. Denied the promised supplies to survive Armageddon, we wait for the blinding light and loss of sight before we melt like candle wax. Ah Lavender's Blue dilly dilly, Lavender's Green. The words of the song I loved as a child comes to mind. Our virgin skins falling off, bloodless like potato peel scattered to the floor and our bones char and flake in the wasteland's fireball.

The past, spread inside the mushroom cloud, expands like vast yellowing sheets of gelatine: the nightmares of black holes in the snow, the Odessa steps littered with the dead bodies and the white umbrella tilted like a fallen moon; red-eyed fiends and bogeymen folded up in the cracks in the walls who endlessly determine who may speak, who can eat soap-cake, who will live, who die. The gulags, the barbed wire, the gas ovens.

I want my mother. Leonard wants to adopt me, but can't comfort me. After his affair with Theresa's mother, he makes it up to me. I have already stolen his name Saunders. But now with the sirens going off all over London, the futility of Leonard's recent proposal to adopt fills me with sadness. The interrogation in court is something I want to forget—*Has he been a good father to you? Do you have a legacy he might want to take from you?* Mine, the faultless performance, trained by Portia: *the quality of mercy is not strained your Lordship. I beg you, do not cut the pound of flesh, but grant me citizenship. Don't you know London belongs to me? I have taken it into my heart. The river Thames runs in my blood.*

And no one asked me if I was prepared to take this man to be my official father. No one tells me my father, the Berliner, is still alive. I wait for them to tell me, give me a choice. I have betrayed my real father. I have scorned his name. Did they fear his refusal? Did the Berliner know? Did he care? *But it is for the best,* I can hear Grandmother say, *to tell her nothing.*

Then that awful night, a reenactment of times past in Germany. The police hammering the door, demanding the alien Heike report at the station every month so that her whereabouts be known.

'Len, Len, what shall we do?' Leonard consulted his mother. Pragmatic Grandmother. The solution is simple: Leonard must adopt Susanna and British citizenship will be conferred upon her automatically.

Like a blessing. A benediction: to be a pilgrim, a Londoner, because I won't allow Germany to have anything to do with me anymore, because there would always be a London, my London growing like a tower from the swampland of the dark river. And in any case my Berliner never came to find and claim me. One day I will stand before him without a word. I am steadfast in my patience. I will wait for him to come to me. I will step forward with my arms at my side. He will take a step, open his arms and draw me to him.

But now here I am, my feet walking upon England's pleasant green, cramming chips into my gob from a newspaper with the sickening report on the Eichmann trial and Yuri Gagarin's flight into space, chatting up boys outside the school gate, walking home and blushing and flirting under the gaze of admirers: Michael and David and Geoff, but never unfaithful to my secret love.

And my mother crying at Herr Stern's funeral, his throat eaten away by cancer and holding the hand of Edith Stern in the synagogue and Leonard sneaking home after a meeting with his latest conquest, all reduced to a tiny five pointed star through the lethal membranes of a radioactive cloud and all the jabbering on the airwaves between the Home Service, Radio Luxemburg and Outer Space sucked up in the single black flute of the London siren like a humming-bird's beak thrust deeply into the exotic flower.

Stillness.

The air is thick with sour carbon monoxide. Then it's over. The sirens all over London die down. Nothing. People still breathing. A blackbird, singing solo. A bus droning in the distance. High up a plane scores a patch of blue sky. Someone has spliced the running film. The two ends, the past and present, are stuck together again and the film runs on. Clickety-click. Clickety-click. Knock. Knock. Knock. A staccato rapping.

We open the door. The sports mistress stands there with her hair windswept and tussled. A frantic look in her eyes. We rally round. It is the British thing to do. Hockey sticks spring from cupboards and down on the field presided over by ancient horse chestnuts, we run, stoic, tight-lipped and determined, the icy wind lashing our bare legs, and there we swing our sticks into air, regardless of safety, and thwack the ball across the frozen, mud-rutted field.

There is an invisible wall across the city of my divided heart. Two letters arrive in the morning post, one is an official letter from the German Embassy and the other is from Lotte. With intense excitement, my mother announces that Lotte intends to visit London in September with her son Fabian, if his college timetable allows. Enclosed is a small passport photograph of Fabian. On the back he has signed it in blue ink: *Liebe Fabian*. I know the photo is for me. My mother says I will have to sleep on the sofa in the sitting room, so that Lotte and Fabian can use my room.

'Oh, that's fine,' I say as casually as if I really couldn't care less if they come or not. At night I creep into the sitting room and rifle through the writing bureau to find Lotte's letter. By the light of the full moon, I find the photograph of Fabian tucked in the folds of the letter and steal it for myself. I put it in my book of John Donne's poetry: *Goe and catch a falling star, Get with child a mandrake root...* I take Fabian's photo everywhere and whenever I have a private moment, close my eyes and kiss his lips.

As soon as Leonard wakes up, he goes into the sitting room and changes the day calendar on the writing bureau. He never puts the radio on. My mother likes it quiet in the morning. She likes to hear the remains of the dawn chorus. But Leonard always changes the calendar. This is especially important to him, marking the days, months and seasons. He never forgets. Then he pads into the kitchen and puts the kettle on the stove and lights the gas with a pop. I can hear him laying the table for breakfast. Afterwards, he makes his way to the bathroom to shave. From time to time, he sloshes the razor around in clear water in the bowl. Sometimes he sharpens his razor on a leather strap hanging behind the bathroom door. Then he rinses his face and makes snorting noises. He always shaves in his house trousers—as my mother calls them—and a white vest. He oils his thinning hair, combs it back and smooths it down with his other hand. I notice he is growing his sideburns and putting on weight.

Toilette complete, he changes into his office suit trousers, a blue shirt and tie, and puts his suit jacket on the back of the hall chair. He returns to the kitchen to make tea in a brown pot warmed for some seconds first and when the tea is brewing, covers the pot with the knitted, multi-coloured tea cosy. We have strong tea from a red tea caddy with *Mazawattee* printed on it. It is kept on the top shelf of the larder. Inside the tin is a broad metal spoon with a handle in the shape of a bust of Boudicca with THE FESTIVAL OF BRITAIN embossed on her tin helmet.

Leonard shuffles into my room with a full cup and saucer in hand. He never knocks on the door and never spills any in the saucer.

'Time to wake up, girl,' he always says, putting the tea down on my bedside table. He likes to pause and read the titles of my books.

'Thank you,' I reply from a deep dreamless sleep, reluctant to drink the tea, and to wake. I want to ask him not to bring me tea and wake me up, but I never have the heart. I can hear him taking tea into my mother and talking to her. On Sundays, he makes us a boiled egg. He shows me how to place three eggs into cold, salted water and bring the water to boil for precisely four minutes. Each egg would then be rinsed under the cold-water tap. Even though I consider myself a young woman, and my mother is almost forty-three, he cuts up the bread and butter into soldiers for each of our plates. On the side of each plate, he leaves a little pyramid of salt. When he has finished his egg, he turns the fragile, empty shell upside down and says, 'There you are, girl. Have another boiled egg.'

Even when I was small I always knew it was a gentle

trick of his. I never wanted to spoil his moment of fun so I would pretend I was naïve and tap the empty shell with my spoon and fake deep disappointment with cries of woe. I could be such a little music-hall actress when I wanted.

Occasionally, I would do it to him. He probably would have clowned around more if I hadn't been such a miserable, homesick, spoilsport of a child.

Now I'm seventeen and he still sometimes plays the egg trick but with an ironic twist, hiding the real boiled egg behind the teapot. 'There's yours, girl. Eat up.' I can always tell when it isn't the real egg because when you tap the spoon on the shell , it has a thinly textured sound. The real thing sounds like stone. 'Oh you!' I say on discovery. I know this little game is a reminder of how hard he tries to bridge our estrangement and it upsets me, but I don't let him see.

These mundane, domestic certainties form a soothing pattern. It's the solution to angst, the creation of *Gemutlichkeit*—comfort and cosiness—an investment in love so easily overlooked. I remember the absurdity of my mother's insistence she made Leonard's sandwiches for work, even when they were not talking to each other during long and murderous months as my mother punished him for his gambling and philandering. Even when his suitcase remained for weeks in the hall, she folded his sandwiches in greaseproof paper for him to slip inside his briefcase. It was as if violent breaches in the family web, a web of magic, had to be continuously re-spun, the web of appearances and domestic rituals, secrets and lies, bound in a sticky cocoon left undisturbed whatever cost.

And on this day, mid-November 1962, I listen to

Leonard's morning ritual as I lie in bed, the cup of tea left to grow cold on my bedside table. I'm taking a day off school and luxuriate in extra time in bed. On this day, my mother and I are summoned to attend a meeting at the German Embassy at 11.30am. It is an opportunity for Fräulein Heike to bring her German passport for an informal relinquishing of her German citizenship, and yet another denial of the existence of a stranger, my father whom I have never set eyes upon, whom I have never met, the father I love, the Berliner. When the letter arrives, the very same day Lotte had written with dates of her future arrival, my mother is filled with joy and consternation all at once.

'Len, Len, what does it mean?' She shows him the letter at the breakfast table from the German Embassy calling for my attendance.

Leonard takes the letter from her hand and reads it carefully. 'Nothing, girl. They're just being friendly.' My mother does not look convinced. 'Maybe it's all to do with officialdom, keeping up their records, that kind of thing. You know what the Germans are like. Everything has to be done properly according to the rule book.'

'Can I see?' I think I have a right since the letter concerns me. Once I've read the letter, written in perfect English, I speak up. 'Couldn't we just say thank you very much we're unable to attend. We could make up some excuse like we're away or something. We could just *send* my German passport. I don't see the point of wasting a whole morning going up town for a quick handover!'

I picture myself at the moment of relinquishing my wretched Germanness. I have to admit despite my protestation it would be a welcome excommunication from the German race. A deliverance. My tainted blood cleansed. A brand-new identity. A new beginning. The feeling of being an interloper, an imposter would free me from the guilt of Germany's past, my mother's past. I picture myself reaching over a desk and dropping my old green passport into the open hand of an official wearing a uniform, because like women, Germans like uniforms, and from that moment, everything German will be blitzed out of my head. Except the knowledge of my father, Oma and Opa, my mother and Lotte and Fabian as well as Tante Minnie and Frau Kurtis and Ilse and her baby and cousins and… these I will keep safe inside me.

'I think we must go to the Embassy,' my mother says after some thought. 'It would be rude not to go, Len. I don't want to lie. They find things out you know.' My mother was becoming anxious. 'We will go very smart, Susie. We will look respectable. You know what the Germans are like!'

'You always look respectable,' says Leonard. But I know there is more to it than that. My mother has pride. She wants to show the bigwigs at the Embassy how well she has done for herself as an immigrant, thanks to the kindness of the Londoners. She doesn't want them to pity her for making mistakes, her homesickness, the years in squalid bed-sits, years of having to put up with her philandering wastrel of a husband.

We discuss what we should wear. My mother keeps changing her mind. A tweed suit, or a new winter coat. A fur hat. But on the morning, she sprays her permed hair with lacquer and puts on her best camel hair coat and red silk scarf, chosen she says because red is the colour of London. I am saved from wearing my school uniform and don a blue wool coat over a pale blue shift dress. My mother thinks it is too short, but I tell her this is the 60s look and everyone is showing their knees these days.

'You look nice Mum. Very English with the pearl necklace,' I venture.

My mother smiles. 'This isn't for me. You're the one! You must look modern and pretty.'

Now that I have passed my GCE exams and have started A level History and Biology we both feel progress is being made. I have a secret desire to become a nurse and travel the world saving the sick, but I know my mother wants me to go 'up town' and work in the city. She would like me to be a secretary or office clerk and live the life of a sophisticated young lady. I haven't told her I declined to take the shorthand and typing course at school, preferring more academic subjects, English being my favourite. My mother has left housekeeping. When Mr. Stern died, Edith Stern emigrated to New York and sold up. My mother now has a good clerical job in a small publisher in Wimbledon. Her English has much improved. I'm a little nervous now. I'm not sure if going to the German Embassy is a good idea. I am officially a British subject. I don't understand why I have to personally hand over my German passport. It seems a silly ritual.

As I brush my teeth, I stare at myself in the bathroom mirror. Aren't I a typical south London girl, through and through? I have all the credentials surely—I'm educated in the English language and literature and well-read for my age. I once recited 'The Lamb' by William Blake and many

382

occasions read passages from the Bible in church when I attended St. Catherine's, and I'm adequately familiar with English customs and manners, thanks to my past mentors, namely Grandmother and Ida, and numerous landladies. I saw Queen Elizabeth II at the top of East Hill in a horse and carriage, wearing a yellow hat, and waved the paper Union Jack. I know all the English kings, Saxon and Norman, and studied Egyptology and the causes of the First World War. And hadn't Mr. Newman delivered the daily news at assembly about atomic bombs and the Iron Curtain and unrest in Africa? In addition, I've made my own investigations about the rise of the Nazi Party and how the Nazis persecuted and murdered Jews and caused the Second World War, leaving me in awe of the English nation, because the English saved Europe from the fascists; they liberated the concentration camps; returned democracy and decency to Germany. They saved the world.

I want the English to save me, if they will. I understand that humanity is not about doing what you want to do, but what you have to do. Bearing all this in mind, I tell myself I'm ready to face the Germans. Hating the Germans is something I can't do. Of course, I loathe the Nazis. But hating the Germans will always be acceptable among the xenophobes. As enemies come and vanish, the last vestiges of racism will unequivocally be conferred upon the Germans. I'll have to get used to it. But I don't want to. Leonard peeps his head around the bedroom door. 'You decent girl?'

'Yeah, are you off to work now, Dad?'

He walks into the room while I stand awkwardly by my

bed. 'You look very smart. Now turn round and let me see.' I oblige and twirl.

'I'm not looking forward to this,' I confess.

'It's just a formality, girl. These diplomats like to exercise a bit of power. It might have got up their noses you've chosen to be British. Just a bit of tribal competition! I'm off now.' He leans towards me and offers his cheek. 'Look after your mother, girl.'

'Of course I will, Dad.' I peck him on the cheek. I feel awkward in his presence. He pats my shoulder. I don't know where my feelings for him have come from. Everything I felt about him in the past, anger and resentment, is mixed with a kind of love that comes from familiarity and dogged perseverance. I'm still not comfortable whenever he gives me attention and we barely communicate. He is my mother's choice, one she may have often regretted, but he has stayed with her. I was never the reason for his betrayal or loyalty. He had wanted her, and I was part of the package, but excluded from his desire. I knew this, but for her sake I tolerated him. The heart has its own force and that is why I felt love for him.

# Lüneburg 1946/47

## Extract from Sophie's diary

November 8th—It's about six years since the war started, but it seems like a lifetime ago and the person I used to be no longer exists. Germany is a wreck. It can never recover. There are ruins and devastation everywhere. My mother went blind the moment she read the news that Erich is dead. He was shot by Partisans in Yugoslavia in retreat. I was in the kitchen shelling peas. She screamed and ran down to the field and screamed his name to the sun just setting. The whole sky was blood red. I tried to comfort her, but she pushed me away. I ran back to the house because Heike was playing on the kitchen floor by herself. The doctor said my mother's blindness is caused by shock. In time she will recover her sight. She makes me angry though because she won't accept sympathy.

Tia has just returned from Munich. She said the railway station is a skeleton. She said the Americans down south are behaving badly, smashing up houses and partying all the time and getting young girls into trouble.

One night Klaus turned up. We told each other things. We were honest. Both of us terribly changed. It was no good. He visited my parents before he left for Berlin. He told them he was going to divorce me for adultery. I'm sad and hurt at first that he blamed me for our failure. But he knew about Leonard somehow. Maybe he just guessed. Maybe he guessed about Hans. Our marriage would never have worked. We both got swept away during the war when everyone was looking for love and excitement. He told my mother he will continue his training to become a teacher. I have his address and will do what he asks. I'll send pictures and news of little Heike. It is the least I can do, and I'm touched he cares about her. I'm always sad when I think about him and wonder if we could have made a good marriage together. We think we are in charge of our lives but mostly we are not. We are just swept away by events and can do nothing but salvage what we can. Loss and gain.

Went to the local cobbler to get my shoes patched again. Everyone in Lüneburg looked pale and strained and half starved.

Lotte and I get through the weekly ration too fast: black bread, quarter pound of butter and half a sausage. We go into the woods to find mushrooms and when I go home my Dad always gives us a turnip or potatoes, although this winter's crop is poor, and hoards come into the fields at night to steal. We just about manage with the extras Lotte can bring home from what she can steal from the Naafi leftovers.

November 13th—Officially I'm a free woman. Klaus has divorced me. It all went through without difficulty. I agreed to be the guilty party so it could go through quickly. I had to say I've had many affairs with other men. I also had to promise to give him regular news about Heike. He is living in Berlin again with his cousin. His street is Holzendorffstrasse in Charlottenburg, most of which is demolished. He has lost his entire family in the Berlin bombing. His parents died in the bombing raid and his two brothers never returned from Russia. I feel terrible for him. I still have feelings for him.

November 16th—Thank God for my dearest Lotte. She works hard at the Naafi place set up in the converted aerodrome. She cleans up all the mess there, but often comes home with coffee and tea, corned beef and detergent. It is still impossible to get anything. The shops are empty. Women are giving themselves for a cigarette. We have been brought to the lowest of the low. I must take care of my parents who don't seem to be getting over Erich's death. My mother's sight has not improved although we hope it will in time. Dad has got a guard dog. The potato and cabbage fields have been constantly plundered. Frau Kurtis was thrown a dead baby from a refugee travelling on an open lorry. She did the kindest thing and buried it in her garden in a place marked with a cross. She took to her bed afterwards for days and my mother had to nurse her back to health. Everyone said it was the shock.

I am the good housewife again, just as I tried to be in Gütersloh. I wonder what happened to the Franenarzts and often think of the little boys I loved and cared for. I have written to them, but the post is impossible, and I hear nothing. Those were happier times in some ways. I hear nothing from my colleague Liska or any of the other recruits who trained with me in Lübeck and worked with me in Paris.

Every day is a struggle. While Lotte works and cleans, I look after Heike and little Fabian. They like to play together in the bedroom, but it is so cold in there. Lotte waits to hear from Wolfgang. Every day people appear and disappear. I must write sparingly as I don't have many pages left in my notebook.

November 20th—The ground is frozen solid. We put the garlic and onions in very late but just in time. The potato crop we stored has rotted. I helped cut away some of the bad bits and we cooked piles of peel and saved pieces for stews and soup. Helped Papa put in tulip bulbs and other spring flowers for his stall. Heike is unwell with a chesty cough and grizzles all the time. I've been impatient with her. She just won't settle or play with Fabian. Neither seem to have an appetite.

Lotte went to a Naafi dance. She looked attractive in my blue dress, which I don't feel the need to wear anymore. I live on cigarettes. I know I should try to eat but nothing is appetizing. I've heard from Klaus. He has invited me and Heike to Berlin, but we can't go. She is not well enough to travel and the trains are full of refugee orphans from the East returning to Germany. Too dangerous to travel by freight train. I've said I'll bring Heike in the spring. I have too much to do here although I have no will to go on with this wretched existence. But it's the same for everyone.

November 23rd—German ex-POWs played the British servicemen in a football match today. Lotte insisted I went with her to watch Colin Peters, whom she had met at the Naafi dance, play just outside the former Luftwaffe airfield. Then Captain Saunders, or Leonard as I now call him, said he would be there too. There was rain and freezing fog in the morning, but it brightened up later. Little Heike and Fabian played in piles of dead leaves. None of the

Englishmen speaks much German, but we managed a few words in English and I met Colin Peters for the first time. He is gallant and affectionate towards Lotte, which makes her happy.

Later Lotte told me Captain Saunders would like to marry me. He was very taken by my striped socks, the first time he saw me. I wear them to death as we can't get nylons here. I bought them in Paris when I was stationed there, and I'm amused to think that's what first attracted him to me across the football field. Len is considerably older than I am. He is quite handsome with dark hair and blue eyes. I suspect he may be married though, and I'm not in the right state of mind for romance or talk of marriage again. Anyway, I think he is pushing his luck. I need all my energy for survival.

December 6th—Found candles at home and Papa said I should take them. He gave us rabbit stew with carrots, which I took home in Mum's old pot with the lid tied down with string firmly placed in the basket on the bicycle. Lotte ate most of it after the children had their fill. She told me last night she is afraid she is falling in love with Colin Peters. She told me in the dark while we lay in our beds. I didn't know what to say because I kept thinking about Wolfgang. Maybe he is in some camp thinking of her. Maybe he is dead. As we lay in the silence I know she felt guilty. Then she said, Sophie don't think badly of me. I said I didn't. But the truth is, I couldn't help feeling deeply depressed. I felt even worse when I discovered it is because of Colin Peters we have tea, coffee, sugar and spam.

Heike is much better and eating a little bread and she

drank all her milk today.

December 18th—Heike's birthday. Three years old. I cycled over with her to visit my parents. Mum made her some biscuits and Frau Kurtis came over with a small doll she had knitted for Heike. She brought her granddaughter Ilse, an orphan. Both her parents were killed in a bombing raid in Hamburg. Ilse played with Heike all afternoon in Erich's room upstairs. Mum and I plaited straw dollies rather later in the year than usual and Frau Kurtis unstitched a little jacket and put in false seams so it would fit Heike as she grew. She looks so sweet in it.

Cycled home in the dusk worried I wouldn't get back before the curfew, but made it just in time to get the tea ready for Lotte and Fabian who had been out with the Englishman. She gave Heike old pieces of chocolate for her birthday. Fabian had a lovely time playing football with Colin Peters over at the former Lüneburg Luftwaffe base. The Tommies aren't supposed to mix with German women, but they all do. In any case, boys need a father figure, Lotte said.

I couldn't help asking: what if Wolfgang turned up? What then? Without hesitation she said Wolfgang would be the one she would choose because he is Fabian's father and she still loved him. I felt calmer after she told me that. I don't know why. It isn't any of my business.

Christmas Day. We all rose late. Even Heike and Fabian slept past nine. First we walked to Lotte's mother's house. She had candles along the windowsill and a little holly tree in a pot decorated with paper angels, silver stars, and tinsel.

It looked so pretty I started to cry. Lotte gave us English cigarettes, and chocolate bought from the Naafi stores with her wages, although it is strictly forbidden. We toasted bread by the open fire. The smell of pine wood burning was beautiful.

Then we sang *O Tannenbaum* and other songs to the children and played games with them before cycling to my parents' place full of aunts and cousins who managed to find all kinds of things to give away. I think, said my mother, all the lofts are empty of everything. Papa looked sad tonight. He is missing Erich. The church bells have been ringing all day, if it wasn't St. Johannis, it was St. Michaelis and then the glockenspiel at the town hall joined in, but the true spirit of Christmas has long gone.

The streets were empty of the English. Lotte said they were having one big party in their compound and hoped to get very drunk. Lotte likes a tipple, but drink makes me ill. I think I have a sensitive stomach. I smoked too many cigarettes and stayed at home with my parents and slept with Heike in my bed. We kept each other warm. I couldn't help myself, but I began to cry when I knew she was asleep. What kind of future can I make for her?

January 18th 1947—Today is my birthday. I decided to let it slip away. Freezing cold. We sit indoors with our coats on. A little more meat to be found in the shops, but the queues are so long we could die before we get a portion.

Len or Leonard comes almost every evening. He brings something for us without fail. He has learned to say: *Ich liebe dich*—I love you—and writes it down on the cigarette packets he gives me. I'm warming to him. He seems solid, strong, reliable and caring. He promises me a different life in England. I point to Heike, meaning he must include her. Ja Ja, he says. I'm tired, resisting him. I think sometimes: why not? What do I have to look forward to here? Poverty, cold, potato picking and being unloved. Lotte thinks I should pack my bags in readiness. She would leap at the chance, she said, if Colin Peters asked her, but he doesn't. Her love is more desperate than mine. She is more passionate, the way I used to be. I know she is disappointed Colin never speaks of their future together. My feelings are dulled by past experiences. My needs are different after my loss of Hans and Klaus. I'm not the same. Everyone has changed.

January 30th—Snow. More snow upon snow. Frost-bitten fingers and toes. Scour forests for kindle wood trying to avoid other bands of people with the same idea. Small armies with shovels and saws intent on sawing off lower branches of trees.

Len and I are engaged. He is returning to England soon. He is taking his mother's advice. If he de-mobs too late, there will be no jobs left at home. I am to follow with Heike and will decide after a few months in England whether or not I agree to marry Len. I have a little money saved but Lotte has helped me buy decent clothes for Heike, some second hand boots and a wool coat. Len has brought me nylons and Lotte has given me a pair of new shoes and a skirt and blouse. By the time I have paid for the train fare and ferry ticket, I will have nothing. This is the risk I am taking.

I wrote to tell Klaus that I will write from England with

a forwarding address with news of Heike from time to time, as promised. He wrote to say he was bitterly disappointed in me, but not wholly surprised I had betrayed him and my country. I was angry. How dare he judge me in that way? Lotte and I agree we owe our country nothing.

February 3rd—Cycled home in the snow with Heike in the seat behind me, her little round face bright red in the cold. This time I knew I must tell my parents I would be leaving for England soon. Both happy to see us. My Dad has made a wooden rocking horse for Heike for when she visits in future, which delighted her so much. I didn't have the heart to tell them we were departing soon. Afterwards I felt sick and threw up in the snow on the way home.

February 12th—Worried the snow will prevent us from travelling to England next week. I'm scared of the future. Lotte gives me strength; she said there is no future here for anyone. I have packed a new suitcase, more like a trunk that I found second hand on the black market. Everything is ready, including my passport with Heike's details. Maybe the English will not let us into the country. Len will be meeting us at Dover. Will go tomorrow and say goodbye to my mother and father. It breaks my heart. Poor Dad is beside himself with worry about everything, and Mum's sight is still poorly. What kind of daughter am I to desert them?

February 13th—Came away from home again without telling them. My Mum cuddled Heike on her lap and said,

'I don't know what we would do without you and your Mummy.' How could I tell her after that? I managed to take a few photographs of me and my brother from my mother's dresser drawer and hide them in my bag to take to England. All the other photographs had to be destroyed because we were in our Hitler Youth uniforms.

On leaving home, I felt wretched, and ill. Stomach cramps all along the lane past Frau Kurtis's house, praying she wouldn't come out to have a chat or give me eggs as she often does. Could barely walk. Hanging onto the bike because Heike was in the child's seat, I threw up in the snow again. Heike was very quiet on the way home. She was not her usual self at all, as if she sensed something. Maybe I should write to Len and tell him it is impossible for me to arrive in England owing to illness or a change of circumstance. But he has been so good to me and loves me and I do have strong feelings for him. Above all, I have Heike's future to consider. It will be a fresh beginning for us both. We can come to life again and put the past behind us. But I don't know if I can do this.

# London 1962

My mother chain smokes on Putney Station platform waiting for the train to Victoria. We are at least thirty minutes early. She likes to arrive at stations ridiculously early. She can't help herself. The mere thought of missing a train causes her distress. I walk up and down the platform feeling responsible for her. You can hear the track zing into life when a train is on its way. In the carriage, my mother smokes another cigarette. It doesn't suit her. I'm worried she will contract lung cancer. She doesn't want the window open because the rush of air would spoil her hairdo. In any case there's damp in the air, which would make her hair-do frizzy. She has the same style as our Queen Elizabeth, short and curled under with two kiss curls above her temples.

I sit in a fug, looking out of the filthy train window. London is desolate and dirty, the track rising above the backyards of stacked, black houses, loaded with old iron, broken sheds and boxes of empty bottles and rubbish. For miles there's not a single tree; this is a forest defeated but weeds flourish from crevices of old walls, and along the clogged guttering. Wildflowers and weeds grow sickly, starved of fresh air and light. Many of the dismal houses with damp streaks down their corroding walls are begging for demolition, held up by the houses either side with sunken roofs and unstable, ramshackle lean-tos. Wet washing, the only sign of human life, is strung across narrow backyards and across public balconies, barely stirring.

In stark contrast, the German Embassy in Belgrave Square comprises three elegant Georgian houses made into one. The impressive marble hallway commands a hushed respect. Once the door closes behind us, the roar of London is muffled and distanced like an underground river. A man approaches, stiff in his shiny suit and silk yellow tie. He doesn't smile but shows us nervously into a small waiting room with a pink damask sofa and a glass coffee table with English and German magazines. He gestures that we should sit. 'You will not wait long,' he says in a clipped accent, and with a little bow of his head, leaves the room. My mother raises her eyebrows and remains standing. She sighs loudly. 'Why are we put inside this little room?'

'I suppose you did remember to bring my passport?' I ask.

'Of course I did, Susie. How long must we wait in here?' She looks at her watch as if she has an immediate appointment and I have answers to her questions. Her nervousness unsettles me.

As she speaks the door opens. A different gentleman in a black suit and tinted glasses leads the way. The soles of his supple calf shoes squelch on the marble floor. We find ourselves in the circular hall again with rooms going off and a central staircase branching to the left and right. Above, a domed glass ceiling diffuses the harsh light, and it pours down in narrow shafts.

'One moment, please,' murmurs the gentleman as he knocks gently on one of the baroque double doors. My mother and I flinch simultaneously when the pair of doors crack open and we're invited inside by another official who is about forty, urbane, and smiling to show his gold teeth. 'Thank you, Herr Ratke,' he says, dismissing the man with the calf shoes who retreats into the hall.

'Please come in Mrs. Saunders und Fräulein. Do take a seat. Herr Bade will be with you very soon. He has been delayed but you will not have to wait long. Maybe you would like coffee or tea perhaps?'

We both say no thank you. We find it unnerving being shuffled from one person to the next.

'Then if you will excuse me. Do take a seat.' He makes a flourishing movement with his arm, and discreetly leaves, closing the double doors behind him. My mother and I stand in a lavishly furnished drawing room with wing chairs, Persian carpets, and an enormous mahogany writing desk with silver inkpots, three ivory telephones and an array of immeasurably sad wooden pencils lined up perfectly and sharpened to splendid points. The walls are decorated with paintings of mountains and woodland scenes in dark oils encased in elaborate gilt frames. The French windows look out onto a walled garden of tangled rose beds carved in the bright green lawns washed and dewy as if all the colours had been freshly painted and were running into each other. Silver birch trees have not yet loosened their fading leaves.

My mother sits on a yellow sofa. She gives a little cry of displeasure as she sinks into the feather cushion. A glass topped coffee table is graced by a blue china bowl crammed full of white roses.

'Delft ware,' said my mother looking at the bowl admiringly. 'The roses. Just look! Ah, so lovely.'

I sit opposite her on a wide stool covered in white silk.

I lean forward to smell the roses. I can feel the scar on my leg prickling through my stockings. 'They are perfect. They look unreal.'

I will remember this room, I tell myself, for the white roses, their luminous petals and delicate stamens and the scattering of yellow pollen on the glass.

The door opens again. 'Do forgive me ladies.' It's Herr Bade, a tall blonde man in a light jacket and a silk cravat in his late thirties. He holds out his hand, bows his head and ever so faintly clicks his heels—old fashioned gestures that cause me to stifle a grin. My mother and I stand to show our respects, unsure what was going to happen next. After the handshakes he says, 'Do let me ring for some tea, Mrs. Saunders, Fräulein?'

'No thank you,' replies my mother, flashing him a charming smile. He gestures we should sit again. My mother hesitates, preferring not to, but relents when Herr Bade sits at one end of the yellow sofa sinking into a comfortable level. I resume my place on the stool and stare at the roses, aware I'm showing too much of myself. My dress keeps sliding up my thighs and without appearing ungainly I pull it down as far as I can, and I cup my knees with my hands. But Herr Bade and my mother are too engrossed in their own conversation to care a stitch about me. Herr Bade slips into German and my mother's fluency returns instantly.

Wanting to affect a cool nonchalance, for surely it must be obvious that my old mother tongue is of little concern or interest to me, I look down at Herr Bade's shoes. Unlike his counterpart's they're made of brown suede with two toggles on each upper sole. My mother and he are talking in animated tones, the German enjoying her attentions, puffing out his chest, his eyes wandering over her.

I relent, out of boredom, and tune in to their conversation. He's talking about Germany, how it has Phoenix-like, risen out of the ashes to become a wealthy European state. He talks about the Berlin Wall, President Kennedy's support and how the West Germans have faith in the American president's fight against the oppression of the Communist East. He speaks about the horrors of life in East Berlin, the Stasi, the surveillance and starvation. In contrast, the economic miracle of West Berlin is a model for all Europeans. But Germany, he warns, is in danger of falling into the evils of materialism. There must be another miracle to restore the nation's soul and spirit. My mother remains perfectly composed, not saying a word. The past has taught her it can be perilous to express a personal opinion.

As I watch Herr Bade in full flow, showing off, full of national pride and very much taken by my mother, I wonder at this condescension in lecturing her. His eyes do not leave her face while she maintains a faint smile. The conversation continues, now desultory. Herr Bade wants to know where she was from in Germany, and where she lives now. They exchange home-town stories, laughing lightly at each other until the moment when my mother wants to get away and reaches into her handbag for my passport.

I feel light-headed. At last! The terrible burden of being German will be lifted. I watch the passport leave my mother's hand and rest in his. He stands, 'Ah *danke...*' My mother and I rise too, and we move into the centre of the room creating a small circle ready to shake hands and take our leave. Herr Bade flicks through my passport as if the applicant is no longer on this earth and looks up to address me. I can smell his expensive soap. With a slight bow, and yet another soft swish of his suede heels, he hands me the dark green German passport with the black eagle stamped on the front.

What was this? A game of pass the passport? Instantly, I look across at my mother for some sign or instruction, flabbergasted. She smiles wistfully, abandoning me to the moment. I offer the passport to Herr Bade. Has there been some misunderstanding? I throw him a quizzical look. Then he takes the passport from me and returns it to my mother. 'I must beg your pardon, Fräulein,' he purrs. He flashes a sympathetic smile to my mother who puts my German passport back into her handbag.

'You see, Heike,' he says in immaculate English, 'I have to congratulate you on the acquisition of your British nationality, but I want you to know that you will always be welcome in your homeland. In our eyes you will always be German.'

He pauses for a long moment, and I blush. 'We must look to the future. One day perhaps it will be important for you to be a German citizen too. We will never turn you away.'

I stare at a button on his jacket; I am a person cursed. I'm dumbfounded and ungrateful. My mother looks at me with a sense of achievement. I'm a fraud, because I have done nothing to make her proud of me. That dreadful desolate feeling returns from when I learnt that my father is alive after all, and the bluebottles scurried across Oma's kitchen table.

I look beyond the memories and my mother to the metallic light falling on the seared trees in the Embassy Garden, and I think of when I believed the sun was a soft, spongy thing, seeping yellow glue onto the windowsill.

Then I become aware of Herr Bade and my mother talking and laughing again, as if this has all been a conspiracy, a little joke between them at my expense. We are led outside into the hall and Herr Bade softly closes the door to the drawing room where he remains, while the attendant with the squelchy shoes approaches, and thanks us for coming, and wishes us well and for a safe journey home.

'Madam, please I beg you,' he says finally, opening the door to the street and stepping back to allow us to pass. My mother thanks him and we call, 'Goodbye! Goodbye! Auf wiedersehen!' over our shoulders, but the door has already closed, and the city noise drums in our ears.

'Quick, Susie, let's go home.' Together we walk briskly down the street on the way to Victoria Station. There's an urgency in our step as if any moment Herr Bade might come running out to insist we return.

'I'm glad that's over,' I say.

A cloud bursts and it rains. My mother opens her umbrella. A pungent earthy, fetid smell of rain on London pavements wafts into the air. I love that smell. The heavy drops pitter-patter on the taut umbrella and run down to stream from the spokes. I feel a sadness well up again. The visit to the Embassy teaches me we are deluded to imagine we can escape the past and be set free to embark on a new beginning. However much my mother hopes to prevent my contamination, it is futile. But she seems satisfied that the morning went well.

My mother once followed her thirteen-year-old daughter home, rejected, ignored, watching the rain soak her clothes and hair. She never uttered an angry word against me. This was not about forgiveness, or indulgence. It was about fear. Silence is better than trying to whitewash or make excuses. For that I admire her. Although this meant, up to that point, she had denied me my true father, and because of that, I know it is possible to love someone with an intense, burning anger. It is a destructive place to be. Our unconditional love for each other is evidence of what is to become, a life-long complicity.

But I don't realise that just yet. For the moment we are together. In the heavy rain we make our way to Victoria Station and my mother lifts the umbrella higher to cover my head. I take her arm. I still don't know her, but this time I'll keep close to her side.

# Endnote

Page 295—The instruction never again to wear black was a code to remind my mother to be careful about her origins, and to do nothing to draw attention to herself. Her Polish surname on her birth certificate may have been why she was called up to serve in the Luftwaffe, and her friends from home were not.

# Endnote

Page 295—The instruction never again to wear black was a code to remind my mother to be careful about her origins, and to do nothing to draw attention to herself. Her Polish surname on her birth certificate may have been why she was called up to serve in the Luftwaffe, and her friends from home were not.

Lightning Source UK Ltd.
Milton Keynes UK
UKHW041429211022
410868UK00014B/266